Favorite Internet sites

Sites	Comments
www.SuperJobSearch.com	gateway to 1,000s of job opportunities
www.pobox.com	own your own e-mail address
www.mapquest.com	details on getting to any address

Favorite e-mail addresses

Addresses	Comments
supersearch@pobox.com	address to Jamenair Ltd.

Favorite Internet sites

Sites	Comments

Favorite e-mail addresses

Addresses	Comments

Favorite Internet sites

Sites	Comments

Favorite e-mail addresses

Addresses	Comments

SUPER JOB SEARCH

T.M.

SUPER JOB SEARCH

™

**THE
COMPLETE
MANUAL
FOR JOB-SEEKERS
& CAREER-CHANGERS**

By Peter K. Studner

JAMENAIR LTD.

SUPER**JOB**SEARCH ®

Although the author and publisher have exhaustively researched all sources to ensure the accuracy and completeness of the information contained in this manual, we assume no responsibility for errors, inaccuracies, omissions or any other inconsistency herein. Any slights against people or organizations are unintentional.

This publication is designed to provide information in regard to the subject matter covered. It is sold with the understanding that neither the author nor the publisher is engaged in rendering legal, accounting, employment procurement or other professional service. If legal advice or other expert assistance is required, the services of a competent professional person should be sought.

Published by JAMENAIR LTD
Post Office Box 241957
Los Angeles, California 90024-9757, U.S.A
e-mail: jamenair@pobox.com

Library of Congress Cataloging-in-Publication Data
Studner, Peter K.

SUPER**JOB**SEARCH ®
Biography: p.
Includes index.
1. Job-hunting.
2. Career changes.
3. Title.
HF5382.7.S78 1987 650.1'4 86-50476
ISBN 0-938667-04-1 Softcover

A selection of the Macmillan Book Clubs
Third Edition
Seventeenth Printing

Special Thanks

This book has been created with the able assistance of John Kane, programming specialist; Stanley Fidel, telemarketing consultant; Elaine Rockett, Maggie Kleinman and Richard Sherer, editorial assistants; and Annie Studner, research coordinator.

I also wish to thank all my candidates who have contributed much to my understanding of this important subject.

Dedication

Annie Studner
Jacques Petoin
Helen Goldye
Vida Stuart

and

My Network

Contents

Foreword to the Third Edition

Whether you have just started a job search or have been looking for some time without success...this book is for you.

Just 1% of the people leaving companies, either voluntarily or otherwise, receive outplacement assistance. This statistic inspired the writing of *Super Job Search*, the first self-directed outplacement program of its kind available to everyone. Since its original publication, more than 100,000 copies have been sold. A fully adapted version is now in its second edition in Great Britain and in 1997, *Objectif Emploi* was released in both France and North America to assist French-speaking job-seekers looking for careers in Canada and France.

The letters and calls we have received over the years are testimony to the fact that *Super Job Search* does indeed provide advice that radically reduces job-search time and helps people make career changes into more productive, interesting and, in many cases, higher paying activities.

Career management and job search have radically changed since this book's original publication. Never before has so much information become available about companies, industries and people. The Internet has become an indispensable tool for all job-seekers in obtaining information. E-mail through the Internet has sped up and deformalized the process of communications.

Yet, with all these changes, there are still some fundamentals that have remained: People get jobs from people; what takes place in an interview decides whether an applicant will be a finalist; the winning candidate will always be the best prepared.

As a result of coaching and training thousands of candidates using *Super Job Search*, I have developed new tools to facilitate networking, create eye-catching model letters and resumes, and improve interviewing techniques that grab the attention of deciders. This Third Edition incorporates these changes and new tools. Regardless of qualifications, outstanding candidates will always get the best offers. *Super Job Search* will help you to become an outstanding job-seeker.

To the Job-Seeker:

Getting the right job with a good salary requires know-how and organization. Reducing the time for your search means working with proven techniques. Whatever the reasons that led you to your search, you need to mobilize all your creative abilities and market yourself in the most attractive package possible to win the best of jobs. *Super Job Search* will show you the way step by step.

Almost every job-seeker has access to a personal computer, modem and laser printer which facilitate and increase communications to companies and target decision makers. With the exponential increase in posted mail and e-mail, it is no longer effective to follow the old prescription of sending your resume to 500 or 1,000 companies, sitting back waiting for calls, interviewing, and then choosing a job from two or three offers. Today's competitive job market requires a candidate to be proactive in reaching deciders.

Super Job Search responds to new challenges in the marketplace and problems facing today's job candidate. It combines elements from more than 30 years of successful job-search experience along with the successful campaigns of thousands of candidates who have been using these techniques. These techniques have helped job-seekers win meaningful positions with annual salaries ranging from $20,000 to more than $4,000,000. *Super Job Search* offers the nuts and bolts of finding not just a job but, whenever possible, a step up the career ladder.

To the Career-Changer:

People occupy jobs unhappily for a number of reasons: They did not have an opportunity to choose a job that matched their skills and interests against career goals; they are in dead-end positions that are boring and unproductive; they are underpaid and underemployed; they have outgrown their original career interests; they do not subscribe to company policies or the direction in which the company is moving; they cling to their jobs strictly because of a paycheck. If you are one of these, this book will have you create a *Super Job Search* that will bring a job of joy back into your life.

To the Mature Person Reentering the Job Market:

Do you wish to return to the workforce after a long absence? Getting back into the job market requires planning to identify the special skills, interests and accomplishments that will provide the opportunity you seek. Your next job will not come from a degree or experience from bygone days. It will come from understanding your abilities and accomplishments, and matching them to your field of interest.

This book will help you uncover your real talents and market yourself into a job of fulfillment rather than just any situation that comes along.

Peter K. Studner
Los Angeles, California
e-mail: studner@pobox.com

Introduction

HOW TO USE THIS BOOK

A well run, self-placement campaign can cut your job search time in half...or better. But more importantly, a well prepared job search will keep you focused on what you really want: career advancement in lieu of just a slot to fill.

Behind every great job offer are great interviews! This book will show you how to generate and conduct the kind of interviews that produce winning jobs.

The SUPER SEARCH program consists of seven training sessions plus additional homework assignments. To get the best results, do each exercise in sequence. Skipping an exercise means losing part of the benefits. You are strongly advised not to begin interviewing before completing the seven-day program and practicing the techniques.

The idea of practice is so important that I have included a bonus for users of the SUPER SEARCH program. Please refer to the registration form at the end of this book. By registering your purchase, you will have an opportunity to meet a partner or partners with whom you may practice.

Millions of people change jobs every year, so you are not embarking on *Mission: Impossible.* Your mission is to identify the position you really want, mobilize your personal resources and sell yourself in a way that achieves your objective. Sound simple? It is—if you follow each of the steps outlined in this manual for your personal placement.

BEFORE YOU BEGIN

Success is rarely an accident. Luck or chance is certainly an element in making changes in life. Preparation balances the chance factor so it is more in your favor. Eddie Cantor is credited with saying: "The harder I work, the luckier I get." This is absolutely true in job search.

Job search is a full-time job. This means five days a week with no less than six hours of work per day. Less than this and you are only fooling yourself that you are looking for a new job.

You are embarking on a self-marketing program. While many of the ideas may be new, give them a chance to succeed.

What makes the difference between success and failure? Consider the following true story:

Bill had a good job in a *Fortune 100* company. He was terminated after 18 months as part of a general layoff. It was the first time he had ever been fired, and aside from the severe blow to his ego, he was worried that he would not get settled quickly and in a job where he could develop his career.

Since his entire department was let go, he had four competitors from his own company—all with the same approximate qualifications and all looking for similar work.

Bill explained his concerns and we discussed a SUPER SEARCH. He said, "Tell me what I have to do to complete the program and I'll do it to the letter!" Bill impressed upon me that he meant business.

Bill developed his career goals and we discussed in depth his accomplishments. He identified his strongest skills and interests. At the end of the third day we completed his resume on a word processor. That afternoon he was researching and listing his target companies.

After Day 6's telemarketing session, Bill was on the phone, calling people who could act as referrals (bridges) to the companies he wanted to approach.

When we completed Day 7's training on interviewing and negotiations, he had an interview with one of his target companies.

Three days later, after lots of networking, he had an offer. He called me, concerned: "This isn't my first choice. They want an answer this week. I don't want to lose this opportunity, but I think another interview I had could produce a better job for me in the company I really want. What will I tell them?" Bill's favored company was not in a hurry.

The company making the offer did not have a job description and their offer was based on a verbal outline of the job. They were tailoring the job to Bill's skills (which represents the true power of networking!). I suggested that he offer to help them make a job description so everyone would be sure of the position's responsibilities, authority and expected results. This could buy him a week during which he could pursue his number one choice.

The company agreed and became even more enamored of Bill as a result. Meanwhile, Bill was able to meet again with choice number one. At last they

made him an offer. The salary was slightly *less* than the other company (though higher than his previous job), but the potential was much more promising.

Bill accepted the offer from his first choice, two-and-a-half weeks after he had finished his SUPER SEARCH program. He was a happy and successful man. Choice number two made a standing offer: If his new job did not work, they would find a spot for him.

Bill's success was no accident. He worked hard on the same exercises you have in this manual. While we reviewed his options and strategies together, all the decisions and action came from Bill. We role-played different scenarios for the difficult questions you will find in Chapter 8. By the time Bill finished his training, he had confidence and knowledge and, as a result, was better able to sell his product: himself.

Why was Bill so successful?

- He worked more than 40 hours per week on his search.

- He was tenacious and committed.

- He did his exercises in detail and took the time to think about their consequences on his life and career goals.

- He was aware of his strong points and how they could benefit his target companies.

- He researched information about the companies and the people he wanted to meet.

- He took the initiative in calling people to make appointments.

- He wrote thank-you letters for each meeting.

- He kept in shape mentally and physically. Sure, he was anxious, but he turned that energy around to work for him. No grass grew under his feet.

- He was smart enough to ask for advice when a decision was needed.

- He practiced with the other terminated members of his department. They met regularly to discuss companies and strategies.

You have in this manual all the training I gave Bill—plus some extras. It is now up to you. But before you begin any of the exercises, I urge you to read the entire book cover to cover. You will understand better the importance of each step and how it will help you toward your goal.

THE PROGRAM

DAY 1
Assessment: Getting to know yourself.
Goal-Setting: Defining your career direction.

DAY 2
Accomplishments: Discovering what makes you great.
                                   Uncovering your skills.

DAY 3
The Resume: Creating your special calling card of
                                   accomplishments. Being remembered.

DAY 4
The Market Plan: Where the jobs are and how to
                                   approach them. Setting time priorities.

DAY 5
Networking: The art of penetrating the hidden job
                                   market. Loaded with opportunities.

DAY 6
Telemarketing Yourself: The power in using the telephone to
                                   arrange interviews.

DAY 7
The Interview, Negotiation   Selling yourself. Making it a win-win
& Action Plan: salary.

CHAPTER 1

Getting Started

ou're out of work! Let go, just finished school, quit—for any number of reasons you need employment.

If you have just finished school, getting the right job means setting your career course and following a plan. That plan should take into account your present and future goals.

You have spent considerable time learning skills. The real challenge has arrived: Where should you apply your talents for the greatest professional benefit? The exercises in this manual will help you focus on the position that will best serve your career needs and set criteria for the type of company where you will want to market your potential. You will be picking your next job instead of having any job pick you. Preparing a career plan today and sticking to it can save you years of wasted time.

Layoffs account for a majority of the unemployed because retrenchment is often a solution to reduced profits. Cutbacks are common and, unpleasant as they are, we read about them all the time.

But there are other reasons for discharges. We live in a society where lawsuits fly in every direction and companies have had to become more sensitive to the hiring/firing process. Today's labor laws favor the employee's rights, so it is not easy for employers merely to "unload" someone they do not like. Usually a well documented file is needed to justify action. Is there such a file on you? Now is a good time to examine what you were doing, consciously or unconsciously, to feed it. It is important to stop and analyze now before moving ahead.

ATTITUDE

When we *feel* we are going to win, we do. Your attitude during this period makes all the difference in finding a new job quickly. It is perfectly normal to have feelings of doubt, lack of confidence, anxiety, fear, rejection, concern and worry. You need someone to talk to about these feelings. They must come out if you are to go on to the next phase. If your company has paid for outplacement, use your counselor to ventilate these emotions. If not, discuss them with a close

friend, relative or, perhaps, a counselor. But do not carry your garbage around on your back. Get these feelings behind you. Throw them out!

How quickly you pass through this stage of letting off steam will determine how soon you will go forward. You cannot argue with facts; you must deal with them. If you are out of work, that is a fact, and you must now organize all your resources to get on with your life. You (and perhaps your family) depend on your ability to put the past in its proper place and move on.

Some candidates try to work over the past through a lawyer. If there is a genuine case, why not? However, you may need your former employer's cooperation in your search. How does this reference sound: "Oh yes. John. You know, he is suing the company over his discharge...!" Be prepared for this kind of remark or temper your litigious feelings. Perhaps negotiations out of court can bring a better settlement for you and assure the good reference you may need.

After the smoke has cleared from your exit, you need to get down to basics:

• What do I tell my family and friends? Tell the truth. You were let go and are putting together your resume and action plan. No need to go into heavy detail, but rather a realistic appraisal of the situation with emphasis on what you are doing about it. Remember, your attitude will determine theirs.

• Do not ask anything of people until you have at least read this book. You will then know what to ask. Right now you need to focus on what you want. Later, you will want to discuss your resume and target companies with as many people as possible. In discussing your availability, you have nothing to be ashamed of; the highest and mightiest have been fired from good jobs.

BUT, when you get moving on your job search, leave all disparagers on the outside. There can be no defeatists in a successful job-search program. You are going to get resettled! That is a fact. How soon and into what job depend on you.

Here are five suggestions to keep you from giving in to depression and feelings of failure:

1. Keep in good physical shape with regular exercise. It is a good idea to have a physical, while you are still covered by health insurance. If you have been playing tennis or some other sport regularly, keep it up. If you have been neglectful about exercise, now is a good time to begin. It can be anything from jogging early in the morning to a brisk walk before going to bed.

2. Have someone to talk to regularly. It is good to discuss your meetings and progress as you go along. Feedback is important, and exchanging experiences will make your search easier and more productive.

3. Get enough sleep and nourish your body. Some people try to save money on food. That is foolish. You can eat properly and be economical at the same time. Any doctor will tell you that skipping meals or cutting back on essentials in your diet can contribute to depression and even bring on illness. So be smart: Treat your body to what it needs, not only during job search, but beyond.

4. Maintain a balanced social life. During this transition time, it is especially important to maintain contacts with friends. You will need to give your brain a rest, and nothing helps more than getting out and being with people. They also will contribute to your program, as you will see.

5. Devote time to your job search every day! No one can promise you a job, but if you maintain a continuous search, you will be surprised and encouraged with the results.

YOUR FINANCIAL SITUATION

Before commencing your search, you need to examine your financial situation and make use of some techniques that will help you save time and money.

We are all used to having a certain amount of cash and credit at our disposal. When the job ends, the problem of having money still flowing out comes as a shock. We never realized how much we depended on that regular paycheck.

Sometimes we are faced with expenses that previously were covered by the company, like automobile expenses and health insurance. When employment stops, it is an opportunity, as well as a necessity, to take stock.

Many companies extend salary beyond the termination date (severance pay), depending on job level and longevity with the firm. But let us assume that you have only a few weeks' salary coming.

The first thing you must do is file for unemployment insurance. Many candidates think this is a degrading and shameful thing. Nothing could be further from the truth. This insurance has been paid for and if you are out of work, by all means collect what you have accrued. You never think twice about medical insurance reimbursement, do you? You have as much right to collect unemployment benefits, so apply.

Since these programs are regulated on the state level, eligibility and payout requirements may vary. Even if you are collecting severance pay, find out what benefits apply and what formalities are required. Doing this now will prevent delays in receiving checks.

About health insurance: Most insurance plans offer a standard grace period (usually 30 days) after which there is often a provision for converting the company's group insurance plan into an individual policy. However, this conversion is sometimes accompanied by a hefty rate increase, so do not accept it without first checking around with other insurance services like Blue Cross/Blue Shield and health maintenance organization providers (HMOs).

For your protection and peace of mind, you will want yourself and family covered for major medical expense at the very least, and it is well worth your while to investigate the alternatives. Do this investigation as soon as you know you will be out of work, not at the last minute, or you will risk a gap in coverage.

Controlling Your Budget

You need to make a budget. You must review all your expenses (outflow) on a monthly, quarterly and yearly basis, and list whatever income you will have from your last job, possible part-time work, insurance, savings and investments. If you have been living beyond your means, you will have to do some belt-tightening.

If you are heavily in debt, you will need to examine the possibility of disposing of some of your assets. Stop buying on credit. If you use credit cards, be sure you will have enough cash at the end of the month to cover your payments. However, before taking any action, complete the following forms so that you can be selective in your action:

The FAMILY NET WORTH form permits you to see how your assets and debts are distributed. It will help you make decisions should you wish to rearrange your debts or assets.

The SOURCES OF INCOME schedule pinpoints your income. To be effective, you should make projections and then track the actual figures, showing any surplus or deficits. This review should be made on a monthly basis; if necessary, you can revise your projections as you go forward.

Listing JOB-CAMPAIGN COSTS helps you itemize expenses related to your search that are tax deductible. Your monthly job-search cost should be carried over to the MONTHLY DISBURSEMENTS PLANNER.

The MONTHLY DISBURSEMENTS form shows all your current monthly obligations. Once they have been listed, you can see which ones you should pay immediately and which ones can be stretched or delayed until you are working again. When you expect to stretch or delay a payment, discuss this *in advance* with the creditor. Most companies will work with you if you explain the circumstances and make regular, if token, payments. Take the initiative in this—do not make them come after you. Protect your credit rating.

To control your finances and to augment slender means during your search, you do have a few options:

1. Part-time work.

2. Taking out an additional mortgage or loans on important assets.

3. Selling off assets. The last form shown is RAISING CASH FROM SALE OF ASSETS. A list of your assets and their market values will help your planning. In all probability you will be resettled before such drastic measures become necessary. This book is about taking control. By preparing in advance, you will eliminate unpleasant surprises. Keep in mind that, aside from raising cash, selling off assets that are not fully paid for is a way of reducing expenses.

FAMILY NET WORTH

ASSETS

Cash	$ _____
Savings Accounts	_____
Stocks	_____
Bonds	_____
Real Estate, Home	_____
Other Real Estate	_____
Automobile(s)	_____
Notes Receivable	_____
Cash Value—Life Insurance	_____
Jewelry	_____
Paintings	_____
Silver	_____
Household Furniture	_____
Antiques	_____
Other Assets _____	_____
Other Assets _____	_____
Other Assets _____	_____
Total Assets	$ _____

LIABILITIES

Current Bills Due	$ _____
Notes Payable	_____
Taxes Payable	_____
Mortgage, Home	_____
Mortgage, Other Property	_____
Balance Due, Vehicles	_____
Balance Due, Installment Purchases	_____
Other Debts _____	_____
Other Debts _____	_____
Other Debts _____	_____
Total Liabilities	$ _____

Net Worth = Total Assets - Total Liabilities = $ _____

Total Liabilities + Net Worth = $ _____

SOURCES OF INCOME

MONTHLY PLANNER

	Projection Mo _____	Actual Mo _____	Surplus (Deficit)
Salary	$_____	$_____	$_____
Severance Income	_____	_____	_____
Unused Vacation Pay	_____	_____	_____
Other Company Benefits	_____	_____	_____
Retirement Income	_____	_____	_____
Unemployment Compensation	_____	_____	_____
Interest from Savings	_____	_____	_____
Dividends from Stocks	_____	_____	_____
Dividends from Bonds	_____	_____	_____
Rental Receipts	_____	_____	_____
Tax Refund	_____	_____	_____
Interest from Loans	_____	_____	_____
Interest from Insurance	_____	_____	_____
Collection of Debts	_____	_____	_____
Earnings—Spouse	_____	_____	_____
Earnings—Children	_____	_____	_____
Earnings—Part-Time Job	_____	_____	_____
Borrowing on Life Insurance	_____	_____	_____
Other _____	_____	_____	_____
Other _____	_____	_____	_____
TOTAL INCOME (A)	$_____	$_____	$_____

List all sources of income without the sale of any assets or incurring any new debts. Use the above form to *plan* each month (projection), then indicate the *actual* figure for the month and note the *surplus or deficit* for the following month's planning.

ESTIMATED JOB-CAMPAIGN COSTS

PLANNER
(watch for duplication in other monthly disbursements)

Computer Cost	$ _____
Computer Supplies	
Ribbons	_____
Paper	_____
Disks	_____
Software	_____
Stationery	_____
Subscriptions	_____
Reference Books/Materials	_____
Copy Expenses	_____
Telephone	_____
Answering Machine	_____
Parking	_____
Gas, Service, Repair	_____
Mileage	_____
Other Travel	_____
Postage	_____
Outside Word-Processing Costs	_____
Printing Costs	_____
Restaurant Costs	_____
Other _____	_____
Other _____	_____

**TOTAL ESTIMATED
JOB-SEARCH COSTS (C)** $ _____

Be sure to discuss the deductibility of these costs with your accountant. Add the total into your ANTICIPATED DISBURSEMENTS PLANNER, line (C). This will help you see what cash reserves you will need for your search.

ANTICIPATED DISBURSEMENTS

MONTHLY PLANNER

	Projection Mo _____	Actual Mo _____	Surplus (Deficit)
Current Bills Due	$_____	$_____	$_____
Installment Loan Payments			
Interest On Loans			
Mortgage Payment			
Rent			
Heating			
Electricity			
Water			
Telephone			
Home Insurance Premium			
Property Taxes			
Domestic Services			
Household Needs			
Personal Needs			
Automobile Loan Payments			
Auto Insurance Premiums			
Gasoline			
Automobile Maintenance			
Life Insurance Premiums			
Medical Insurance Premiums			
Food			
Clothing			
Drugs & Medical Expenses			
Laundry & Dry Cleaning			
Child Care			
Tuition Expenses			
Taxes			
Subscriptions, Magazines			
Club & Ass'n Dues			
Professional Fees			
Entertainment			
Contributions			
Travel, Bus & Taxi			
Other Travel			
Job—Campaign Costs * (C)			
Gifts			
Miscellaneous			
Other Disbursements _____			
Other Disbursements _____			
Other Disbursements _____			
TOTAL DISBURSEMENTS (B)	$_____	$_____	$_____

* watch out for duplication   (C) see summary on previous form

List all monthly expenses. Use the above form to *plan* each month (projection), then indicate the *actual* figure for the month and note the *surplus or deficit* for the following month's planning. This list will help you choose which expenses to cut.

RAISING CASH FROM SALE OF ASSETS

(if and when absolutely necessary)

ESTIMATED INCOME

Automobiles $ _____

Rental Property _____

Boats, Planes, Sport Cars, Snowmobiles _____

Secondary Residences _____

Recreational Vehicles _____

Camera Equipment _____

Jewelry _____

Musical Instruments _____

Paintings/Other Art _____

Stamp, Coin or Other Collections _____

Antiques _____

Home _____

Salable Equipment _____

Furniture _____

IRA and/or KEOGH Account(s) * _____

Other Salable Assets_____ _____

Other Salable Assets_____ _____

Other Salable Assets_____ _____

Other Salable Assets_____ _____

**TOTAL POTENTIAL
ADDITIONAL CASH RESOURCES** $ _____

*Early conversion of IRA or KEOGH accounts will mean some penalties. Check with your accountant before making withdrawals.

The above list shows you a potential means of raising cash. You should decide which assets would go first in case of need. With good planning and action on your part, it may never come to this.

You now can figure your MONTHLY CASH FLOW. This should be done for several months in advance so you can prepare your financial planning.

MONTHLY CASH FLOW

SUMMARY

	Projection Mo_____	Actual Mo_____	Surplus (Deficit)
BEGINNING CASH BALANCE	$ _____	$ _____	$ _____
(+) TOTAL INCOME (A)	_____	_____	_____
(—) TOTAL DISBURSEMENTS (B)	_____	_____	_____
ENDING CASH BALANCE	$ _____	$ _____	$ _____

Total Income figures come from line (A) and Total Disbursements come from line (B) of previous schedules. The name of this game is to keep in a positive cash position at all times.

Only spend what is necessary and eliminate all that is merely useful. While your search may take only a few weeks, you should be prepared for it to take several months. Delay that new sofa or vacation until after you are resettled in a new job. It is important not to keep your family in the dark. Bring them into the discussion and let them help. Do not shut them out; give them the chance to share the burdens and you will see some extraordinary cooperation.

Your budget should, however, include recreation. Remember what that word really means: re-creation. You cannot go through a job search without some diversion and outside activity; it just does not have to be expensive.

After you have listed all your expenses and income, you may want to sit down with your accountant or financial advisor to see what else is possible and how you will have to adjust your living standard during this transition period.

Part-Time Work

In your financial review, you may come to the conclusion that, while you are looking for a permanent job, you still have to bring your income up to break-even. Since you are in transition, part-time work is preferred to selling off important assets. A part-time job is better than taking a full-time, meaningless position and stopping your search for the right job altogether. Your part-time job should still allow you to devote a minimum of 25-30 hours per week to job search.

The part-time work you seek could be an extension of your present skills, though it may not be as remunerative. One candidate had prior experience as a computer salesperson. While looking for a new full-time position during the week, he was able to work in a computer store on weekends.

If you have financial and accounting skills and you are out of work at the beginning of the year, you might be able to find temporary work as a tax preparer. Similarly, if you have computer skills, you might register with temporary agencies that specialize in this field. One executive with excellent computer skills needed extra work and was able to generate income doing detail spreadsheet work for a consulting firm. This part-time job developed into a full-time position. We will discuss the part-time job in depth in Chapter 9.

HELPFUL HINTS

Telephone

Get a telephone credit card. While your local telephone company will provide you this service, you can do much better at considerably lower rates, for example, call VoiceNet, 1-800-377-1490. Keep a record of calls made for tax-deductible expenses against your search.

There are many services offering long-distance calls at reduced rates. Try for one that charges by second intervals rather than by the minute.

An answering machine is vital. Many times it is better to have the machine pick up calls instead of your family. It will easily outdo the best efforts of your four-year-old. You can obtain excellent units at less than $50 where you can retrieve your messages away from home. A word of advice: Cute and clever messages can convey the wrong impression.

If your telephone must also serve the needs of your spouse and children, think about putting in an extra line. Reserve one for family use and the other for business calls—which will have the maximum chance of being unobstructed.

Some people prefer to have one line with the Call Waiting feature. If you can get used to the idea of having a clicking sound while you are talking, it can help you get off of a less important call to check if the other call is job related.

When people call you to help you with your search, do not delay in getting back to them. A little courtesy goes a long way.

For senior executives who want their calls immediately, consider obtaining a cellular phone with call waiting and voice mail. The cost of a cellular phone is less expensive than having a live message service and will permit you to be in constant contact with your job market. The voice mail feature will let you know what calls are waiting to be returned. If you obtain a cellular phone, be sure to put it on your resume with the heading Cellular/Messages.

Expenses

Speak to your accountant about deductible job-search expenses and how they will be treated under the new law. If they are deductible, they must be properly documented should you ever be audited. Get into the habit of writing on each invoice or receipt the name, date and purpose. Be sure to include tips and parking fees.

Using credit cards will postpone payments and reduce the need to carry cash, but is not recommended unless you pay off your charges every month. Credit-card borrowing is one of the most expensive loans you can get. This should not be one of the extended payments referred to earlier. If you frequently eat in restaurants or stay at hotels, investigate obtaining a Transmedia Network credit card, 1-800-422-5090. Transmedia offers you a 20% reduction on thousands of restaurants and hotels; the card is free.

You will need a good calendar. Use one with a 5" x 8" format with one page devoted to each day. This gives you space to enter your appointments and any notes or comments. Be sure to include:

a. Name of the person you are going to see.

b. Time of appointment.

c. Telephone number.

d. Address and perhaps directions if you are not sure. Internet users should go to <www.mapquest.com> for detailed door to door directions with maps.

e. Who referred you to this person. This is important!

By following the above procedure, you will have a quick reference for key information. You do not need a good memory if you have a good system!

It is useful to tape receipts and invoices to pages of a spiral notebook. You will have a chronological file and ensure that nothing gets lost. Keep it simple but up-to-date.

Another spiral notebook is useful for notes during and after each interview. By keeping this information, you will build a chronological history that can supplement any other files you may wish to keep.

Begin accumulating job advertisements for positions of interest. Major sources will be the Internet and newspapers like *The Wall Street Journal*. Most of the *Journal's* want ads appear on Monday, Tuesday and Wednesday. To get the *Journal's* national listing of classified advertisements, you may wish to purchase *The National Business Employment Weekly*, which is available at many newsstands. For information about subscriptions, call 1-800-568-7625. Your local library may also carry these papers.

ARRANGING YOUR FINANCES

Sources of Income:
- severance pay
- vacation pay
- bonus
- interest
- dividends
- rental income
- retirement income
- tax refund
- salary from spouse or children

First Priority Expenses:
- rent
- mortgage
- food
- utilities
- job-search costs
- prescription drugs
- medical
- insurance
- telephone
- current bills due
- household needs
- personal needs

Cutting Monthly Costs:
- negotiate delays on loan payments
- buying only necessities
- no credit purchases
- refinancing debts
- disposing of assets on which you still have heavy debts to pay

Raising Additional Cash:
- selling assets
- part-time work
- drawing on retirement funds
- borrowing on insurance

In addition, you should be reading local papers and even the *Sunday New York Times,* which is distributed in many cities. Many of its want ads are nationwide in scope.

If you are considering relocation, you should investigate the local papers in your area of interest. You can arrange directly for a limited subscription, or perhaps a friend or relative can send you copies. Check which newspapers are carried by your local library.

Professional magazines and trade publications can also provide useful job leads, so be a regular reader. This should be part of your routine research.

Clip job ads of interest and place them in another spiral notebook, one to a page, leaving space for notes about each. Above each ad, identify the source and date.

Written Communications

You will need access to a typewriter or, better yet, a word processor. Every contact you make, especially interviews, should be followed with a short letter (we will discuss this later).

The most expensive approach is to use an outside secretarial service; the most practical is to use a personal computer (PC). If someone in your family owns a PC or if you have been considering buying or renting one, now is the time to investigate. There are also plans that allow you to apply a portion of rental toward purchase.

It is a buyers' market for personal computers. Discuss your needs with an expert. If you have absolutely no knowledge about computers, call your local high school or computer store and find out how you can be put in touch with a local IBM Users Group. Go to a meeting and ask the president of the group for the name of a reputable consultant who can advise you on how to get organized in the least expensive manner. A good consultant will know where the best and most reliable bargains are in town. A few hours with a consultant can make your entry into the personal computer world much easier. Aside from helping you with your job search, your personal computer can make record-keeping at home less of a chore.

Even if you never learn to type, there are easy-to-use (and fun) programs on the market that can teach you in a few hours how to turn out impressive letters and resumes.

Your job search will entail meeting lots of people, and keeping track of contacts can be so much easier using an organized program that stores all your information, sorts it, and provides you with what you need, when you need it. A basic computer setup, which costs less than $1,000, can do all this and more. It may be tax deductible, as well.

CHECKLIST

☐ 1. Answering machine

☐ 2. Telephone credit card

☐ 3. Low-cost long distance service

☐ 4. FAX machine

☐ 5. Cellular telephone

☐ 6. Record of all receipts

☐ 7. Subscriptions to newspapers/magazines

☐ 8. Collection of ads (note source & date)

☐ 9. Personal computer (modem, printer)

☐ 10. Internet access

☐ 11. Stationery

☐ 12. Personal business cards

☐ 13. Medical insurance

☐ 14. Unemployment benefits

☐ 15. Target company list

☐ 16. List of everyone you know

☐ 17. Calendar

☐ 18. References

CHAPTER 2

Assessment/
Goal-Setting/Strategy

here is something lacking in the entire job-search process that begins the day we look for our first job. Did you really plan the job you have or had? Or was it a chance situation that appeared to be a good opportunity at the moment?

Have you given thought to what really turns you on at work and what is missing from your professional life? If you are unhappy in your work, can you identify what it is you would like to change? No matter what led you to read this book at this moment, you have a golden opportunity to get back on your critical career path.

What information do you need to make the right decisions?

- Your personal job interests

- Your knowledge and experience compared to your job interests

- Your preferred work environment

- Your likes and dislikes in past positions

- Your weaknesses and strengths

- Your ambitions, today and in the future

The exercises you will perform should be done with care and thought. The information you create will help focus your search, give you a better understanding of yourself and provide a yardstick to measure different job offers.

JOB PREFERENCES

The first exercise is listing ALL possible jobs that could be of interest. Your list may be quite long and varied; that is okay.

Once your list is complete, it should be ranked in order of interest, personal knowledge and experience.

Let us look at an example of an accountant who works for one of the Big Eight accounting firms:

Positions of Interest	Interest	Knowledge	Experience
Partner in Accounting Firm	2	1	2
Vice President of Finance	1	2	5
Financial Consultant	3	1	3
College Instructor	4	2	5
Controller	2	2	5
General Manager	1	4	5
Vice President Administration	3	3	3
Vice President Marketing	1	5	5
Executive Recruiter	2	2	2
Private Accounting Practice	1	2	4
Owner of a Business	1	5	5
Internal Auditor	2	4	4

The grading score:

1 = Highest Interest, Greatest Knowledge, Strongest Experience
2 = Above-Average Interest, Good Knowledge, Good Experience
3 = Average Interest, Some Knowledge, Some Experience
4 = Some Interest, Little Knowledge, Little Experience
5 = Little Interest, No Knowledge, No Experience

Our accounting candidate has a varied list of possible jobs. Since he has been working in an accounting firm, his first thought was to continue in the same direction, with the ultimate goal of reaching partner level.

However, while he is very well informed and highly trained for that position, his interest level is only above average; it is not his number one preference.

Looking at his positions of highest interest we have:

Positions of Interest	Knowledge	Experience
Vice President of Finance	2	5
General Manager	4	5
Vice President Marketing	5	5
Private Accounting Practice	2	4
Owner of a Business	5	5

Our candidate has five choices for his number one interest, but he must take into account his lack of experience and knowledge. While he may have a passion for one or more on his list, his lack of immediate skills will be the determining factor. Going one step further, if his desire is really strong, he can learn the needed skills either at school or by working his way up through another organization, or both.

If additional education is required, financial and time factors have to be taken into consideration. While he has created a dream list of jobs, at some point practicality must take charge.

Continuing with his original list, there are four radical career changes:

Positions of Interest	Interest	Knowledge	Experience
College Instructor	4	2	5
Vice President Marketing	1	5	5
Executive Recruiter	2	2	2
Owner of a Business	1	5	5

He will have to talk to people in these positions, ask questions and get the information he needs to make a decision. This is one aspect of networking and will be discussed in Chapter 6.

An advantage of networking will be the feedback he gets with respect to his preferences. Are there jobs available today that will satisfy any of his projected goals? Are these jobs located in his geographic area or will a move be necessary? It is only through research that he can evaluate his interests, knowledge and experience for the career he prefers. This preliminary study and evaluation can prevent wasted time and effort spent in looking for a job that may not be.

He also has given high preference to a private accounting practice and/or ownership of a business. Both would require financial reserves and staying power. A discussion with someone already in those situations can provide him with information on the problems and pitfalls others have experienced.

Here is the intangible factor each person must confront: What personal sacrifices am I prepared to make to achieve success?

Using the example of our accountant, you should now prepare your list of Positions of Interest and then rank them for evaluation.

Once your list is made, it will become apparent which position you want to target as number one. For this position, consider what skills you have and what additional ones you will have to develop. Are jobs available in your immediate market?

You may have other positions on your list that interest you but you are not sure of your qualifications. You will want to learn more about these positions by meeting people who can furnish you information.

POSITIONS OF INTEREST

Positions	Interest	Knowledge	Experience
1.			
2.			
3.			
4.			
5.			
6.			
7.			
8.			
9.			
10.			
11.			
12.			
13.			
14.			
15.			

Selected positions from the above list to research:

1. _____

2. _____

3. _____

4. _____

My number one preference (at this time):

1. _____

1 = Highest Interest, Greatest Knowledge, Strongest Experience
2 = Above-Average Interest, Good Knowledge, Good Experience
3 = Average Interest, Some Knowledge, Some Experience
4 = Some Interest, Little Knowledge, Little Experience
5 = Little Interest, No Knowledge, No Experience

WORK ENVIRONMENT

Writing out what you liked and disliked previously will help you evaluate potential jobs in terms of personal preference. For example, if you prefer a large company with a structured work environment, this is important to note. It will help you single out specific companies for your target list. With this exercise in hand—and taking into consideration that no situation is perfect—you will be in a position to measure the importance of environmental conditions versus the total opportunity at hand.

Sample Listing of Favorable Work Attributes

The Company

- Consistent growth
- Internal promotion opportunities
- Team spirit
- Excellent products and services
- Good surroundings
- Modern facilities
- Well-established management policies
- Security
- Suggestions encouraged
- Genuine interest in everyone's advancement
- Challenging environment
- Sound structure and policies
- Motivation
- Reputation for honesty and fair play
- Educational opportunities
- Good benefits
- Management responsive to individual problems
- Modern management
- Good location

The Job

- Good salary
- Defined authority
- Good interpersonal relations
- Chance to be creative
- Adequate time to do a good job
- Travel
- Opportunity for promotion
- Interesting fellow employees
- Independence
- Defined responsibility
- Chance to build a team or work on an existing one
- Clearly defined duties
- Opportunity to learn
- Effective communications
- Challenging work

Our candidate filled out his forms and we can see what is important to him:

LIST ALL THE THINGS YOU DID NOT LIKE IN YOUR PREVIOUS JOB TO AVOID IN YOUR NEXT (and rank them in order of maximum dislike):

1. No room for advancement (3)
2. Very political (2)
3. Slow on decisions (4)
4. Too much overtime (1)
5. _____
6. _____
7. _____
8. _____
9. _____
10. _____
11. _____
12. _____

LIST ALL THE THINGS THAT YOU LIKED IN YOUR PREVIOUS JOB (and rank them in order of preference):

1. Very respected firm (2)
2. Structured (5)
3. No lack of business (3)
4. Have some good friends (4)
5. Learned a lot (1)
6. Modern offices (6)
7. _____
8. _____
9. _____
10. _____
11. _____
12. _____

NOW, LIST ALL THE THINGS THAT YOU WOULD LIKE TO BE INCLUDED IN YOUR IDEAL JOB (and rank them in order of importance):

1. Opportunity to learn (2)
2. Good salary (1)
3. Chance to advance (3)
4. Large company (6)
5. Nonpolitical (7)
6. Minimum overtime (4)
7. Close to residence (5)
8. Modern facilities (8)
9. _____
10. _____
11. _____
12. _____

We can draw several conclusions from the above:

1. The candidate is ambitious. Money, personal growth and advancement are his prime objectives.

2. He likes modern facilities and wants to avoid a politically charged atmosphere. He feels protected in a large and structured company.

3. With these preferences, it appears that being a vice president of finance in a large, modern company would have appeal. Being in his own private practice, while intriguing, may not actually be such a good idea. He would not be paid as much in the beginning and could count on heavy overtime. Both of these factors, which represent typical start-up sacrifices, go against his preferences. So, it was easy for him to make his first choices either vice president of finance in a large organization or continuing in public accounting.

Now, define your environmental preferences using the same form:

LIST ALL THE THINGS YOU DID NOT LIKE IN YOUR PREVIOUS JOB TO AVOID IN YOUR NEXT (and rank them in order of maximum dislike):

1. _____   7. _____

2. _____   8. _____

3. _____   9. _____

4. _____   10. _____

5. _____   11. _____

6. _____   12. _____

LIST ALL THE THINGS THAT YOU LIKED IN YOUR PREVIOUS JOB (and rank them in order of preference):

1. _____   7. _____

2. _____   8. _____

3. _____   9. _____

4. _____   10. _____

5. _____   11. _____

6. _____   12. _____

NOW, LIST ALL THE THINGS THAT YOU WOULD LIKE TO BE INCLUDED IN YOUR IDEAL JOB (and rank them in order of importance):

1. _____   7. _____

2. _____   8. _____

3. _____   9. _____

4. _____   10. _____

5. _____   11. _____

6. _____   12. _____

In the above listings, be sure to include environmental factors, human relationships and company policies as well as the specific characteristics of your job.

WEAK AND STRONG POINTS REVIEW

The next exercise will help you evaluate your strong and weak points. One purpose is to alert you to possible pitfalls you may encounter in an interview and permit you to prepare answers in advance to potentially embarrassing questions.

By reviewing your weaknesses, you can see what areas need work in terms of control, education or outside help. Better to face up to a weakness and work on it than to let it interfere with your career.

Before doing your list, look at how our accounting candidate filled out his:

STRENGTHS:

1. Natural number sense

2. Able to handle more than one job at a time

3. Good with people

4. Able to teach others

5. Fast learner

6. _____

7. _____

8. _____

9. _____

10. _____

WEAKNESSES:

1. Impatient - want to get the job done fast

2. Too modest at times

3. Not enough attention to my career

4. Afraid to take risks _____

5. Stutter under pressure _____

6. _____

7. _____

8. _____

9. _____

10. _____

If this candidate had an inquiry during an interview as to his weaknesses, he could easily mention his impatience and modesty. These both have reflections of strengths. Impatience could mean that he likes to get a job done and does not appreciate delays. Modesty (or self-effacing) could mean that he is not prone to spend a lot of time blowing his horn. Humility is a virtue. For his problem of stuttering, getting help at this time can be an important contribution to goal achievement.

His strengths are certainly something to be disclosed in an interview. Accountants who have natural abilities to teach, who are able to handle mixed work loads and who catch on fast are valuable employees.

Take a moment and list your strengths and weaknesses.

STRENGTHS:

1. _____

2. _____

3. _____

4. _____

5. _____

6. _____

7. _____

8. _____

9. _____

10. _____

WEAKNESSES:

1. _____

2. _____

3. _____

4. _____

5. _____

6. _____

7. _____

8. _____

9. _____

10. _____

Do not be discouraged by your weaknesses; we all have them. Admitting to what may be wrong is your first step toward improvement.

You will discover that a weakness is often nothing more than an excess of a strength. Control the excess and you have eliminated the weakness! For example:

STRENGTHS	WEAKNESSES
▶ Strives for excellence	▶ Demands perfection
▶ Modest	▶ Self-effacing
▶ Leadership	▶ Too bossy
▶ Fast	▶ Impulsive
▶ Takes risks	▶ Gambler
▶ Economical	▶ Cheap
▶ Tenacious	▶ Overbearing
▶ Negotiator	▶ Compromiser
▶ Stickler for detail	▶ Compulsive

Address yourself to your weaknesses and, wherever possible, turn them into strengths. Being aware of your inner feelings is half the battle.

AVOIDING EMBARRASSMENT

While your previous work experience is fresh in your mind, it is important to list ALL THE THINGS YOU DO NOT WANT TO BRING UP IN AN INTERVIEW! It is easy to talk too much about the wrong subjects. An interview can be going very well when suddenly you volunteer some unnecessary information and there it is: your foot in your mouth. This can be prevented.

By writing out a list of things you do NOT wish to blurt out to an interviewer, you will know in advance when to keep quiet. You will not be thrown by a sudden question.

Review this list from time to time, reminding yourself to keep these matters between you and God. You may be asked about some of them by an interviewer, so you will need to have some answers prepared. But do not volunteer negative or embarrassing information. The following is a sample list of potentially dangerous subjects. Take a moment to review it before completing your own list.

SUBJECTS I WOULD LIKE TO AVOID
BRINGING UP IN AN INTERVIEW

1. Salary - at least in the beginning

2. Problems with a former employer

3. Psychological problems

4. Financial problems

5. Medical problems - mine or family

6. Drinking problems

7. Divorce(s)/domestic problems

8. Former bankruptcy

9. Smoking problems

10. Racial or religious matters

11. Politics

12. Age

13. Handicaps

14. Automobile accidents/traffic violations

15. Human rights issues

16. Lawsuits

17. Grievances of any kind

18. Arrest record

19. _____

20. _____

21. _____

22. _____

23. _____

24. _____

25. _____

GOAL-SETTING

The *Random House College Dictionary* defines GOAL as follows: "The result or achievement toward which effort is directed; aim; end. The terminal point in a race...."

The question you have to ask yourself is: "What do I want to do in life and am I willing to go for it?" Your goals must include the skills you need to accomplish what you set out to do. Otherwise, goals may be nothing more than dreams. Having a dream is okay, too, and realizing a dream is a thrill. But you are directing your efforts toward goals at this time.

Most people have given little thought to this question. Ask some of your friends what their goals are for the present, medium- and long-term future, and see what answers you get. By making a conscious effort to keep in mind what you really want, you will be in a better position to steer your life the way a captain moves the tiller of a boat.

The dictionary includes in its definition that a goal is the terminal point in a race. For your goals, keep in mind that it is not arriving that counts so much as the trip. Being happy on a day-to-day basis while you are seeking some medium- or long-term objective is better than achieving a momentary victory.

Many people strive to be Number One in a business or company. They devote long hours, make sacrifices and slowly move up the ladder from entry level to supervision and then into management. When they finally arrive, is it really what they wanted? Without continuous evaluation, a person risks setting an objective that no longer is appropriate a few years later. Then, rather than rethink the position, he or she continues drifting away from the intended purpose and happiness.

You are now in a position to devote some time to thinking about why you are on earth and what you want to do with your life. Once these objectives are put on paper, determine how your career can help you realize your dreams.

In deciding where you want to be, consider factors such as family growth, physical comforts, intellectual challenge, creativity, financial security and personal power.

Here is how our accountant candidate stated his goals for the next five years:

One year from now...

Family Growth: <u>Marry Pam—no children for a while.</u>

Physical Comforts: <u>Move to a larger (higher rent) apartment.</u>

Intellectual Challenge: In a public accounting firm, work with larger clients, or become vice president of finance of a small- to medium-size company.

Creativity: In a public accounting firm, perhaps some marketing for new clients. As vice president of finance, ensure that the company has all the accounting systems up to date.

Financial Security: Would like to be making at least $50,000/year plus car allowance.

Personal Power: In a public accounting firm, be at manager level, have a few people under me. As vice president of finance, have entire department under my responsibility.

Three years from now...

Family Growth: One or two children, no more.

Physical Comforts: Own home, three weeks' vacation.

Intellectual Challenge: Specialize in health-care accounts if in a public accounting firm. As vice president of finance, move up to more decision-making in the company.

Creativity: Public accounting, be responsible for a sector of marketing. Vice president of finance, help company grow and participate more in corporate development.

Financial Security: Earning between $75,000 to $85,000/year plus.

Personal Power: Public accounting, have a department under my direction. Vice president of finance, be admitted to the executive committee.

Five years from now...

Family Growth: No change.

Physical Comforts: Trip to Europe.

Intellectual Challenge: In public accounting, become a partner in charge of health-care clients. As vice president of finance, get involved in mergers and acquisitions.

Creativity: Public accounting, set policy for marketing and hiring a team. As vice president of finance, continue to grow with the company.

Financial Security: Earning more than $100,000/year.

Personal Power: Public accounting, become a senior partner in firm. As vice president of finance, move up to senior vice president or even executive vice president.

He is not sure which direction he wants to pursue. He is focused on either a vice president of finance job in industry or continuing in public accounting. These goals and objectives will be important to refer back to when he finally confronts a live opportunity.

In setting your own goals, you may also have multiple career possibilities. Taking time now to think about being in one or the other of them can help you focus on what you really want to do versus what is possible in the present job market.

NOW, LIST YOUR GOALS FOR EACH OF THESE:

One year from now...

Family Growth: _____

_____

Physical Comforts: _____

_____

Intellectual Challenge: _____

_____

Creativity: _____

_____

Financial Security: _____

_____

Personal Power: _____

_____

Three years from now...

Family Growth: _____

_____

Physical Comforts: _____

_____

Intellectual Challenge: _____

_____

Creativity: _____

_____

Financial Security: _____

_____

Personal Power: _____

_____

Five years from now...

Family Growth: _____

_____

Physical Comforts: _____

_____

Intellectual Challenge: _____

_____

Creativity: _____

_____

Financial Security: _____

_____

Personal Power: _____

_____

These goals are a measure of your value system as you are today. Expect that they will change. Keeping this list handy will let you see these changes and allow you to alter your gameplan to satisfy new goals as they evolve. Change is a natural force. Awareness of your own development will keep you focused on what is important (and most comfortable) for you.

You are now in a position to begin shaping your future.

STRATEGY

When beginning your search, several factors should be examined simultaneously. These are:

1. What about geographic considerations?

2. What is the vertical market and how can it be approached?

3. What is the horizontal market and how can it be approached?

4. What about a complete change of profession?

5. What are the problems in looking for work past age 55?

6. What about buying or starting a business of my own?

7. What about an international job? How can I find out more about this market?

Geographic Considerations

If you are the second breadwinner in your household, you may have some restrictions on your ability to move, especially if your spouse has a good position. For you, geographic planning is critical. Once the number of companies in your industry and within your geographic limits is exhausted, you may need to think about other types of work that utilize your training and experience.

Many candidates have been opportunity-driven, which means wherever the best job was located was where they wanted to go. This is a healthy attitude. Remember, you can always say "No" to an offer. But get it first!

GEOGRAPHIC CONSIDERATIONS

1. Search within 1 to 1-1/2 hours from current home.
2. Search within your state.
3. Search within a grouping of states.
4. Search within the U.S.A.
5. Search international.

- How are you handling each of these considerations?
- Which search will you be making?
- What is your gameplan?

The Vertical Market

The vertical job market involves moving up or down from your present level. Let us look at some possible examples:

YOU ARE	IN A SMALL, MEDIUM OR LARGE FIRM	YOUR TARGET	IN A SMALL, MEDIUM OR LARGE FIRM
Sales Manager	Large	V.P. Sales	Medium or Small
President	Small	V.P. Division	Large
Programmer	Medium	Supervisor	Medium or Small
Production Manager	Large	Prod. Director	Medium or Small
Section Head	Large	Supervisor	Medium or Small
Buyer	Large	Purchasing Agent	Medium or Small
Regional Manager	Large	Country Manager	Medium or Small
etc.			

The key decision here is, do you want to continue working in a large firm or would you feel better being in a smaller operation? There are pros and cons for both, and this question merits your serious consideration. When in doubt, place it on your research list for information networking.

The Horizontal Market

The horizontal market means moving from one industry to another while moving up or down in the hierarchy. Here are some examples:

PRESENT INDUSTRY

(current direction)		(new direction)
Chemicals		Hospitals—Private
Pharmaceuticals		Hospitals—Public
Equipment		Clinics
Supplies	**Healthcare**	Retirement Homes
Import/Export		Veterans Administration
Training		Government
Market Research		Management Consulting
Product Development		Teaching

Consider a candidate from the healthcare industry who was part of a group dismissal. He previously held a market research position. At the time of his layoff, his geographic area was saturated with people looking for healthcare market research positions. By looking at the horizontal market, it became quite apparent that there were many parallel industry sectors he could approach where his experience would help land an interesting position. And he did—as a consultant for one of the large accounting firms that was expanding into healthcare.

While looking up and down, you should also be looking at other related industries that may have a need for your skills.

Complete Change of Professional Activity

There comes a time in almost every career when one thinks: "If I had it to do over again, I would have been...."

Changing professions today is not as uncommon as it was years ago. People burn out and need a change. People have new interests and want to pursue them. There is nothing wrong in making a change.

Some examples of career changes:

Past Position	**New Activity**
Executive Recruiter	Sales Manager

Past Position	New Activity
Consultant for an accounting firm	Chief Executive in a sporting goods firm
Chief Scientist in a high-tech firm	Stockbroker
General Manager of companies	Consultant/Writer
Businessperson	Writer
V.P. Human Resources	Outplacement Counselor/Recruiter
Printing Executive	Marketing Consultant
Medical Doctor	TV Educator

If you are contemplating a career change, be sure of the ground before you. You should investigate as many aspects as possible of the prospective profession before going ahead. In your research networking, you will talk to people already in that profession and learn what it will take for you to make the transition. What are the tradeoffs? Most likely, you will have to make some sacrifices; what are they? Do you have staying power until you can earn enough to support yourself and your family? A little brainstorming will provide you with a long list of questions. With informed answers, you can feel comfortable about making the change.

You might even be able to arrange a tryout by sitting in with someone to see what they do all day long. Other considerations are: What additional training will be needed? Are any licenses required? Are they difficult to obtain? What professional help can you expect along the way? If your critical path involves a radical job change, plan it.

Transferable Skills

As we mature in the work place, jobs come and go. What we learned as young professionals may be totally obsolete today. We can all think of industries and professions that have gone by the wayside. The telex and typesetting industries are good examples; they have been replaced by the facsimile machine and desktop publishing, respectively.

People coming out of declining industries need to get in touch with their basic skills and look at new possibilities. The difference between a later career change and just starting out is that you will be able to learn faster from previous experiences. Fortunately for all, there are many courses, workshops and seminars that can teach us what is required to start over.

Getting Restarted Over 55

If a candidate genuinely believes that he is too old to find employment, he is guaranteed to fail. If you are over 55, out of work—either through retirement or otherwise—and want to return to work, you may have to go through some adjustment. Today there are more young capable people on the market than ever before. Competing with this group on its level is not only foolhardy but downright depressing.

But, keep in mind what older candidates DO have to sell. Experience, of course! Job-seekers over 55 therefore need to look at themselves differently; emphasis must be placed on skills and experience. With the right skills, any candidate at any age can obtain employment. The problem is not one of age, it is one of identifying what the market needs, assessing your skills, enhancing or adding to those skills and marketing yourself as a solution in search of a problem.

If you can find a problem that you can resolve, and with the self-marketing skills you are learning in this manual, you will be in a better position to make a sale.

Never mention that you are "retired" or are "financially settled." Project an attitude that your job search is your number one priority. Be open to different work proposals. Later, you can always select, but get the offer first.

Your resume should show a long list of accomplishments, and be directed to a company concerned more with solid, dependable experience than age. A functional type of resume is ideal for this kind of presentation. (More about this in Chapter 4.)

Selling your experience requires all the job-search techniques in this manual. Strategies may vary. Here are some ideas that you will want to consider:

- Seek problems. Applying your experience to a troubled company can provide affordable solutions for small companies' problems.

- Be willing to consider an immediate short-term assignment rather than holding out for a long-term job. Many short-duration jobs have blossomed into permanent situations as a result of top performance.

- Try offering your services with remuneration based on performance. You will be making an offer that is hard to refuse while gaining the chance to prove your worth.

- If you were working in a department or division that had a specialty that another company could use, you can offer your know-how and, perhaps, bring in a team made up of former associates. Think of competitors or companies that could profit by your knowledge and contacts.

- If you have talent for marketing or sales, you can offer your services for a territory or product not presently covered.

- One technique for showing your expertise creatively is to write a report on an industry, market or product. If the report includes new and valuable information, it could be saleable. Find your subject using research interviews. A good idea may be worth an advance from one or more companies.

- You can work for several companies as a part-time consultant. Your service would be affordable and your earnings would multiply.

Consulting

With pressure from investors to increase revenues and decrease costs, companies have been in a perpetual payroll downsizing mode for the past 15 years. While the economy is improving today, it is clear that companies will continue to operate with tight payroll budgets to keep profit margins up. Although many people have been impacted by these sweeping cuts in personnel, this mass exodus of jobs has given way to a significant rise in consulting opportunities. The reduced payroll budget has been satisfied, but the work still needs to be done. The loophole for company managers has been to hire outside talent, often the very people who were discharged, as consultants. The funds to cover these expenses are not coming from the payroll account!

We have experienced an increasing number of candidates going into consulting. Oftentimes, they report higher yearly earnings from consulting than their former employment. Being a consultant, you can:

- Sell your expertise to a number of clients, minimizing the danger of being totally out of work when you lose one account.

- Often get more money.

- Have freedom to arrange your own work schedule.

- Work from your home.

- Become published in your field.

- Add to and modify your services according to the needs of the market.

- Make alliances with other consulting firms for referrals.

- Expand your territory internationally.

- Not be concerned about age—people now need your know-how.

- Avoid getting caught up in company politics.

Becoming a consultant means that you have to think differently about your professional activity. You need to focus clearly on what the market needs and how you are going to present your skills. Marketing your services will take the same training that you will find in the networking, telephone and interviewing chapters of this manual.

Putting Together a Consulting Brochure

If you have decided to break away from a traditional job and venture out on your own, perhaps a consulting service based on your years of experience in a given field is the way. At times this may be the only option a candidate has considering age, job availability and competition. This works well for the following professions:

Accounting, financial planning, real estate appraising, product design, sales representation, human resources, training, translations, writing, art direction, illustrating, computing/programming, real estate sales, purchasing, security, environmental control, waste management, recruitment, desktop publishing, marketing, manufacturing....

To advertise your business, a simple brochure works better than a resume. However, you will find it easier to create your first business brochure after you have completed your resume. You should collect competitive brochures of people already in this business and you will see what looks good and what needs improving. From your resume, a brochure can follow. A typical brochure can be put together from letter size stationery as follows:

Panel 1

This is the cover of your brochure. It shows the name of your company, e.g., John Smith & Company, John Smith Associates, John Smith Consultants. Underneath the name of your company should be the main theme of your company's activities, e.g., Accounting, Desk Top Publishing, Medical Products Development....

Immediately thereafter should be the key areas of service that you provide followed by your address, telephone, e-mail, facsimile number and Internet site. On the bottom of the cover can be a slogan, if appropriate for your business.

Panel 2

This panel is your biography. It is different from a resume in that it is more of a narrative than a detailed chronological summary. It should highlight your education, years of experience and qualify you in the reader's eyes as an expert in your field. Remember, everything you say should be easily verified. You will note from the samples on the following pages that a brochure biography is written in the third person as if someone was presenting you.

Panel 3

This is a good place to list testimonials or references. Request recommendations from former clients, companies or individuals who have used your services to give you quotable quotes. Wherever possible, it is wise to indicate the source of your reference. If you do not have references that you can include right away, then you can add an additional summary of products or projects that you have worked on.

Sometimes you may wish to include a checklist for the reader, highlighting problems that he may have that you can resolve.

Panels 4/5/6

List the benefits in working with your company. The "Why should I use your company?" has to be evident. Your business will do one or more of the following for your customers:

Increase sales	Improve reliability
Lower costs	Improve morale
Increase profits	Improve employee skills
Improve production time	Develop new business
Do more for less	Expand internationally
Provide part-time expertise	Solve problems
Improve quality	Relieve anxiety
Improve safety	Eliminate stress...

Under each heading listed on the cover, enumerate what services are provided for that category. To emphasize your ability to be of help, you can add accomplishments to show what you have done in the past. Lastly, you may wish to include a statement as to guarantees, and offer your first consultation at no charge.

From this simple format, which can be done easily with a word processor and desktop software, you can print your first business brochure. Check with your local paper supplier. There are paper manufacturers that provide designer papers in small quantities made for this type of brochure already creased for folding to fit in a business size envelope. The manufacturer also offers matching stationery and laser cut business cards that you can print on your home printer. A laser printer is recommended. You need not spend a fortune on printing costs to test-market your concept. Using this approach, you can tailor your brochure to the markets you are prospecting.

Even with the best of brochures, all the principles concerning networking and selling yourself still apply. No matter what business you choose, you must learn to become a salesperson of your services.

Getting More Help

Starting your own business has many facets. You are encouraged to get outside information on business plans, types of businesses to investigate (one of the best reference guides for business ideas is the *Yellow Pages*), managing your finances and setting up your home or initial office. Get additional help from your bankers, the Small Business Administration, Chambers of Commerce and extension courses.

An International Job

It probably is exciting to think about living and working in Paris, London or Rome.

There was a day when American management was regarded as the pinnacle of business leadership around the world. However, in the last twenty years, the numbers of foreign-born students educated and trained in American universities has shot up exponentially. Today, you can find large numbers of foreign-born MBAs from Harvard running businesses in remote areas around the world. The heyday of Americans working abroad is over.

New tax treaties between the IRS and equivalent agencies in foreign countries have all but eliminated the advantages. Tax-exemption laws have swung in every direction, making tax liability unsure for the overseas employee. Exchange rates have fluctuated up to 100 percent and more, while inflation, even though officially reported at a single digit, is in reality out of control.

If you are interested in living and working abroad, learn about the local tax laws in the country of your choice and then see what the IRS position is. Ask around about any anticipated changes in legislation. *This is very important.*

Visit the country that interests you and gain experience first hand. Find out what it costs to live there, how foreigners are regarded in the domestic labor market, what jobs would be open and how to apply, and how difficult it will be for you to learn the language.

While you are traveling, check with the local American embassy and find out if there is an American Chamber of Commerce or American club where you can meet U.S. citizens already working in the market. Talk to these people and ask questions. You will learn more from them than any book on the subject.

Another source of international jobs is the U.S. Department of Commerce. If you are interested in a government-sponsored international job, contact the Department's International Trade Administration. Ask what opportunities are open and how to apply.

A special caution: Unemployment is rampant around the world and particularly in Europe. Be careful of any agency or advertisement claiming it can get you an international job. *Before getting involved with any such agencies, always check their references.*

Layout for Preparing Your First Business Brochure
Chief Financial Officer

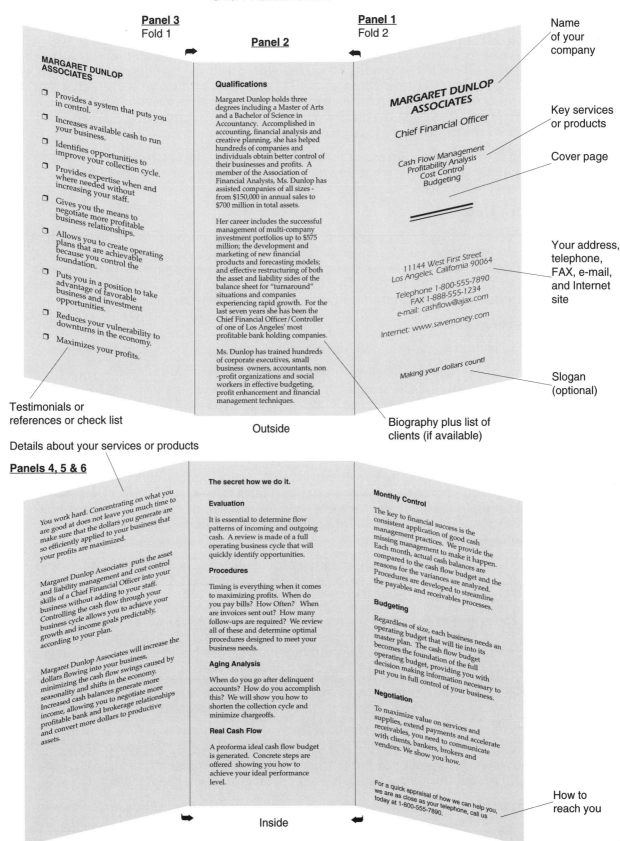

Panel 3
Fold 1

Panel 2

Panel 1
Fold 2

Name of your company

MARGARET DUNLOP ASSOCIATES

☐ Provides a system that puts you in control.

☐ Increases available cash to run your business.

☐ Identifies opportunities to improve your collection cycle.

☐ Provides expertise when and where needed without increasing your staff.

☐ Gives you the means to negotiate more profitable business relationships.

☐ Allows you to create operating plans that are achievable because you control the foundation.

☐ Puts you in a position to take advantage of favorable business and investment opportunities.

☐ Reduces your vulnerability to downturns in the economy.

☐ Maximizes your profits.

Testimonials or references or check list

Qualifications

Margaret Dunlop holds three degrees including a Master of Arts and a Bachelor of Science in Accountancy. Accomplished in accounting, financial analysis and creative planning, she has helped hundreds of companies and individuals obtain better control of their businesses and profits. A member of the Association of Financial Analysts, Ms. Dunlop has assisted companies of all sizes - from $150,000 in annual sales to $700 million in total assets.

Her career includes the successful management of multi-company investment portfolios up to $575 million; the development and marketing of new financial products and forecasting models; and effective restructuring of both the asset and liability sides of the balance sheet for "turnaround" situations and companies experiencing rapid growth. For the last seven years she has been the Chief Financial Officer/Controller of one of Los Angeles' most profitable bank holding companies.

Ms. Dunlop has trained hundreds of corporate executives, small business owners, accountants, non-profit organizations and social workers in effective budgeting, profit enhancement and financial management techniques.

Outside

MARGARET DUNLOP ASSOCIATES

Chief Financial Officer

Cash Flow Management
Profitability Analysis
Cost Control
Budgeting

11144 West First Street
Los Angeles, California 90064

Telephone 1-800-555-7890
FAX 1-888-555-1234
e-mail: cashflow@ajax.com

Internet: www.savemoney.com

Making your dollars count!

Key services or products

Cover page

Your address, telephone, FAX, e-mail, and Internet site

Slogan (optional)

Biography plus list of clients (if available)

Details about your services or products

Panels 4, 5 & 6

You work hard. Concentrating on what you are good at does not leave you much time to make sure that the dollars you generate are so efficiently applied to your business that your profits are maximized.

Margaret Dunlop Associates puts the asset and liability management and cost control skills of a Chief Financial Officer into your business without adding to your staff. Controlling the cash flow through your business cycle allows you to achieve your growth and income goals predictably, according to your plan.

Margaret Dunlop Associates will increase the dollars flowing into your business, minimizing the cash flow swings caused by seasonality and shifts in the economy. Increased cash balances generate more income, allowing you to negotiate more profitable bank and brokerage relationships and convert more dollars to productive assets.

The secret how we do it.

Evaluation

It is essential to determine flow patterns of incoming and outgoing cash. A review is made of a full operating business cycle that will quickly identify opportunities.

Procedures

Timing is everything when it comes to maximizing profits. When do you pay bills? How Often? When are invoices sent out? How many follow-ups are required? We review all of these and determine optimal procedures designed to meet your business needs.

Aging Analysis

When do you go after delinquent accounts? How do you accomplish this? We will show you how to shorten the collection cycle and minimize chargeoffs.

Real Cash Flow

A proforma ideal cash flow budget is generated. Concrete steps are offered showing you how to achieve your ideal performance level.

Monthly Control

The key to financial success is the consistent application of good cash management practices. We provide the missing management to make it happen. Each month, actual cash balances are compared to the cash flow budget and the reasons for the variances are analyzed. Procedures are developed to streamline the payables and receivables processes.

Budgeting

Regardless of size, each business needs an operating budget that will tie into its master plan. The cash flow budget becomes the foundation of the full operating budget, providing you with decision making information necessary to put you in full control of your business.

Negotiation

To maximize value on services and supplies, extend payments and accelerate receivables, you need to communicate with clients, bankers, brokers and vendors. We show you how.

For a quick appraisal of how we can help you, we are as close as your telephone, call us today at 1-800-555-7890.

How to reach you

Inside

CHAPTER 3

Accomplishments

e hear the word "accomplishment" more and more in our everyday language. When someone does something exceptional, people take note. Getting a new job requires ammunition, and this ammunition will come from prior experiences in which you have excelled. This chapter is devoted to uncovering your collection of skills as translated into deeds: your accomplishments.

Accomplishments are the key to your resume, interview and ultimate job offer. We buy something when we are convinced we need it, and the same marketing principle applies to job search. Your ability to show what you have done and what you can do for a prospective employer determines his interest in hiring you over someone else.

What is an accomplishment? It is something you personally did that improved a situation, solved a problem and/or made a contribution either in value or substance.

Your list of accomplishments should cover your entire school and work history. Every experience you can think of that made you stand out or feel good or brought recognition from others should be included. Your list may be very long, and that is good since you will want to reorganize this list in several ways. The first task will be to identify the skills that went into the accomplishment. The second will be to use your accomplishments to create your resume. The third will be to draw upon this reservoir of successful experiences during the interview process.

Think back over your first job experiences. You may have been in school or have had a summer job or contributed to a school project. Carry your list through each job you have had since you began your professional career.

Your list of accomplishments should include instances in which:

1. You solved a problem or handled an emergency situation.

2. You created or built something.

3. You developed an idea.

4. You demonstrated leadership in the face of challenge.

5. You followed instructions and realized a goal.

6. You identified a need and satisfied it.

7. You contributed actively to a decision or a change.

8. You increased sales or profit or reduced costs.

9. You helped somebody realize his objectives.

10. You saved time and/or money.

11. You received an award or special commendation.

Assign numbers or values to the accomplishment and state explicitly what happened as a result of your action. If sales increased by $1 million, or costs came down by 18 percent, or efficiency improved by 33 percent—saving $575,000 over two years—say so!

Here are some other examples:

Sales Accomplishments:

- Realized two new markets for the company's products adding $2 million in new sales over 18 months.

- Launched a new line of products that captured 63 percent of the market in 18 months.

- Designed a marketing plan that increased sales from $8 million to $22 million.

- Hired and trained a new sales team that increased sales by 20 percent and margins by 15 percent.

- Expanded company's customer base by 80 percent and increased sales by 200 percent to more than $10 million through expanded trade show participation.

- Negotiated new distributors in the Western United States resulting in a 40 percent increase in sales the first year.

Financial Accomplishments:

- Installed a new computerized accounting system that saved 50 percent over previous methods and cut the reporting cycle by three weeks.

- Developed a standard cost system to permit better forecasting and provide more accurate controls on operating budgets.

- Provided a realistic means of determining true operating costs by product, thereby permitting appropriate price increases and elimination of unprofitable lines. Savings were in excess of $2 million the first year.

- Reduced audit expenses by 25 percent through better record-keeping.

- Designed and implemented an inventory recording program that saved two days from prior methods and eliminated counting errors.

- Provided weekly cash-flow analyses for management to improve better control of financial resources.

- Negotiated a line of credit one point lower than former lending rates for an annual savings of $150,000.

- Set up a revolving line of credit to replace a fixed-interest loan with a net savings of $200,000.

Manufacturing Accomplishments:

- Reduced costs by 22 percent, saving the company $1.2 million the first year.

- Cut product launching time by six months.

- Found new sources for raw materials, saving 10 percent on purchased materials and amounting to more than $560,000 the first year.

- Negotiated a new union contract within the company's objectives and with no lost time.

- Reduced work force by 12 percent with no loss in production.

- Increased productivity by 22 percent, which helped increase sales by $2 million for the year.

- Introduced a CAM system that cut manufacturing costs by 15 percent and reduced new product development time by two months.

THE ACCOMPLISHMENT

1. What was the problem?

2. What did you do?

3. What skills did you use?

4. What was the benefit for you?

5. What was the benefit for your company?

Your accomplishments will come from:

- Performance

- Savings

- Profits

- Sales

- Efficiency

- New business

- Handling an emergency

- Creativity

- Excellence

- Inventing

- Finding

- Expanding

- Teaching

- Restructuring

Service Accomplishments:

- Processed more than 25 orders per day, resulting in a daily increase of reported sales of $60,000.

- Increased the number of sales calls in the Western States by 15 percent (through reorganization of territory), which added 22 percent to sales the first quarter of the fiscal year.

- Reduced annual operating costs by $3.1 million through better deployment of warehouse facilities.

- Organized press conferences for top management and regional conferences with attendance in the thousands.

- Restructured the employee communications program for a *Fortune 500* company with 38,000 employees.

- Organized three major health-care industry fairs for business and senior-citizen communities in Los Angeles to increase hospital recognition, resulting in a greater demand for the hospital's services and physicians.

- Developed strategic planning for more than 20 hospitals and 10 subsidiaries to maximize return on investment.

- Increased telephone handling capacity for incoming calls by 25 percent.

- Successfully recovered $4.5 million in past-due accounts.

General Management Accomplishments:

- Turned around to profits nine operating divisions in eight months, reversing losses in four countries.

- Provided 33 percent of total corporate profits with only 6 percent of the company's total sales.

- Sold off two divisions that were losing money for a net gain of $588,000.

- Increased sales and profits by 18 percent and 20 percent, respectively, over three years.

- Acquired two subsidiaries that increased the company's profitability by $500,000 the first year.

- Expanded company's activities in Europe, providing export sales of $750,000 over three years at margins higher than domestic levels.

Personnel Relations Accomplishments:

- Hired and trained entire sales team that realized its goal of $1.2 million sales in the first 12 months.

- Set up a management incentive program that contributed to a profit increase of 12 percent the first year.

- Launched a company newsletter, which improved morale.

- Added a computerized data base for employee records, providing better controls with fewer personnel.

- Initiated a safety program that reduced accidents by 12 percent in the first three months.

- Created a management review system as a basis for a new bonus program, resulting in a 10 percent profit increase.

A "good" accomplishment will do one or more of the following:

▶ Increase performance	▶ Improve employee relations
▶ Decrease costs	▶ Improve reliability
▶ Increase profits and/or sales	▶ Streamline operations
▶ Reduce time	▶ Improve strategic planning
▶ Increase efficiency	▶ Turn around losing operations
▶ Expand client base	▶ Eliminate waste
▶ Lower unit costs	▶ Improve working conditions
▶ Provide better controls	▶ Identify and solve problems
▶ Permit better decision making	▶ Solve emergency situations
▶ Help management to manage better than it did before	▶ Introduce new talent through recruitment
▶ Make things more beautiful or functional	▶ Provide service where it did not exist before

The following is a list of ACTION WORDS that can help you write your accomplishments.

VOCABULARY OF ACTION WORDS

Advertising & Promotion

Accounted for	Influenced	Persuaded	Represented
Convinced	Launched	Promoted	Secured
Generated	Marketed	Recommended	Sold
Improved			

Communications

Approved	Edited	Moderated	Presided
Counseled	Facilitated	Participated	Served as
Demonstrated	Instructed	Presented	Wrote
Disseminated	Interviewed		

Creativity

Arranged	Devised	Invented	Reshaped
Conceived	Enabled	Originated	Resolved
Created	Enhanced	Packaged	Solved
Designed	Formulated	Refined	Structured
Developed	Innovated		

Management

Administered	Exceeded	Managed	Retained
Attained	Executed	Masterminded	Revised
Conducted	Expanded	Obtained	Strengthened
Contracted	Headed	Organized	Supervised
Controlled	Implemented	Performed	Trimmed
Coordinated	Incorporated	Produced	Turned Around
Directed	Initiated	Reduced	Undertook
Enacted	Instituted	Repositioned	Was Responsible for
Established	Maintained		

Negotiations

Assured	Evaluated	Mediated	Proposed
Closed	Investigated	Negotiated	Sorted
Determined			

Public Relations & Human Resources

Advised	Employed	Handled	Motivated
Balanced	Facilitated	Hired	Recruited
Collaborated	Grouped	Integrated	Sponsored
Consulted	Guided	Monitored	Strengthened
Counseled			

Research & Analysis

Automated	Differentiated	Investigated	Solved
Classified	Equated	Related	Synthesized
Determined	Experimented	Searched	Theorized
Developed			

Resourcefulness

Accomplished	Diverted	Improved	Solved
Awarded	Eliminated	Pioneered	Strengthened
Corrected	Identified	Rectified	Surpassed

Technique & Authority

Analyzed	Computed	Improvised	Reviewed
Arranged	Decreased	Increased	Revised
Budgeted	Distributed	Indexed	Scheduled
Catalogued	Enlarged	Leveraged	Singlehandedly...
Compared	Examined	Redesigned	Synthesized
Compiled	Expanded	Reorganized	Systematized
Completed	Generated	Restructured	Verified

In listing your accomplishments, include as much detail as possible. Later, when you are working on the resume, you will tighten the description to keep verbiage low. The objective now is to identify and list these accomplishments.

SKILLS

Behind every accomplishment are the skills you used to achieve it. By illuminating your accomplishments, you show a potential employer how your skills can be applied to his business. When he hires you, that is what he is buying!

Look at the ACTION WORDS above and find the skills you used in each of your accomplishments. Skills can be broken down into several areas; the following are a few examples.

Relationships with people:

▶ Selling, negotiating, persuading
▶ Leading, delegating, directing
▶ Supervising, instructing, guiding
▶ Educating, training, communicating
▶ Selecting, recruiting, motivating

Handling information:

▶ Analyzing, reviewing, organizing
▶ Communicating, copying, synthesizing
▶ Creating, designing, compiling
▶ Computing, calculating, collecting
▶ Filing, comparing, storing

Working with systems:

▶ Operating, running, setting
▶ Driving, piloting, directing
▶ Manipulating, controlling, correcting
▶ Creating, designing, producing
▶ Repairing, maintaining, restoring

Do not neglect skills or talents that you have never considered as income-producing. Are you good at building things, writing, public speaking, raising money for your church or painting (just to name a few)? Usually what we enjoy, we do well! We see examples all around us of people who have tapped into their natural talents and gone on to extraordinary careers.

However, having a skill is not enough. You must have the desire and the will to use it. This is where many talented people fall by the wayside. Achieving a mind-set that disciplines talents and develops them is an important part of building a career. No one can do this for you.

The better your skills, the more valuable you are in the marketplace. For new entrants in the job market, your skills will be identified from school projects, courses in which you excelled, hobbies and part-time work.

In the following exercises, identify specific skills that went into each accomplishment. These are the skills you will draw upon in an interview.

Example:

Accomplishment: Hired and trained a new sales team that increased sales by 1.2 million the first year.

What problem were you solving? Existing sales team was not meeting its sales objectives, company was losing money.

What skills and talents did you apply personally? Selecting a winning team, developing people by establishing training programs, identifying and solving problems, leadership.

Now use the following format for your accomplishments:

1. Accomplishment:

What problem were you solving?

What skills and talents did you apply personally?

2. Accomplishment:

What problem were you solving?

What skills and talents did you apply personally?

3. Accomplishment:

What problem were you solving?_____

_____

What skills and talents did you apply personally?_____

_____

4. Accomplishment:_____

_____

What problem were you solving?_____

_____

What skills and talents did you apply personally?_____

_____

5. Accomplishment:_____

_____

What problem were you solving?_____

_____

What skills and talents did you apply personally?_____

_____

6. Accomplishment:_____

_____

What problem were you solving?_____

_____

What skills and talents did you apply personally?_____

_____

7. Accomplishment:_____

What problem were you solving?_____

_____

What skills and talents did you apply personally?_____

_____

8. Accomplishment:_____

_____

What problem were you solving?_____

_____

What skills and talents did you apply personally?_____

_____

9. Accomplishment:_____

_____

What problem were you solving?_____

_____

What skills and talents did you apply personally?_____

_____

10. Accomplishment:_____

_____

What problem were you solving?_____

_____

What skills and talents did you apply personally?_____

_____

11. Accomplishment:_____

What problem were you solving?_____

_____

What skills and talents did you apply personally?_____

_____

12. Accomplishment:_____

_____

What problem were you solving?_____

_____

What skills and talents did you apply personally?_____

_____

13. Accomplishment:_____

_____

What problem were you solving?_____

_____

What skills and talents did you apply personally?_____

_____

14. Accomplishment:_____

_____

What problem were you solving?_____

_____

What skills and talents did you apply personally?_____

_____

15. Accomplishment:_____

What problem were you solving?_____

_____

What skills and talents did you apply personally?_____

_____

16. Accomplishment:_____

_____

What problem were you solving?_____

_____

What skills and talents did you apply personally?_____

_____

17. Accomplishment:_____

_____

What problem were you solving?_____

_____

What skills and talents did you apply personally?_____

_____

18. Accomplishment:_____

_____

What problem were you solving?_____

_____

What skills and talents did you apply personally?_____

_____

19. Accomplishment:_____

What problem were you solving?_____

_____

What skills and talents did you apply personally?_____

_____

20. Accomplishment:_____

_____

What problem were you solving?_____

_____

What skills and talents did you apply personally?_____

_____

CHAPTER 4

The Resume

 n the last two days, you have gone into great detail about what you really want to do and what skills and accomplishments you can use to support your job search. Now we are going to gift-wrap the package.

First of all, understand that the concept of a resume is a myth. Without it, job searchers feel insecure because there is nothing to validate their existence. Without it, the interviewer feels insecure because there is nothing to verify and no script to follow—especially if the interviewer does not know how to interview!

THE REAL PURPOSE OF A RESUME

FACT: The resume is used more often to eliminate than to hire. Consider the ad that draws 400 resumes. What is the first task of the personnel analysts? To cut the pile down to as few as possible! Why? Because many applicants are not qualified but send a resume anyway, hoping it will attract attention. Second, many applicants who do qualify do not know how to market themselves correctly. Third, no one has time to interview 400 candidates. Finally, resumes do not get jobs; people do.

The exercise of creating a resume, however, is valuable. A well-written resume will:

- Fix in *your mind* your skills, accomplishments, work history and education.

- Assist you in networking and getting referrals.

- Provoke interest and get an interview.

- Facilitate a face-to-face presentation.

- Prospect for you outside your geographic area and generate interviews.

The resume is above all a calling card—after the fact—to remind the interviewer who you are. So here is the dilemma: You must create something you hope will be little used, but create it in such a way that if it is used, it will help your campaign!

When a resume is submitted in answer to an ad, you should know that the odds can be more than 400 to one against your being chosen—even for an interview! Suppose you had to select your resume out of a field of 400. How would it stack up? What can be done to put the odds more in your favor?

GETTING READY

Work Experience and Accomplishments

Begin by making a detailed chronological list of your total work experience. This is for your own reference. As simple as it may seem, this list will keep you from forgetting something important in your professional history just when you need it.

Working backwards, complete the following form:

1. Most recent employment: From_____To_____

Company name: _____

Company main address: _____

Your work location (if different from above):_____

Your title: _____

Your superior, name & title: _____

You were responsible for:_____

Your key accomplishments were (refer back to Chapter 3 and indicate appropriate

numbers): _____

Starting salary: _____ Finishing salary: _____

Extra benefits: _____

What attracted you to this job? _____

What was your reason for leaving? _____

Who can be a good reference for you? _____

2. Next most recent employment: From _____ To _____

Company name: _____

Company main address: _____

Your work location (if different from above): _____

Your title: _____

Your superior, name & title: _____

You were responsible for: _____

Your key accomplishments were (refer back to Chapter 3 and indicate appropriate

numbers): _____

Starting salary: _____ Finishing salary: _____

Extra benefits: _____

What attracted you to this job? _____

What was your reason for leaving? _____

Who can be a good reference for you? _____

3. Next most recent employment: From _____ To _____

Company name: _____

Company main address: _____

Your work location (if different from above): _____

Your title: _____

Your superior, name & title: _____

You were responsible for: _____

Your key accomplishments were (refer back to Chapter 3 and indicate appropriate

numbers): _____

Starting salary: _____ Finishing salary: _____

Extra benefits: _____

What attracted you to this job? _____

What was your reason for leaving? _____

Who can be a good reference for you? _____

4. Next most recent employment: From _____To _____

Company name: _____

Company main address: _____

Your work location (if different from above): _____

Your title: _____

Your superior, name & title: _____

You were responsible for: _____

Your key accomplishments were (refer back to Chapter 3 and indicate appropriate

numbers): _____

Starting salary: _____ Finishing salary: _____

Extra benefits: _____

What attracted you to this job? _____

What was your reason for leaving? _____

Who can be a good reference for you? _____

5. Next most recent employment: From _____To _____

Company name: _____

Company main address: _____

Your work location (if different from above): _____

Your title: _____

Your superior, name & title: _____

You were responsible for: _____

Your key accomplishments were (refer back to Chapter 3 and indicate appropriate

numbers): _____

Starting salary: _____ Finishing salary: _____

Extra benefits: _____

What attracted you to this job? _____

What was your reason for leaving? _____

Who can be a good reference for you? _____

6. Next most recent employment: From _____ To _____

Company name: _____

Company main address: _____

Your work location (if different from above): _____

Your title: _____

Your superior, name & title: _____

You were responsible for: _____

Your key accomplishments were (refer back to Chapter 3 and indicate appropriate

numbers): _____

Starting salary: _____ Finishing salary: _____

Extra benefits: _____

What attracted you to this job? _____

What was your reason for leaving? _____

Who can be a good reference for you? _____

7. Next most recent employment: From _____ To _____

Company name: _____

Company main address: _____

Your work location (if different from above): _____

Your title: _____

Your superior, name & title: _____

You were responsible for: _____

Your key accomplishments were (refer back to Chapter 3 and indicate appropriate

numbers): _____

Starting salary: _____ Finishing salary: _____

Extra benefits: _____

What attracted you to this job? _____

What was your reason for leaving? _____

Who can be a good reference for you? _____

8. Next most recent employment: From _____ To _____

Company name: _____

Company main address: _____

Your work location (if different from above): _____

Your title: _____

Your superior, name & title: _____

You were responsible for: _____

Your key accomplishments were (refer back to Chapter 3 and indicate appropriate

numbers): _____

Starting salary: _____ Finishing salary: _____

Extra benefits: _____

What attracted you to this job? _____

What was your reason for leaving? _____

Who can be a good reference for you? _____

9. Next most recent employment: From _____ To _____

Company name: _____

Company main address: _____

Your work location (if different from above): _____

Your title: _____

Your superior, name & title: _____

You were responsible for: _____

Your key accomplishments were (refer back to Chapter 3 and indicate appropriate

numbers): _____

Starting salary: _____ Finishing salary: _____

Extra benefits: _____

What attracted you to this job? _____

What was your reason for leaving? _____

Who can be a good reference for you? _____

10. Next most recent employment: From _____ To _____

Company name: _____

Company main address: _____

Your work location (if different from above): _____

Your title: _____

Your superior, name & title: _____

You were responsible for: _____

Your key accomplishments were (refer back to Chapter 3 and indicate appropriate

numbers): _____

Starting salary: _____ Finishing salary: _____

Extra benefits: _____

What attracted you to this job? _____

What was your reason for leaving? _____

Who can be a good reference for you? _____

11. Next most recent employment: From _____ To _____

Company name: _____

Company main address: _____

Your work location (if different from above): _____

Your title: _____

Your superior, name & title: _____

You were responsible for: _____

Your key accomplishments were (refer back to Chapter 3 and indicate appropriate

numbers): _____

Starting salary: _____ Finishing salary: _____

Extra benefits: _____

What attracted you to this job? _____

What was your reason for leaving? _____

Who can be a good reference for you? _____

12. Next most recent employment: From _____ To _____

Company name: _____

Company main address: _____

Your work location (if different from above): _____

Your title: _____

Your superior, name & title: _____

You were responsible for: _____

Your key accomplishments were (refer back to Chapter 3 and indicate appropriate

numbers): _____

Starting salary: _____ Finishing salary: _____

Extra benefits: _____

What attracted you to this job? _____

What was your reason for leaving? _____

Who can be a good reference for you? _____

13. Next most recent employment: From _____ To _____

Company name: _____

Company main address: _____

Your work location (if different from above): _____

Your title: _____

Your superior, name & title: _____

You were responsible for: _____

Your key accomplishments were (refer back to Chapter 3 and indicate appropriate

numbers): _____

Starting salary: _____ Finishing salary: _____

Extra benefits: _____

What attracted you to this job? _____

What was your reason for leaving? _____

Who can be a good reference for you? _____

14. Next most recent employment: From _____ To _____

Company name: _____

Company main address: _____

Your work location (if different from above): _____

Your title: _____

Your superior, name & title: _____

You were responsible for: _____

Your key accomplishments were (refer back to Chapter 3 and indicate appropriate

numbers): _____

Starting salary: _____ Finishing salary: _____

Extra benefits: _____

What attracted you to this job? _____

What was your reason for leaving? _____

Who can be a good reference for you? _____

15. Next most recent employment: From _____ To _____

Company name: _____

Company main address: _____

Your work location (if different from above): _____

Your title: _____

Your superior, name & title: _____

You were responsible for: _____

Your key accomplishments were (refer back to Chapter 3 and indicate appropriate

numbers): _____

Starting salary: _____ Finishing salary: _____

Extra benefits: _____

What attracted you to this job? _____

What was your reason for leaving? _____

Who can be a good reference for you? _____

Summary of your education:

Elementary school: _____ Year graduated: _____

High school: _____ Year graduated: _____

High school diploma or certificate: _____

College: _____ Dates: _____

Course of study: _____

College: _____ Dates: _____

Course of study: _____

Degrees received: _____ Date: _____

_____ Date: _____

_____ Date: _____

Licenses for: _____ Date: _____

_____ Date: _____

Honors: _____

_____

Special Training: _____

School: _____ Date: _____ Certificate: _____

School: _____ Date: _____ Certificate: _____

Special Talents:

a. Languages: (degree of fluency)

    Written: _____

    Spoken: _____

    Read: _____

b. Other skills: (programming, word processing, writing, etc.)

_____

_____

_____

Associations:

    Professional: _____

_____

    Social: _____

_____

Hobbies/Sports: _____

_____

Congratulations! You have already done a great deal of valuable work and it will make the rest of your job that much easier.

FORMAT OF A RESUME

There are three formats widely used today: Chronological, Functional and a mixture of the two called THE PERFORMANCE RESUME. The resume format you choose should be flexible enough to allow modification depending on the job you are going after.

The Functional Resume

The functional resume presents accomplishments and work experience arranged according to function or responsibilities without real attention to chronological order.

Advantages:

- If you have had a number of jobs in a short period of time, a functional style can help by highlighting skills and accomplishments rather than focusing on your changes.

- If your most recent experience does not relate to the position for which you are applying, a functional resume will focus more on your past strengths.

- If your most recent position is inferior to your earlier jobs, a functional resume will keep this in the background.

- The functional format permits you to group a number of different accomplishments into one area of expertise. The employer can look at your abilities in light of job requirements without thought of titles or former positions.

Disadvantages:

- Employers and personnel managers are used to a chronological presentation of work history. Deviation from this format can arouse suspicion, if not confusion.

- It is not an easy resume to prepare and it must change to match each job objective.

- You must be careful that you are communicating exactly what you intend. You must address the questions: What specialty am I highlighting? How can this employer use me?

JACK WILSON
1234 Fifth Avenue
New York, New York 10017
(212) 555-3344   e-mail: jwilson@aol.com

SALES EXECUTIVE: Ten years' international experience in sales, marketing, advertising, promotion and general management. Hired and trained both the European and Asian sales forces for companies dealing in technical products.

SALES	Increased sales over three years by 22% resulting in a $2.3 million profit increase.
	Launched five new products in Asia and sold manufacturing licenses to Japanese firms.
	Opened sales offices in Japan, France and Germany and fully staffed each.
TRAINING	Recruited and trained 21 salespeople for a line of industrial building supplies. The team outperformed all other sales staff in the company.
MARKETING	Conducted market studies in advance of new product introduction. Supervised collection and interpretation of data indicating the most cost-effective methods to launch new lines.
	Opened new distribution channels in South America, resulting in a 12% increase of sales for the Western Hemisphere.
MANAGEMENT	Singlehandedly surveyed European market and set up sales offices under budget which became profitable six months after opening.
WORK HISTORY	**Director - International Sales** Rockland Industries, New York, New York, 1994-1996
	Director of Marketing White Manufacturing Co., Newark, New Jersey, 1991-1993
	Import-Export Manager Blake Trading Co., New York, New York, 1987-1990
	Salesman for a number of industrial products companies 1980-1987
EDUCATION	**Bachelor of Science**, Marketing New York University, New York, New York

- You may still be asked to give chronological detail when you complete the traditional personnel application.

The Chronological Resume

The chronological resume lists positions by date, beginning with the most recent. Emphasis is placed on recent experience rather than past history, and usually a progression in responsibility is indicated. Each job listing should show: company name and location, dates of employment, job title(s), main responsibilities and key accomplishments.

Advantages:

- This is an easy resume to organize.

- For many years this has been the standard format and consequently it is the most familiar.

- It shows progress made in your field of specialization as well as increasing responsibility.

- If you have been in one company a long time with a number of promotions, it shows stability.

Disadvantages:

- If you have changed jobs frequently, it shows instability and will require explanation.

- Any gaps in employment stand out.

- If you have changed professions or career direction, it may raise questions about your real goals.

- Your key accomplishments are buried in different job situations, preventing focus on your real talents.

- If your last position was not an important one in your career, you may be associated with it anyway.

The Performance Resume

I prefer a mixed chronological-functional format incorporating a powerful up-front section, called The 20-Second Resume, which is designed to attract the reader's attention immediately. It combines accomplishments into functional areas and places up front your greatest accomplishments in relation to the position you are targeting.

JACK WILSON
1234 Fifth Avenue
New York, New York 10017

(212) 555-3344
e-mail: jwilson@aol.com

SALES EXECUTIVE: Ten years' experience in international sales, marketing, advertising, promotion and general management. Hired and trained both European and Asian sales forces for companies dealing in technical products.

EXPERIENCE

ROCKLAND INDUSTRIES INC., New York, New York   1994-1996

   Director of International Sales

Responsible for building materials sales offices located in Asia, Europe and South America with sales of $38 million. Directly supervised a staff of four people. Opened and staffed new sales offices in Japan, France and Germany.

WHITE MANUFACTURING COMPANY, Newark, New Jersey   1991-1993

   Director of Marketing

Directed market support activities for manufacturer of industrial building supplies. Recruited and trained staff of 21, which later outperformed all other company sales groups.

BLAKE TRADING COMPANY, New York, New York   1987-1990

   Import-Export Manager

Conducted market studies keyed to introduction of new products for a construction supplies company. Supervised collection and interpretation of data indicating the most cost-effective methods to launch new lines. Opened new distribution channels in South America resulting in a 12% increase in sales for the Western Hemisphere. Singlehandedly surveyed the European market and set up offices that conformed to plan and were profitable six months after opening.

BC CONSTRUCTION SUPPLIES INC., Mt. Vernon, New York   1985-1987

   Salesman - Supplies

Recruited for overseas markets. Launched five new products in Asia and closed deals for manufacturing licenses to Japanese firms.

STONE MANUFACTURING INC., New York, New York   1982-1985

   Salesman

Responsible for the entire East Coast sales territory as well as for exports to Latin America for a building supplies company. Increased sales by 22%, resulting in a $2.3 million profit increase over three years.

MURPHY SUPPLIES, Brooklyn, New York   1980-1982

   Salesman

Began career in construction materials retail sales and progressed to outside sales representative for the Greater New York area. Voted "Salesman of the Year," 1982.

EDUCATION

NEW YORK UNIVERSITY, New York, New York

   Bachelor of Science - Marketing, 1978

Military Service: U.S. Army, Staff Sergeant, 1978-1980

Advantages:

- It immediately highlights your strengths.

- It is extremely flexible.

- It maximizes your chances of catching a reader's interest.

- You can adapt the resume to suit the job you are going after without sacrificing quality.

- It permits you to display originality in your ideas and manner of presentation.

- You can lead the reader in the direction you want to go in terms of your skills and accomplishments.

- It permits maximum utilization of the ABC principle: Accomplishments (A)= Benefits (B) to be Converted (C) by the candidate to fill a need.

- It permits you to describe yourself in better marketing terms.

Disadvantages:

- Putting together this resume takes know-how.

A GOOD PERFORMANCE RESUME HAS THE FOLLOWING:

+   **Name and address**

+   **Telephone number and perhaps an office, FAX and message number**

+   **An e-mail address and, if appropriate, an Internet home page**

+   **An opening statement that gives a summary of your overall professional capabilities**

+   **Two to four major accomplishments**

+   **A statement that describes the way you like to work, what kind of person you are and your expertise**

Employment History (reverse chronological order)

> Company
> Dates of Employment
> Your Title(s) and Date(s)
> Accomplishments and/or Responsibilities

+ = the 20-Second Resume

Prior Experience (if pertinent)

Education (if pertinent)

> School(s)
> City, State
> Degree(s) or Certificate(s), Date(s)

Affiliations (only if they contribute something directly to your search)

Note: *You should NOT include in any resume:*

> *References or the statement "References Available"*
> *Salary or requirements*
> *Hobbies or sports unless pertinent*
> *Affiliations, if not pertinent to your search*
> *Marital status, number of children, health, age, color, race,*
> *nationality, information about parents, political party, handicaps,*
> *any legal problems....*

+ = the 20-Second Resume

The 20-Second Resume

Most people who read resumes do not! Most resume "readers" glance over the resume and quickly grab onto one or two items of interest and, if the candidate is present, use these items to break into the interview.

One reason is that most resumes are boring—certainly for the reader and probably for the poor candidate as well.

The average attention span of a resume screener is all of 20 seconds! That is not a long time, especially if you have given the reader a two-page resume.

Look at the summary above, which lists the contents of a good performance resume. The elements of the 20-Second Resume are labeled with "+" marks.

Use the following outline:

PERFORMANCE
RESUME OUTLINE

FIRST NAME, MIDDLE INITIAL, LAST NAME   HOME TELEPHONE NUMBER
STREET ADDRESS   BUSINESS AND/OR MESSAGE (if practical)
CITY, STATE, ZIP   FAX, E-MAIL, INTERNET ADDRESS (if available)

+ I.   Opening statement that gives a summary of your overall professional capabilities.

+ II.   ▪ A Major Professional Accomplishment
             ▪ A Major Professional Accomplishment
             ▪ A Major Professional Accomplishment

+ III.   A short description of the way you like to work (management style), what kind
          of person you are and your expertise.

IV.   **Accomplishments**

Specific   ▪ Two or three accomplishments that back up each specific function
Function   ▪
(optional)   ▪
                  ▪

V.   **Professional Experience**
                    (work backwards from your most recent experience)

Company   Dates
City, State

Title

Responsibilities and/or Additional Accomplishments

VI.   **Prior Experience**

VII.   **Education**

College
City, State
Degree(s), Date(s)
Specialization (optional)
Languages (if applicable)
Special Licenses/Permits (if any)

VIII.   **Other Items (only if pertinent)**

Awards/Honors (if any)
Publications (if any)
Patents (if any)
Affiliations

+ = the 20-Second Resume

RESUME REVIEW

I. Your Opening Statement/summary of your overall professional capabilities should lead the reader in the direction you want him to go, e.g., your specialty, your years of expertise. Your objective should be expressed in this single line.

For example:

1. **Nine years of management and consulting experience in strategic and financial planning, financial controls and systems development for leading health-care organizations.**

Or,

2. **A seasoned, versatile executive with a highly successful track record in brand and sales management, market research, consumer promotion, new product management and strategic planning.**

The first example tells us we are looking at a generalist who has worked as a consultant, primarily in health-care organizations. His skills are on the financial side, with strong emphasis on planning.

The second example shows a specialist in sales and marketing who has a lot of experience and has some important accomplishments that he will be telling you about later in his resume. His specialty is in building brand sales performance through market research—advertising with emphasis on planning.

II. Your Two-to-Four Best Accomplishments will now be utilized in the Major Professional Accomplishments section.

Action Words (Chapter 3) are vital in directing the reader to your accomplishments. Accordingly, these words should be chosen carefully.

Your major accomplishments should support by action and deed your claim to fame. Action words punctuate the accomplishment in the reader's mind.

The object here is to convert an accomplishment to a benefit that you hope will be tied to a need. Once the need connection is made, the reader will think of you as someone who can repeat the accomplishment.

III. Following major accomplishments should be a **Short Description of the Way You Like to Work** (management style) and some reflection of your personality.

For example:

1. A creative, articulate achiever with excellent organizational, analytical and interpersonal skills.

Or,

2. A natural leader with strong interpersonal skills who enjoys team work in an environment of creativity and constant challenge.

Items I, II and III make up the 20-Second Resume. In just a few lines, the reader has been told a lot about this candidate. The format shows his years of experience by activity and industry, and implies where the candidate can do the most good for a prospective employer. This top performer is humanized by showing a little about the candidate's personality and preferred management style.

If you work hard on this part of your resume, the rest will fall into place and make it truly an effective selling tool. Your 20-Second Resume will also become the basis of Broadcast Letters, as you will see in the samples found in Appendix B.

IV. In this section, continue with **More Accomplishments**. These will support your work history and reinforce the statements made in your 20-Second Resume.

Some candidates prefer to group their accomplishments into SPECIFIC FUNCTIONS. There is nothing wrong with this, provided the candidate really has some excellent accomplishments to put in each category. This kind of grouping usually is done by people who have been working a long time and have accumulated a number of important accomplishments.

You will find a list of specific functions that you may want to consider if you decide to use these headings on the following page.

V. Professional Experience

Refer to the list you made earlier in this chapter concerning work history. This part should be brief and add only new material, not repeat accomplishments already mentioned. Discuss the size of your company, its sales, key products and number of employees, if there is space. Your final resume *should not* exceed two pages. (Note: A trick to get more information into a resume is to print it in "Elite" type. There is an example of a two-page resume compressed into one page at the end of this chapter.) Refer to the resume samples in Appendix A for ideas.

A Selection of Possible Specific Functions

Engineering and Manufacturing

Cost Effective Planning
Costing
Customer Relations
Facilities Planning
Industrial Engineering
MRP Inventory Control
Performance Review
Product Design

Production Control
Productivity
Project Planning
Prototype Production
Purchasing Management
Quality Control
Setting Standards
Sourcing

Financial

Audit
Banking Relations
Budget Preparation and Control
Cash Management
Cost Control
Credit Management

Divestitures
Financing
Merger and Acquisitions
Strategic Planning
Tax Analysis
Tax Planning

Human Resources

Benefits Program
Compensation Management
Counseling
Employee Relations
Industrial Relations

Labor Relations
Outplacement
Professional Staffing
Recruitment
Training Programs

Management

Contracts Management
Contracts Negotiation
Corporate Planning
Crises Management
Facilities Management
General Management
International

Management Controls
Management Information Systems
Methods and Control Systems
Operations
Problem Solving
Research and Development
Training Management

Marketing, Sales, Advertising and Communications

Account Management
Advertising
Catalog Preparation
Marketing and Sales
Merchandising
New Business Development
New Product Development

Promotion
Public Affairs
Public Relations
Radio, TV and Film
Sales Service
Training

VI. Prior Experience

If you have had a long career with a number of different employers, cut your chronological presentation after going back 15-20 years and combine your experiences into one category, PRIOR EXPERIENCE. Cover your entire work history but concentrate on the most recent events.

The further you go back in time, the less detail you should give. It is important that you focus your reader on recent accomplishments that can be related to immediate need. Being an expert in electronics ten years ago is not the same as being one today.

However, your PRIOR EXPERIENCE may be pertinent if there have not been too many changes in technology, products, manufacturing processes, etc.

Look at two examples of "Prior Experience" paragraphs:

Sales Director for a medical products company. Responsible for 18 reps and sales of $6.8 million. Directed a family-owned pharmacy for three years with an annual sales growth in excess of 20% each year. As a hospital trainee (part-time), maintained all medical supplies inventory for three floors and saved $10,000.

Or,

General Manager for an electric motor firm with sales of $20 million. Foreman for a precision machine shop doing high integrity machining. Draftsman (part-time) while attending school.

These "Prior Experience" paragraphs do not take up much space, yet show that you were active and growing even early on in your career.

Make several drafts of your resume. While you are working, refer to the samples on the following pages. These samples are actual resumes (with minor changes) that produced results in arousing interest for an interview. If you expect more from a resume, you are in for a disappointment. At best, when you send a resume in response to an ad or in a mail campaign, you are only sending a very limited indication of your overall potential.

SOME BASIC GUIDELINES

These rules will help you create your resume:

1. Focus on accomplishments, skills and results.

2. Never include statements or accomplishments that cannot be proven.

JACK WILSON
1234 Fifth Avenue
New York, New York 10017

(212) 555-3344
e-mail: jwilson@aol.com

Ten years' international experience in sales, marketing, advertising, promotions and general management. Hired and trained both European and Asian sales forces for a number of companies dealing with technical products.

- Increased sales by 22%, resulting in a $2.3 million profit increase over three years.

- Launched five new products in Asia and sold manufacturing licenses to Japanese firms.

- Opened sales offices in Japan, France and Germany and fully staffed each.

A versatile sales executive who knows how to create overseas sales, from originating products to opening successful sales offices. A proven professional who has personally sold millions of dollars of products with high profit levels.

ACCOMPLISHMENTS

- Recruited and trained 21 salespeople for a line of industrial building supplies. The team outperformed all other sales staff in the company.

- Conducted market studies in advance of new product introduction. Supervised the collection and interpretation of data which indicated the most cost-effective methods to launch new lines.

- Opened new distribution channels in South America which resulted in a 12% sales increase for the Western Hemisphere.

- Singlehandedly surveyed the European market and set up sales offices under budget which were profitable six months after opening.

EXPERIENCE

ROCKLAND INDUSTRIES INC., New York, New York   1994-1996

Director of International Sales

Responsible for building materials sales offices located in Asia, Europe and South America with sales of $38 million. Directly supervised a staff of four.

JACK WILSON   **Page 2**

WHITE MANUFACTURING COMPANY, Newark, New Jersey   1991-1993

Director of Marketing

Directed all market support activities for a producer of industrial building supplies.

BLAKE TRADING COMPANY, New York, New York   1987-1990

Import-Export Manager

Responsible for construction supplies overseas sales with emphasis on South America and Europe.

BC CONSTRUCTION SUPPLIES INC., Mt. Vernon, New York   1985-1987

Salesman-Supplies

Recruited staff to open overseas markets.

STONE MANUFACTURING INC., New York, New York   1982-1985

Salesman

Responsible for building supplies sales on the East Coast as well as exports to Latin America.

MURPHY SUPPLIES, Brooklyn, New York   1980-1982

Salesman

Started sales career in construction materials retail operations, progressing to outside sales representative for the Greater New York area. Voted "Salesman of the Year" for 1982.

EDUCATION

NEW YORK UNIVERSITY, New York, New York

Bachelor of Science - Marketing, 1978

Military Service: U.S. Army, Staff Sergeant, 1978-1980

3. Keep sentences short and punchy.

4. Your resume should be attractive and easy to read: good spacing, margins and bold printing. Avoid overcrowding.

5. Do not use abbreviations when there could be doubt as to meaning. Be clear and precise.

6. Keep it short. A good resume will be as short as possible, certainly not longer than two pages and, if possible, one page.

7. Do not use personal pronouns (I/we).

8. Use ACTION WORDS to describe each accomplishment.

9. Whenever possible, show results in numbers.

10. Even though referring to the examples here, try to be original. Avoid exaggerations and flowery terms. The world has seen enough of the expression "results-oriented executive!" A little originality will go a long way. (See Larry's resume on page 102.)

11. If you have a sense of humor, let it show a little in your resume. A resume that can reflect your real personality is a wonder. While photos are not generally encouraged, if your physical appearance would be a plus to your candidacy, include a nice, clean-cut snapshot. But do this only after testing the idea with some friends in the industry. Ask how they feel about it.

12. Some people like to show exact starting dates, including the month. The preference is to show only the year you started or terminated a position. If there have been promotions during the period of employment, those dates can be shown in parentheses next to each job title. If you are still on the company's payroll, even though you may not be physically at the office, you can put down starting date to Present, e.g., 1990 to Present.

13. There is no reason to burden a resume with a lot of inconsequential data. There should be only enough information to provoke the reader's interest. Any more only loads it down and can actually do more harm than good.

14. The employer will ask: "Does this person have the kind of talent I am seeking?" If the resume does not convey a certain level of competence in the employer's area of interest, there will be no invitation to interview.

15. Candidates without much work experience, or who are tackling their first job search, must change "Accomplishments" to "Skills" (see Chapter 3).

Example:

Fully knowledgeable in programming using Java.

Or,

Completed with honors five years of French study; fully bilingual, written and spoken.

Or,

Successfully completed course work and two case study problems on refinancing a $20 million company.

Or,

Organized from scratch a company for the sale and rental of sailboats at Marina Del Rey in Summer of '96. It netted $17,500 in just 60 days.

The just-out-of-school candidate is showing his potential in a way that still incorporates the ABC formula: Skills + some Accomplishment (A) = Benefit (B) to be Converted (C) by the candidate—which could fill a need.

16. Test your resume before launching it on the market. Ask your friends, former supervisor (if you can), business associates and others to give you their impressions.

The last exercise will give you some genuine feedback. Keep in mind that you may run into people who will want you to put in such items as personal data, salary and job objective, which were customarily included back in the '70s. Politely sit on those recommendations. But watch out for interpretation. Is your message getting through? That is the key. Is your resume interesting? A boring resume is full of clichés, redundancies and general statements that mean so much they mean nothing.

This exercise also gives you a low-pressure head start on NETWORKING. Networking will be one of your most powerful tools for getting your next job. You can begin it informally with this question: "Frank, I've just completed a draft of my resume, and I value your opinion a lot. Can we get together for a few minutes so I can have your thoughts about it? How about Tuesday at the end of the day?"

Believe it or not, with that first appointment, you are on your way to networking.

You have now put together your accomplishments, you have outlined your job history and you certainly have some thoughts about your 20-Second Resume. Now you can write your first draft resume.

(Items in parentheses are only instructions)

(Name) _____   Residence (   ) _____

(Address) _____   Cellular/Messages (   ) _____

(City, State, Zip) _____   FAX (   ) _____

e-mail (   ) _____

(Opening statement) _____

_____

(Accomplishment) • _____

_____

(Accomplishment) • _____

_____

(Accomplishment) • _____

_____

(Second Statement) _____

_____

Accomplishments
(Specific functions optional)

(Accomplishment) • _____

_____

(Accomplishment) • _____

_____

(Accomplishment) • _____

_____

(Accomplishment) • _____

_____

(Accomplishment) • _____

_____

Experience
(work in reverse chronological order)

(Company Name) _____ (Dates of Employment) _____

(City, State) _____

(Your job title) _____

(Responsibilities and/or additional accomplishments) _____

_____

(Company Name) _____ (Dates of Employment) _____

(City, State) _____

(Your job title) _____

(Responsibilities and/or additional accomplishments) _____

_____

(Company name) _____ (Dates of employment) _____

(City, State) _____

(Your job title) _____

(Responsibilities and/or additional accomplishments) _____

_____

(Company name) _____ (Dates of employment) _____

(City, State) _____

(Your job title) _____

(Responsibilities and/or additional accomplishments) _____

_____

(Company name) _____ (Dates of employment) _____

(City, State) _____

(Your job title) _____

(Responsibilities and/or additional accomplishments) _____

_____

(Company name) _____ (Dates of employment) _____

(City, State) _____

(Your job title) _____

(Responsibilities and/or additional accomplishments) _____

_____

Prior Experience (if appropriate)

_____

Education

(College or University) _____

(City, State) _____

(Degree earned, year *) _____

(Specialization, optional) _____

(Languages, if appropriate) _____

(Special licenses, permits, certificates, affiliations, awards, presentations—only if pertinent)

_____

* If your graduation date or years of attendance go back beyond 25 years, you may wish to leave dates out.

Your resume is a snapshot of you. You must feel comfortable with it as a selling tool. If it does not present you at your best, go over it again (and again if necessary), and get it right.

USING YOUR COMPUTER FOR JOB SEARCH

Computers have become a way of life for everyone. Graduates coming on the job market have been exposed to PCs and MACs at an early age. They usually know several programs including how to navigate the World Wide Web (WWW). However, there are many older workers who missed getting in on the rush to automation and are still novices at the mystique of computers.

The job-seeker and career-changer can use computers for:

- Preparing resumes
- Writing broadcast letters and responding to advertised job opportunities
- Conducting personalized mail campaigns to lists of addresses at one time (mail merge)
- Contact management
- Prospecting for job leads using the Internet
- Responding electronically to job listings
- Using the Internet to obtain information about companies, products, business ideas, locations, and people

Getting Ready

If you are new to computers, now is the time to learn what you need to know to help yourself become more efficient in your job search.

Your first objective is to locate a PC or MAC for training. A friend with a home computer can be a big help to you at this time. There are also job clubs, schools and libraries that have computer rooms for members' use. Your previous employer may let you use a computer after hours. Your objective is to locate a computer that you can try out.

Before going forward with any computer, you must feel comfortable typing on a keyboard. There are programs on the market that make it so easy, you will think that you are playing an arcade game.

► Computers do not need to be expensive, and the purchase could be a tax deduction. It is a buyer's market. Every month there are newer and better units coming on the market. This means that last year's models have already become today's bargains. If you are not familiar with equipment, you should have someone knowledgeable help you make a selection. Bench test used equipment to be sure there are no hidden problems.

A set-up with last year's model computer, monitor, laser printer, and modem should be a fraction of the cost of new equipment and will most likely include lots of loaded software. Be sure to include the latest versions of popular anti-virus and hard disk utilities programs.

If you purchase new equipment, make sure that service is included. Call the company's technical support hotline as if you already had their unit. If they keep you waiting more than 10 minutes or give you the runaround, you should not purchase from that company. A local purchase from a company you know is more prudent.

Learning Programs

Whether you purchase a PC or MAC, take the time to learn the computer's operating system. Everything that follows will be easier and more understandable.

Basic to all your writing needs will be a good word processor. Using a popular program has its merits for your job search and later when you are on the job.

Popular word processors come with a tutorial module. You can save yourself money and time if you follow the tutorial page by page. Unfortunately, most computer users do not take the time to learn the basics and then have problems with crashes and lost data. Do not make this mistake.

Preparing Resumes, Letters and Mail Merges

First and foremost, you need to write an outstanding resume following the guidelines and examples in this manual.

In setting up your resume on a PC or MAC, first type the text into the document. Do not be concerned with formatting at the beginning. Content is your primary concern.

To format your resume, here are some guidelines that will make your life easier no matter which word processor you use.

1. Justify your document to left and right margins.

2. Become familiar with using and setting tab markers. This is preferred to doing tabs manually.

3. Select an easy-to-read font. Popular fonts are Helvetica, Arial, Bookman, and Times. Do not mix fonts or point sizes. Stay with one for the entire document. Most resumes have point sizes of 10, 11 or 12.

4. Use bold and italics sparingly. The more you change a font style, the more confused your document becomes. Beginners have a tendency to use too many fonts. Your resume should be pleasing to the eye, inviting someone to read it.

5. To create additional space on your resume, you can reduce the font size of the spaces between lines. If you do this, be consistent.

6. Always spell-check your documents before final printing.

7. Have at least two people proofread your resume to make sure that it is easy to understand and clear with good grammar.

8. Read your resume and letters out loud. If it sounds good, in all probability it is good.

9. Letters should be short and to the point. The best letters are not more than one page. Never send a resume without a cover letter.

10. Letters to lists of target companies or selected contacts can be done with mail merge. Mail merge commands vary depending on your software. Your word processor tutorial will show you how.

Contact Management

Any successful job search will require meeting a lot of people. Using a contact management program will be a big help.

These programs permit you to enter names, addresses, telephone numbers and other pertinent information about the people you meet. You can use this data later to create mailing lists, telephone directories and even correspondence, directly from the contact manager.

To find the best contact managers, ask around. Some software companies have free demos of their programs that you can try before buying. See page 327 for a free demo offer of Super Search™ Software.

Getting Job Leads Electronically

Every job-seeker and career-changer needs to identify job opportunities. While the highest quality leads come from networking, there is a new, rapidly growing arena where you can obtain job listings from every corner of the globe.

For a number of years, associations and organizations have been using electronic bulletin boards to post job opportunities as well as a multitude of classified advertisements. Using electronic bulletin boards to advertise jobs expanded to major corporations, but for many years this was considered a marginal way of locating job opportunities and was primarily for technical positions. Accessing electronic bulletin boards required a good knowledge of computers plus use of communications software.

This has all changed. With the arrival of friendlier communications software, Windows, faster modems, packaged interfaces, online services, and the Internet, all of a sudden there are thousands of bulletin boards where everyone can find job listings.

The Internet is a massive communications network that began in the '60s. Initially, it was used for communications among research laboratories, the U.S. Defense Department and universities. When the U.S. Government relaxed its controls and the private sector began to encroach on it seriously, many people jumped at the opportunity to access the Internet. As you read this book, millions of people are communicating on the Internet. What makes this communications network so unique is that no one organization controls what goes into it.

It is now possible for someone in Los Angeles to prospect available jobs in Melbourne, Johannesburg, New York, or Paris with any company that has a presence on the Internet, all for the cost of a local phone call.

To better understand this new gold mine of opportunities, here are some common terms that you may run into while approaching the Internet for jobs:

ISP: You will need an Internet Service Provider to gain access to the Internet. The monthly cost for unlimited access to the Internet varies from below $10.00 to $19.95 and should include necessary software to facilitate your getting started. Be careful in selecting your provider. Some companies have over-promoted their services so that it is virtually impossible for their members to sign on. The most popular ISP is America Online (AOL). In late 1996, AOL was plagued with thousands of complaints from unhappy users. Begin your search with your local telephone service and ask around among your more savvy friends for reliable providers.

Modem: To enter the world of electronic communications your computer needs a **mod**ulator/**dem**odulator, an electronic device that will connect you to other computers by telephone and permit the exchange of data. The most common modems have speeds of 33.6 and 56 kilobits per second (kbps). The higher speed is preferred as it will keep your Internet communications time to a minimum by faster downloading.

Browser: This software allows you to ex'amine documents on the Internet. Many services that provide access to the Internet offer software to facilitate your e-mail and Internet searches. For example, America Online (AOL) has a user-friendly interface that permits you to "surf the 'Net" or "navigate the Web" for information and job leads.

The two most popular browsers on the Internet are produced by Netscape Software and Microsoft Corporation. These programs are available on a trial basis, and you can download a version directly from the companies' home pages. Try visiting Netscape's home page at <**http:// home.netscape.com**> and Microsoft at

<http://www.microsoft.com> to see what is offered. Other great WWW addresses for shareware and trial software are **<http://www.tucows.com>** and **<http://www.download.com>**.

Bulletin Boards (BBS): Bulletin boards are computer-based sites run by special interest groups (SIG) to which anyone can connect, provided you have a computer, modem and communications software. In special cases, you may be asked to pay a user fee. Do not give out your credit card or bank account number by modem unless you are 100% sure that the transmission is secure. Always request sample information as to what is being offered before you purchase.

E-mail: Electronic mail is probably the most popular and widely used Internet function. E-mail is a fast, low cost, private, and efficient way to communicate with either one person or thousands. With an e-mail message, you can send resumes, cover letters, files and even photos as an attachment to your communication. When you use a provider to access the Internet, you will be given an e-mail box. For example, I can be reached at **<supersearch@pobox.com>**. A useful tip: Be careful in picking a service where you will become stuck because you have given out their e-mail address to your contacts. To avoid this, contact **<http://www.pobox.com>**. You can acquire an alias e-mail address and then assign to it whichever service you use. Later, you can change your service without changing your e-mail address!

Home Page: Home pages and web sites are synonymous. It is the front door leading to the rest of the information within that site. Almost every major company today has a web site address where you can visit, obtain information, perhaps apply for jobs and leave your personal comments. It is not difficult to create your own web site and everyone from students to the President seems to have one. You do not need a home page or a web site to go visiting others who do.

Listservs & Mailing Lists (Discussion Groups): Once you have become adept at using e-mail, you will want to communicate with others who share your interests. Electronic discussion groups, or mailing lists, are one way to do this. Since all electronic discussion is conducted by e-mail, it is commonly called a mailing list group. Your communications to and from these groups will be through your e-mail box.

Download: Downloading is copying a file or document from another computer to yours. When you discover a web site with job leads of interest, you can download that document (save as) and read or print it later when you have terminated your web communication.

File Transfer Protocol (FTP): FTP is software that permits copying files between computers. You will use this software to obtain job leads and send letters and resumes in reply to advertised jobs of interest.

File Transfer Protocol Site: FTP sites are libraries that provide files you can download containing documents and software.

Hypertext Transfer Protocol (HTTP): This is the prefix used for all web home page addresses.

Search Engine: A web site that assists you in locating information on the Internet. Some of the popular ones are Altavista, Yahoo, Lycos, Dejanews, Infoseek and Webcrawler to name a few.

Uniform Resource Locator (URL): This is an address of a web site or file library. For a list of popular URLs loaded with job-search opportunities, visit our site, <**http://www.jamenair.com**>.

▶ If you are new to the world of electronic communications, you should contact an online service like America Online. In addition to having access to the Internet, you will find a wide range of proprietary services including shopping, weather reports, news, games, financial services, magazines....

Some of these services offer a trial period where you can have a number of free hours hookup. Take advantage of these offers to get acquainted with using the Internet.

There is a proliferation of Internet related magazines that publish the best suppliers to the Internet. The list keeps growing and you will do well to obtain a few issues when you are ready to get started.

Some schools, libraries and job clubs have an Internet connection that is free or at a minimal charge to members. Investigate locally where you might find an Internet terminal that you can try.

Keep in mind another valuable feature about the Internet—the possibility of obtaining information about companies. When using your browser software, you can do a search by company name.

Having a good resume on hand is essential before approaching the Internet. When you can send your resume by modem, prepare in advance a text version (*.txt) using your word processor. You may be requested to fill out an e-mail form resume. It is best to think out your replies before submitting.

Your e-mail communications to companies and recruiters about any job should follow the examples in this manual. Keep communications short with emphasis on your achievements.

General Thoughts About Resumes

One prominent firm needed to recruit middle managers. To find out what was available on the market, the company placed an ad in *The Wall Street Journal* and received several hundred responses. Looking through the replies, management was able to throw away almost 70 percent—because the candidate had not really read the advertisement. There were resumes badly reproduced on photocopy machines, form letters and no cover letters—in short, only paper in an envelope without a prayer of acceptance.

If you are going to take the trouble to answer an advertisement or write to someone and enclose your resume, be sure that your letter and resume represent the best you have to offer. Any compromise and you are only wasting your time and money, and will be adding frustration when your campaign does not seem to be producing interviews.

One candidate had been searching for quite a while. "Larry's" major interest was radio advertising sales and he was having trouble advancing in this industry. He was not making people take notice of his skills. Larry is 29 years old, single and well educated, but has had several job changes in a short period of time. His resume did not convey his true skills in salesmanship. After all, to sell radio, he first had to sell himself!

After a review of his goals, accomplishments and targeted companies, Larry decided to try a mailing of his resume with a personalized cover letter. The challenge was to create a resume that would generate interviews.

The resume on page 102 was mailed to 60 targeted companies, produced eight interviews and resulted in four job offers, which landed Larry a bigger network job. Of course, the resume only helped Larry get an interview. His talents in communicating his skills won him these offers. If you were a network sales executive in need of additional sales talent, would you want to meet Larry after receiving his mailing?

REFERENCES

Work on your references now. Try to have a reference for each work situation in your resume. When your resume is completed, you will want to talk with each of these references, asking their permission and cooperation. Go over your resume with the individuals and discuss the kind of recommendation they will give you. The best references are people who will stick to what you did at work and discuss you factually. You do not need long-winded, subjective reviews. A good rule of thumb is not to overkill with exaggerations, which will only force an inquisitor to look further.

The best question your reference can ask you is, "What do you want me to say?" At that point, go over the elements of the job you are after and discuss in detail your accomplishments. Anyone who can back up your accomplishments will be a good reference.

When putting together your reference list, think about persons who might give you a bad or so-so report. While you may have some excellent references, it is possible that people not on your list may be contacted. This is a good time to go back and mend broken fences.

By asking for help from someone with whom you have had problems in the past, you are complimenting them and, at the same time, recognizing that they are important in your life. Time heals bad feelings, and since you are also part of that person's history, there is reason on both sides to try to regain mutual respect. Abe Lincoln was credited with saying, "I destroy my enemies by making them my friends."

While you may not put these people on your reference list, you will know that, if they are contacted, your chances for a more favorable report will be improved.

Sample Resume: *"Elite Type"* printed on a Near Letter Quality printer.
Because of type size, entire resume is on one page.

LARRY BROWN   **(310) 555-6789**
123 Fourth Avenue
Torrance, California 90500

A salesman's salesman...give me a rope, and I come back with horses.
Products - hardware, software, advertising, radio, notions and craft products....

- SOLD $750,000 in personal computers in 10 months with a 33% gross margin.
- RANKED #2 out of 110 salespeople (#1 was the boss's son).
- SOLD country music radio advertising to a Mercedes auto dealer - 1st time ever.
- INCREASED radio station's ratings by 20% in one summer.

A SUPER ACHIEVER - articulate, quick and entrepreneurial marketing/sales professional in search of a challenge and real opportunity.

EXPERIENCE

C.B.A. BROADCASTING   1994-Present
Orange, California

Account Executive
- Responsible for Country XFB-FM radio advertising sales to local retailers.
- Generated five to six new accounts per month.

MICROLAND   1992-1994
West Los Angeles, California

Senior Marketing Representative
- Opened the way for Teledyne's purchases from MICROLAND.
- Responsible for sales of computers and related equipment to small, medium and large buyers. Received IBM counselor sales training.
- Salesman of the Month, many times.
- Produced, wrote, executed and hosted a televised talk show about computers in the Los Angeles area.

WRIGHT COMPUTER CENTERS   1991-1992
Beverly Hills, California

Sales Executive
- NUMBER 1 sales performer in the center.
- LEADING producer for the sales of training, service contracts and other value added sales.

YOUNG HOME SEWING COMPANY   1990
Mid-Atlantic Territory, Washington DC

Territory Sales Representative
- LED sales division after only three months in the company.
- RECEIVED presidential award for reopening business with Craftworld.
- SELECTED to test market automated bar coding ordering procedure.
- TRAINED in Xerox methods of selling.

EDUCATION

NEW ENGLAND COLLEGE
Henniker, New Hampshire and Arundel, Sussex, England

Bachelor of Arts with honors in Business Administration, 1989
(Financed own education)

MELINDA R. STRONG, RN
1234 Highland Avenue
Los Angeles, California 90000-1234

(213) 555-5555

A highly successful healthcare educator/trainer with more than 20 years' experience in nursing who has developed and delivered training programs in perioperative nursing, CPR, instrument utilization and RN first assistant preparation for more than 500 doctors, nurses and medical staff.

Expertise includes the development, implementation and evaluation of programs; selection and orientation of personnel as well as budget and resource management.

ACCOMPLISHMENTS

PROGRAM DEVELOPMENT

Designed a post-graduate perioperative nursing program for Registered Nurses to develop skills in scrubbing and circulating in the operating room.

Constructed a RN first assistant program for Registered Nurses to practice an expanded perioperative role.

Developed the tool to train-the-trainers for the successful implementation of computerized intraoperative documentation.

Revamped the Quality Assessment and Improvement Program for the operating room that contributed to a successful JCAHO survey (October, 1995).

SELECTION OF STAFF

Instructed and mentored experienced Registered Nurses to become perioperative nursing clinical instructors.

TEACHING AND PUBLIC SPEAKING

Prepared and delivered more than 50 presentations from 1989 to 1995 on Perioperative Nursing, Designing RNFA Programs, Operating Room Management, CNOR Review Courses and Staffing for leading medical centers.

MANAGEMENT

Managed operations and budgets for the endoscopy support team providing support services for 50-75 procedures per week. Directed night shift Registered Nurses, Surgical Technicians, Logistics Technicians and the Instrument Technician. This included coaching, counseling and evaluating performance.

PROFESSIONAL EXPERIENCE

Huge Medical Center, Los Angeles, California

1993-1996

Assistant Director of Nursing
OR Services for Perioperative Education

MELINDA STRONG   **Page Two**

USA Health Corporation, Los Angeles, California   1985-1993

   Clinical Nurse Specialist (1988-1993)
   Nurse Teacher Practitioner (1985-1988)

Veterans' Administration Medical Center, Long Beach, California   1985

   Head Nurse

Veterans' Administration Medical Center, Washington, DC   1980-1985

   Staff Nurse-Operating Room

George Washington Hospital, Washington, DC   1978-1980

   Staff Nurse-Operating Room

Veterans' Administration Medical Center, Washington, DC   1975-1978

   Staff Nurse

EDUCATION

University of California, Los Angeles, Los Angeles, California

   Registered Nurse First Assistant Certificate, 1991
   Post Graduate Nurse Educator Certificate, 1987

Georgetown University, Washington, DC

   Master of Science in Nursing, 1985
   Bachelor of Science in Nursing, 1975

Special Training: Laser Safety & Instructor, Cardiopulmonary Resuscitation

REGISTRATION/CERTIFICATION

Certified for Professional Achievement as a Registered Nurse First Assistant (CRNFA, Certification #912345)
Certified Nurse Operating Room (CNOR, Certification #812345)
Registered Nurse, California (RN312345)

AFFILIATIONS

Association of Operating Room Nurses (AORN), 1978; Operating Room Council of California (ORNCC), 1995; Association of Surgical Technologists of Southern California, Chapter 100, Member, 1993

PUBLICATIONS

Contributed a section on orthopedic clinical applications, *The RNFA: An Expanded Role*, Second Edition, J. Robinson, 1995, published by Medical Publishing Company

You should keep your references up-to-date on your search progress. If distance is a problem, a short telephone call at a convenient time can do a lot of good. Once your references know your objectives, they also may have network contacts to suggest. With good preparation, you can assure quality backup support for your campaign.

To help you in your discussions with references, keep in mind the following:

- If your reference is from a former employer, the caller will want to know the circumstances of your departure. Have this worked out. Some typical reasons are: management change, closing of a division or department, company relocated, merger or acquisition made your job redundant.

- Anticipate that your reference will be asked to discuss your strengths and weaknesses. Refer to Chapter 2 regarding weaknesses that may be only excesses of your strengths.

- How long has the reference known you? In what work situation were you associated?

- A reference can be asked how you might fit into a new organization. One of the most frequently asked questions is: "Would you rehire this person?"

- Though trying to help, some references may in fact provide negative input. For example: "John is a great achiever, though he suffers fools badly." While being complimentary, the reference was telegraphing the message: "Watch out! John may not get along with everyone on the team!" Try to review in advance what they are going to say. If you stress that you need their help, supportive references should be willing to follow your suggestions.

- People who make reference checks do not always call the person you indicate. A good researcher will call your reference but also ask the reference if there are others in the company familiar with your work.

- If you have had a managerial position, you may want to include a few references from people who worked for you. They can give a different perspective of your skills and leadership abilities.

- Along with professional references, you will need some personal character testimonials. Pick people you can count on and who know you well enough to support your candidacy.

- After an interview, you should be quick to alert your references to expect a call. Carry your reference list with you at all times!

- Some interviewers ask for references right away in the discussion. It is preferable not to produce your references until you really have a job in view, though this is not always possible to control. It is best to be prepared.

Use the following form to organize your reference list:

PERSONAL & PROFESSIONAL REFERENCES

1. (Name) _____

(Company) _____

(Position) _____

(Address) _____

(City, State, Zip) _____

(Telephone) _____ FAX ( ) _____ e-mail _____

(Former company & position where you knew this person, if appropriate. Example: Former Vice President, Manufacturing, XYZ Company) _____

2. (Name) _____

(Company) _____

(Position) _____

(Address) _____

(City, State, Zip) _____

(Telephone) _____ FAX ( ) _____ e-mail _____

(Former company & position where you knew this person, if appropriate. Example: Former Vice President, Manufacturing, XYZ Company) _____

3. (Name) _____

(Company) _____

(Position) _____

(Address) _____

(City, State, Zip) _____

(Telephone) _____ FAX ( ) _____ e-mail _____

(Former company & position where you knew this person, if appropriate. Example: Former Vice President, Manufacturing, XYZ Company) _____

4. (Name) _____

(Company) _____

(Position) _____

(Address) _____

(City, State, Zip) _____

(Telephone) _____ FAX ( ) _____ e-mail _____

(Former company & position where you knew this person, if appropriate. Example: Former Vice President, Manufacturing, XYZ Company) _____

CHAPTER 5

The Market Plan

It is Day 4 of your program. You are now ready to develop a marketing strategy that will include all the information and priorities you have put together. There are two factors that will govern the speed and efficiency of your search:

1. Be prepared to spend at least six hours a day on your search. Of this time, you must use at least four hours or more on the search activity that will produce the best chances for an interview: Networking. Preferably, all of your written communications will be done at times when it is not practical to meet with people (evenings, weekends, holidays).

2. Consider carefully your target geographic area. Are you certain the jobs you want can be found here? RESEARCH INTERVIEWS may be required to uncover the jobs you want to prospect. How many of the companies you are interested in have operations in the area in which you wish to live? We will be developing your target company list a little later.

WHERE IS YOUR NEXT JOB COMING FROM?

Your first priority is to create as many interviews as you can—and, from those interviews, get others. This road will lead you to someone who has a need for your skills.

Where are the best sources of leads?

According to the U.S. Department of Labor*, for blue- and white-collar workers, people get jobs from:

12.2%	Agencies
13.9%	Ads
63.4%	**Informal** (Job-seeker uses personal contacts to generate a job = NETWORKING)
10.5%	Other (from trade union and Civil Service help)

*(Reference: *Job Seeking Methods Used by American Workers*, U.S. Department of Labor, Bureau of Labor Statistics, Bulletin No. 1886, 1975.)

Another study** for professional, technical and managerial positions shows:

8.9%   Agencies

9.9%   Ads

74.5%   Informal (Job-seeker uses personal contacts to generate a job = NETWORKING)

6.7%   Other (from trade union and Civil Service help)

In addition, of those who found jobs through personal contacts, 43.8 percent had new positions created for them.

Looking at the above figures, the logical conclusion is that seven out of ten jobs come from personal contact. Nevertheless, some job-searchers are quite successful by pursuing other, more familiar job-search techniques. Any number of variables contribute to a successful job search. Pursue them all—but spend proportionate amounts of time and effort on the activities that produce interviews. Look at the "classic" job-search options:

Help-Wanted Ads

If you pay attention to newspaper publicity, you would think that classified ads are the number one way to get a new job. But, advertised openings produce only 9.9-13.9 percent of job opportunities. If you are spending more than 10 percent of your time in this area of job search, you are wasting energy that should be applied to more productive methods—like networking.

You know that advertising works, or people would neither advertise nor reply. But to what extent does it work? For the average job-searcher, getting a job through an ad is a little like winning a beauty contest.

Here is an example:

A company wanted a vice president responsible for European operations. They advertised in *The Wall Street Journal* and received 200 replies. Twenty resumes were retained and the candidates interviewed. The selection then was narrowed down to 12. These 12 were interviewed again. Six were retained. After further and more extensive interviews, two finalists remained. The two were interviewed by more than 25 executives in the company and one was selected. The entire process took more than five months!

Moral of the story: If you go after an advertised job, keep in mind the odds, which can be as high as 400 or 500 to one. Weigh those odds against running into a job opportunity every 12 to 16 interviews through networking, where there are not as many competitors, if any!

** (Reference: Granovetter, *Getting a Job: A Study of Contacts and Careers*, Harvard University Press, Cambridge, 1974.)

Should you answer ads? Of course, but selectively, so that it does not take you away from your number one priority: *networking*.

Analyzing Ads.

Blind ads. The advertiser is not identified and the wording often is ambiguous. Is this a real job? It may be nothing more than an executive recruiter testing the water. The toughest job an executive recruiter has is not finding candidates but finding assignments, so they can be engaged either on retainer or contingency to find candidates. Recruiters spend most of their time networking—just like you will—meeting company executives in all the same ways you will (associations, clubs, sports, conferences, seminars, alumni meetings, parties, interviews), to cultivate the people who give out job-search missions.

One method some recruiters use is to find out who might be interested in leaving a job, because that person's employer then represents a possible mission. They do this by placing an ad, and someone looking for a change responds.

The recruiter places an ad for a vice president or president, with a very broad definition. For example, this is an ad from a recent newspaper:

PRESIDENT/C.E.O.

Experienced executive, reporting directly to the Board of Directors, to take charge of young growing sales and development organization. Must be a self-starter with some knowledge of all facets of business including production, finance, personnel, sales and marketing. Submit resume and salary history to: L.A. TIMES BOX..........

The advertiser, who may be a recruiter (or just a company browsing), will use a box number at the newspaper. (The identity of box holders is heavily protected.) If it is a recruiter, there may be no president's job open, but through this vague ad the recruiter will soon identify a number of *employed* vice presidents or presidents who are anxious to make a change. Suddenly, there is a market for the recruiter to cultivate. He now knows someone in that organization who is actively seeking a change—and most likely before anyone in the company knows.

Most recruiters are too busy and too ethical to use such methods. Unfortunately, the few that do use this technique make it difficult for the others.

What does this all mean to you? A blind ad that looks like a dream job may be just that: a dream concocted by someone just fishing.

It could also be a recruiter who simply needs to fill his data base with a number of people from a given sector of business or specialty.

The reasons for legitimate blind ads placed by firms are:

- To maintain secrecy from both competitors and employees (especially if the company is planning to make a surprise replacement).

- To shield companies with questionable reputations (perhaps with financial problems) that would make recruiting quality people difficult.

- To aid companies in testing the market.

- To protect companies from job-seekers who do not meet all their specifications.

Be suspicious of any blind advertisement. There are, however, some blind ads that you can track down. If a post office box is used rather than a newspaper box, a call to the post office branch (use the Zip code to help you get a phone number) can give you the name of the box holder. Once you have the company name and their newspaper ad, you can devise an approach.

Complete Ads: When you have a specific ad in front of you and the company name is given, does this mean you want to reply? Not always.

Most companies place their ads through a personnel manager or outside recruiter, or even a resume review service that will do preliminary screening. If your resume or letter contains even one of their criteria for elimination, it may never get to the person who placed the requisition. This is not an indictment of personnel managers, recruiters or screening services; they have to develop methods of evaluating candidates as quickly as possible, and a part of any screening process is to eliminate the poorly written resumes.

You can avoid being screened out in the preliminaries if you bypass the ad completely. If the ad is for a vice president of sales, research the company and get the name of its president. Verify (by telephone) that he is, indeed, still the president. Then figure out your best approach through networking. If, in spite of your best efforts, you cannot locate a referral who can introduce you to someone in the company, you will still make an approach, either by direct phone call or a letter.

Should your letter to the president include a resume? Not necessarily. What the letter should do is address the qualifications described in the ad without making reference to an advertised opening.

Broadcast Letter in Reply to an Ad.

A broadcast letter is your resume in letter form designed to address very specifically a targeted company or opportunity. The 20-Second Resume is the heart of a well-written broadcast letter.

Resumes that arrive spontaneously usually are routed automatically to personnel or human resources for reply. However, a well-written broadcast letter embodying key accomplishments from your resume has a much better chance of:

1. Being read by the person you addressed.

2. Getting a reply.

While a great broadcast letter still may be rerouted, it stands a fair chance of getting you an interview.

If your resume does not meet all the criteria of the job but your skills are in line, this letter can omit chronological employment data and concentrate directly on accomplishments paralleling the company's needs. Cite your management experience, marketing, manufacturing or other skills; your accomplishments can create interest in a meeting. But remember, the best you can expect of a broadcast letter or letter/resume is an interview—which is your primary objective anyway!

Cover Letter Plus Resume in Response to an Ad.

If your accomplishments, work experience and education match the company's needs, your resume can be a strong response, provided the accomplishments in your 20-Second Resume support the needs published in the ad. In other words, rearrange your accomplishments to fit their priorities.

Job searchers soon learn that mail campaigns and answering ads are numbers games and, as in any mail advertising program, interview results of more than one or two percent are considered good!

Look at a typical ad:

> # International Sales Manager
>
> Established aerospace component manufacturing company requires an experienced international sales manager. Successful candidate will select and train international reps; therefore, experience in establishing a rep organization would be a plus.
>
> Knowledge in selling US products to foreign markets a must. BS degree in engineering plus 8-10 years of marketing experience required. Working knowledge of foreign aerospace markets desired. Excellent salary incentives and benefit plans. Please forward resume with salary history to
>
> LA TIMES BOX ....
>
> Candidates will be contacted for interview. All replies will be treated confidentially. EOE-M/F

What can you deduce from the above advertisement?

- It probably is legitimate. It is too precise to be a recruiter just filling his data base, though the interviewing and processing may be in the hands of a recruiter. The equal opportunity employer (EOE) and male/female codes reinforce the assumption that it is a real company with a position to fill.

- Since the reply is to a newspaper box, there is no chance of tracking down the advertiser. If you have a list of aerospace component manufacturers, you might be able to make some discreet inquiries, but chances are the ad is well protected to prevent disturbing current employees. However, if you plan a campaign to presidents of aerospace component manufacturers, you know at least that one of them is looking for an international sales manager. Going by way of the president's office, either through networking or a mail campaign, will certainly be different from going through the vice president of human resources or personnel manager, who will receive at least 100 replies to this advertisement.

- Knowing this, you may want to reply anyway. The ad requests that you forward a resume with salary history. By now you should realize that the salary history is to screen out rather than screen in, so at the risk of being incomplete, ignore the salary history part. What is essential is to get your reader excited about the benefits you will bring to the company (your accomplishments, which they can apply to their *needs*). If the formula (ABC) can be communicated either by cover letter/resume or broadcast letter, you may have a chance at an interview. The goal of this exercise is to receive a call from the company or their recruiter for a meeting.

To organize your reply, reread the advertisement line by line and word by word to fully understand what they are seeking. The needs of the company are:

1. Aerospace Knowledge
2. International Experience
3. Sales Management
4. Training Experience of Reps or Other Salespersons
5. Know-how to Establish a Rep Organization
6. Knowledge in Selling U.S. Products Abroad
7. Bachelor of Science Degree or Better in Engineering
8. Knowledge of the Foreign Aerospace Industry

This company requires an international professional. Experience with off-shore salespeople also is important, as they evidently wish to deal at arm's length with their different markets. On the other hand, they want the candidate to know how foreign markets work even though direct sales by the manager may not be essential.

This is a tall order and, unless you have at least rep experience, international sales accomplishments, an engineering degree, knowledge of U.S. and foreign aerospace industries, and sales management experience, you will be hard pressed to qualify. For illustration, assume you meet the requirements.

How to Write a Broadcast Letter.

To create a broadcast letter using elements from your resume:

Dear (always verify correct spelling of name and title unless you are addressing a blind ad; then use "Dear Sir/Madam" or "Gentlemen"):

Step 1.
Introduce yourself, adapting one or two sentences from your 20-Second Resume.

Step 2.
Lead into key accomplishments—taken from your resume—either in support of the ad you are answering or backing up the position you are trying to approach.

Step 3.
Include a very brief indication of your education, language abilities (if appropriate), and focus the reader on what you feel you can do for this company.

Step 4.
Close your letter with one of the following:

   a. When you write to a specific person, indicate that you will be calling him for an appointment within a few days.
   b. When addressing a box number, suggest an early meeting.

Your letter should be no more than two pages, and preferably only one.

Coming back to the sample advertisement, your broadcast letter must support each of eight criteria with accomplishments.

As with your resume, you should tailor the letter by specifically selecting accomplishments from your 20-Second Resume in support of the company's requirements. Your 20-Second Resume statements may need to be rewritten to conform to the stated needs.

You can include a full resume, but the extra information it contains could be on the screener's "eliminate" list.

While you want to give information, the best reply would be a brief broadcast letter. The following letter is adapted from the 20-Second Resume section of your newly revised resume. Here is how it would look:

Sample Broadcast Letter in Response to the Ad on Page 113.

JOHN JONES
12345 Second Avenue
Santa Monica, California 90403
(310) 555-1234

(Date)

LA Times Box...
Los Angeles, CA 90053

Gentlemen:

For more than 12 years I have been involved in international sales management, with eight years directly in the aerospace industry. Some of my accomplishments have been:

  * Established sales offices in France, Great Britain and Germany for a line of clamps and fasteners, managing a group of 16 sales representatives.

  * In 12 months, obtained 43 percent of the UK market. I personally dealt with the Rolls Royce Engine Company and the Ministry of Defence in obtaining clearances for our products in the UK.

  * In 17 months, was successful in obtaining 45 percent and 27 percent of the French and German markets, respectively, dealing with nearly all local engine and airframe manufacturers.

  * Provided training programs for all European staff, including full briefing on our own products as well as competitor lines.

  * Generated more than $28 million in sales for my company with excellent margins.

Does this sampling of performance match the kind of international sales manager you seek?

I hold a BS degree from UCLA in electrical engineering and speak some Spanish and French.

I feel confident that an interview would demonstrate that my expertise in setting up rep organizations, training, motivating and managing an international sales department would be an excellent addition to any established, growing aerospace company.

At the right time I can provide references to meet your highest expectations and would welcome hearing from you at your earliest convenience.

Sincerely,

John Jones

John Jones

The preceding letter is not a resume, but if you were the screening recruiter or personnel manager, would you want to meet John Jones? Jones' broadcast letter reply addresses only the qualifications asked for in the advertisement, so it is difficult to rule out Jones for some nonrelated activity. Jones' chances of getting a call are good.

The risk in this approach is that Jones did not follow the ad's instructions (which might have eliminated him from the running anyway!). You can try a few replies like the above and measure your success versus those who will be faithful to every request in the ad. Sometimes a little information that is right on target can be more powerful than overkill.

A compromise solution would be to send a revamped resume with a cover letter showing key aerospace accomplishments in the forefront. But it would be better to save the prepared resume as a backup in case Jones is called in for an interview.

Assume that three to six weeks go by with no reply. The broadcast letter obviously was not appreciated. But there is nothing to prevent Jones from sending in a well-constructed cover letter with his revised resume, for the same job again. Chances are his first letter has long since been forgotten, and the fact that he is writing so late will make his second submission stand out. You still should not enclose salary history.

Writing a Cover Letter to Accompany Your Resume.

Suppose you decide you want to send a cover letter and resume instead of a broadcast letter. Here is a basic pattern for your cover letter:

Dear (always verify correct spelling of name and title unless you are addressing a blind ad—then it should be "Dear Sir/Madam" or "Gentlemen"):

Step 1.
Explain the purpose of your letter. You either are writing to express interest in working for their company or in reply to their advertised need. You need not refer to their ad or the fact that you are sending your resume. That is self-evident.

Step 2.
Present your resume.

Step 3.
Highlight some accomplishments directly against their needs.

Step 4.
Close by asking for an interview. If you know the name and company, indicate

that you will be calling in a few days to arrange a mutually convenient time for an interview.

Some pointers:

▶ Keep the letter short.

▶ Focus on their needs.

▶ Do not mention salary.

▶ Sign your letter.

▶ Date your letter but NOT your resume.

▶ Read your letter aloud to see if it sounds right.

▶ Check for spelling errors or typos.

▶ Match your key accomplishments to their needs.

▶ Keep a record of your mailing for follow-up.

There is another example of an advertisement along with a cover letter and resume beginning on page 120.

JOHN JONES
12345 Second Avenue
Santa Monica, California 90403
(310) 555-1234

(DATE)

LA Times Box...
Los Angeles, CA 90053

Gentlemen:

For more than 12 years I have been in international sales, with the last eight in the aerospace industry. I have lived in several countries and worked with both civilian and military establishments in developing sales.

Many of your requirements match my experience and qualifications.

You Require

8-10 years marketing

Selection & training of sales reps

Knowledge of selling US product overseas

Engineering degree

Knowledge of foreign aerospace industries

My Experience

More than 15 years selling & marketing experience

Hired, directed and trained more than 16 sales reps in four countries

Generated $28 million in sales with excellent margins

Graduate electrical engineer

Worked with all Common Market countries

I would be most interested in discussing your needs and look forward to your call.

Sincerely,

John Jones

John Jones

Enclosure

Sample Advertisement "A"
(A Real Ad)

Vice President International Business Development/Operations

A diversified international company, based in San Francisco is currently seeking a key executive to play a major role in its future development.

In this position, you'll be responsible for strategic planning and for identifying, analyzing and negotiating acquisitions, helping us structure business deals and reinvest profits. To qualify, you must have an MBA and 8-10 years' international business and financial/strategic planning experience. You should also have the ability to successfully operate and manage the financial area of a business. This unique international opportunity requires travel to Asia and offers an outstanding salary and strong bonus incentives.

To apply, please send your resume and cover letter to:
Smith & Smith, Inc.,
Recruitment Advertising, Dept. WSAA, ...
San Francisco, CA 00000.

Both S&S and our client are
equal opportunity employers.

Analysis of Advertisement:

Requirements:

1. Strategic Planning
2. Complete Handling of Acquisitions
3. Structure Business Deals
4. Handle Money for Investment
5. Financial Management and Operations
6. MBA
7. 8-10 Years' International Experience
8. Experience in Asia Desirable

To reply with:

- Cover Letter
- Resume (Mixed Performance and Functional Resume)

PAUL JONES
23344 Rochester Avenue
Los Angeles, CA 90034

(213) 555-1234

(DATE)

Smith & Smith, Inc.
Recruitment Advertising, Dept WSAA
Street, Suite XXX
San Francisco, CA 00000

Gentlemen:

I am most interested in your advertisement for an international vice president and feel that my qualifications and experience are well suited to your needs.

You Require	My Experience
International Experience	* More than 20 years international P&L management of which 16 years were overseas.
Strategic Planning	* Opened and successfully managed new offices. * As CEO, established and executed business plans. * As a consultant, have been advising international companies on expansion.
Structuring Business Deals	* Initiated license agreements. * Sold company's products in difficult markets. * Restructured public companies.
MBA and 8-10 Years Experience	* MBA in operations research. * Excellent financial skills. * Managed 20 professionals.
Acquisitions Experience	* Bought and sold assets and companies worldwide.
Knowledge of Asia	* Have worked on licensing, joint ventures, acquisitions and manufacturing projects in Japan, Taiwan, S. Korea, Hong Kong and The Philippines.

I would welcome the opportunity of discussing your needs personally, and I look forward to hearing from you.

Sincerely,

Paul Jones

Paul Jones

Enclosure

PAUL JONES
23344 Rochester Avenue
Los Angeles, California 90034
(213) 555-1234

More than twenty years of progressively increasing responsibilities and challenging general management experience with consumer, medical and industrial products in highly competitive domestic and international markets.

- Turned around and managed nine losing manufacturing/sales divisions into a highly profitable group. Sold off unprofitable divisions with an exceptional capital gain of $588,000.

- Responsible for a sales organization that increased sales from $8 to $22 million.

- Investigated more than 50 major acquisitions. Completed four, resulting in a sales increase of $12 million and a profit increase of $1.1 million by the third year.

Decision-maker and strong manager who has the capacity to analyze and successfully market a broad range of products. Competent in recruiting, training and motivating personnel. Superior interpersonal skills. Excellent microcomputer and hands-on financial management.

SIGNIFICANT ACCOMPLISHMENTS

Sales & Marketing Management

- Quadrupled sales in four years for a manufacturer of precision electric motor components for military and industrial applications.

- Created a marketing strategy that launched a new line of healthcare products in more than 600 hospitals with sales growth of $800,000.

- Developed a creative marketing plan that resulted in multimillion dollar orders for capital goods with secured payment.

Strategic Planning

- Changed expansion goals for a European group of manufacturing divisions and saved more than $2 million in investments while expanding a new activity which became immediately profitable.

- Convinced the board of a public U.K. firm to sell off an unprofitable segment of its business. This had a positive effect on cash flow.

- Redirected marketing objectives and operations of a $500 million major automobile company's parts division to provide better utilization of facilities and savings of $25 million in annual purchases.

- Recommended and carried out the sale of a troubled operating division that resulted in a $2 million capital gain.

International

- Opened new markets for an industrial materials line that gained 63% market share in 18 months.

- Organized and formed direct selling subsidiaries in lieu of sales representatives selling the company's 6,000 catalogued products. Profitability improved by 23%.

- Conceived a turnaround plan for a Belgian subsidiary of a listed U.K. holding company which resulted in a complete return to profitability. Continued as a Member of the Board of Directors.

PAUL JONES   Page Two

Problem Solving

- Directed a new product development team which reduced the time to launch new products from 6 months to 6 weeks.

- Performed major consulting assignments in The Philippines, India and the Far East, resulting in an exchange of know-how and significantly improved performance.

- Turned around a chronically unprofitable multinational manufacturing/sales operation which went from losses to providing the parent company with 33% of corporate profits with only 6% of its sales.

- Set up and managed a financial department of 20 professionals controlling a network of five manufacturing/sales operations on two continents.

EXPERIENCE

Johnson Management Services, Inc., Los Angeles, California   1994-Present
   Management Consultant (Financial Controls, Mergers & Acquisitions, Marketing)

R.J. Resting Corporation, Chicago, Illinois   1991-1993
   General Manager - Europe (Sales/Distribution)

Drexel Industries S.A., Paris, France   1987-1991
   Division Director (Manufacturing/Sales)

Walters Inc., Columbus, Ohio   1985-1986
   Vice President - Europe (Manufacturing/Sales)

R.K. Madison Company, Inc., Pittsburgh, Pennsylvania   1978-1984
   General Manager - Europe (Manufacturing/Sales)

PRIOR EXPERIENCE

As financial manager of a $14 million electronics company, installed a complete computerized accounting department. General manager of a medium-sized distribution company.

EDUCATION

Master of Science, New York University, Industrial Engineering & Business - 1972
Bachelor of Science, New York University, Business Administration - 1971

Served in the United States Air Force, 1st Lieutenant, 1973-1975

Fluent in French, working knowledge of Spanish

AFFILIATIONS

Sales and Marketing Executives of Los Angeles
Franco-American Chamber of Commerce, France and Los Angeles
Financial Executives Association of Los Angeles
Member (Committee Chairman) of the Association of Corporate Growth

Helpful Hints for Answering Ads.

1. Sources for advertisements: *The Wall Street Journal*—especially Tuesday and Wednesday, *Los Angeles Sunday Times, The Chicago Tribune, Sunday New York Times*, industry trade magazines and special publications, all other big-city Sunday newspapers in areas in which you are interested. Check your library for the *Standard Periodical Directory*; this has addresses for all industry newspapers and trade magazines. (See other sources in Appendix C.)

2. If you are going to answer, do it right or not at all. Tossing a resume in an envelope with just a few words or without a letter will not get you where you want to go. If you do not care, why should they?

3. Make a list of all the requirements the ad specifies.

4. Next to each item, write your specific accomplishments that address that need. If you do not meet the most important job requirements, along with three out of five of the other needed experience factors, you should think twice before investing the time for a proper answer.

   Some feel a candidate should answer as many ads as possible, on the theory that if the reply does not fit that particular job, there may perhaps be other situations in the same company. That argument may have been valid in the past when there were not so many replies to every ad. Today, when there are literally hundreds of replies, the chances that your resume can be referred for another post are weak indeed. It could happen, but your main consideration now is using your time to best advantage, and if you cannot justify answering a given ad, do not waste your time.

5. If you are employed and are quietly seeking a change, you risk exposure by replying to a blind ad. It may not be worth the risk.

   There is one way to answer a blind ad without exposing your identity. This is to have someone, a friend for example, write to the advertiser, omitting your name, present employer and otherwise protecting your identity—even by generalizing details of your accomplishments—yet attracting their attention. A sample letter would address the advertised needs and might look something like this:

Gentlemen:

   I know a young person who answers excellently the description advertised for the position of medical product sales manager. This person has all the qualities you are seeking and more.

   For example:

* Has more than seven years' experience selling directly to private and public hospitals with annual sales growth of 20 percent each year.

* A former registered nurse, this person has made the transition to sales and marketing of medical products and knows all aspects of hospital purchasing operations and protocol.

* Has been an outstanding salesperson for several consecutive years.

* Is bilingual in Spanish and English.

* Has trained a number of other salespeople. Each has become an outstanding performer.

   In spite of my friend's exceptional record and performance, present opportunities and personal growth are limited.

   I have been asked to reply to you in confidence and would be delighted to put you in contact with my friend, who will then give you complete details. This person is exceptional and has a track record worthy of your consideration.

   There is absolutely no charge for my assistance and I will, of course, keep all communication confidential between my friend and you. You can reach me at (213) 555-1677 in the mornings or at dinner time.

   Sincerely,

In the above sample letter, even the gender of the candidate is disguised. Since the candidate has had eight years' experience, the letter says "more than seven...." In other words, care has been taken to keep from revealing any identifying information just in case the candidate is from the advertiser's own company. There may be suspicions, but nothing concrete.

The "good friend" approach has its limitations and should only be used when you feel that you *must* answer a given advertisement but do not wish to arouse suspicion that you are looking around. This letter may be put aside if others reply with more precise data.

Another school of thought suggests you put your letter and resume in a sealed envelope and send this letter with instructions on the outside indicating which companies you do not wish to open the envelope! You may not feel comfortable leaving that decision to someone else. Obviously they can do whatever they want and you may never know what happened. Better to not reply.

6. Assuming you are going after the advertised job with a cover letter and a resume, be sure to update your 20-Second Resume to conform to the needs stated in the advertisement.

   Matching your most important accomplishments to the specifications maximizes your chances of a response. From there on out, it is a numbers game with the people who read the replies.

7. In general, the higher your salary objective, the less chance you have of finding a job through an advertisement. High-level jobs are secured through networking and recruiters. Salary levels under $50,000 will have a much better response rate.

8. In most cases, the person who writes the ad is not the person who has requested the search. Often there are errors in priorities due to internal misunderstandings, and the advertised requirements may have little relation to the actual job. There is not much you can do about this other than present your strongest talents. But do not spend time worrying about the reason if you do not hear back.

The Follow-Up.

Keep copies of each ad you answer, your analysis of the ad, your letter and any resumes sent. Your file of replies should be chronological so that, if and when you get a call, you can track down the original ad.

This file also will be useful for following up the ad with another reply if you do not get an answer.

You have examined some of the strategies for answering ads. There is no one right formula. Even with the techniques discussed here, it is difficult to obtain interviews this way. Excellent responses can get drowned in the volume of paper. If you follow all the advice above, you will improve your chances of being called, but remember, the competition is severe. At best, answering ads is an exercise in organizing your accomplishments and your imagination in response to someone's published needs.

Job Hot Lines

Many large corporations, universities, hospitals, and city, state and federal government agencies maintain 24-hour job hot lines with recorded messages listing current openings.

These usually include brief job descriptions, requirements and salary ranges, along with closing dates for applications.

To find out if your target employers offer such a service, check their listings in the white pages of the telephone directory, call their information operators or their personnel offices.

These messages are normally updated weekly and, if you keep up on the changes as they occur, you may be able to target a position before it reaches the classified section of your newspaper.

Executive Recruiters

There are two types of executive recruiters:

Contingency Recruiters.

These work on recruitment assignments without retainer. They sometimes help the client define the position, but more usually work to the job specification they receive from a company. They conduct searches and receive payment only if their candidate is chosen. The company is not under any obligation other than paying their fees if one of their candidates is hired. There is no charge to the candidate.

Contingency recruiters normally work in the lower- to middle-management range, though some work on fairly high-level assignments. A lot depends on the rapport they have with their clients.

Contingency recruiters can work months on an assignment, and submit good candidates, only to lose the placement to another firm that has presented a more acceptable (not necessarily better) candidate. This can be a heartbreaker for a recruiter who has worked hard at identifying good people.

Since contingency recruiters do not have exclusive searches, submitting your resume to more than one could mean that your resume might be presented to the same company by competing firms. The chances of this happening are rare and should not be a deterrent to approaching as many as possible.

Retained Recruiters.

Retained recruiters usually have an exclusive arrangement with their clients and work on middle-management to senior-executive levels. They receive fees for their searches and will continue to submit candidates until the client either is satisfied or calls off the search. Their fees can range from 20 percent to 40 percent of the offered salary, plus expenses. Using a retained recruiter can be expensive for the company, but the results can be worth it.

Part of their work is to help the client create the job description, define the salary package and review the responsibilities of the position. To be successful they need to have a complete specification of what the client wants and an understanding of how the position will fit into the client's organization.

If you are selected as a candidate, the recruiter will make a detailed report highlighting your strengths and weaknesses. The report usually is a composite of your resume and the recruiter's notes after one or more interviews with you. A candidate does not see the recruiter's report. If your network includes some recruiters, be sure to ask for their comments about your resume as part of an advice interview.

Working with Recruiters.

There are some basic concepts in working with recruiters that will save you a lot of time and perhaps anxiety.

1. Recruiters work for their clients; they do not work for candidates. A recruiter will only submit you as a candidate if he feels he can make a sale.

2. When accepting a mission, recruiters sometimes will submit different sample candidates to find out what their client really wants, which may be completely different from the written job specification.

3. When a recruiter tells you that you are a selected candidate, remember you are most likely one of at least three and that the recruiter may be only in the testing stage.

4. If you are out of work, your chances with a recruiter diminish rapidly. Psychologically, clients want to feel that the recruiter is picking a candidate from a field of currently employed and highly successful people who meet their exact specifications. While you want to be listed with as many recruiters as possible, do not count on your next job coming from one of them if you are unemployed. Under the best of conditions, statistics show that recruiters fill less than 15 percent of all jobs.

   On the other hand, once you have your new job, do let all the recruiters in your area and beyond know of your new position and company. Keep the contacts going. If you have any promotions or significant changes in your position, by all means send the information to your recruiter list. This pre-buildup makes them aware that you are a mover and someone to keep an eye on.

5. A successful recruiter fills 10 or more missions per year. Think of the great numbers of people they must interview to fill what may be very difficult specifications.

6. You do not need to send a list of references to recruiters until requested. Reference checks ideally should be made only after you and a prospective employer have agreed in principle on a job. It is not wise to bother your references before you are sure what direction a job opportunity is taking.

7. Most recruiters maintain resumes in data bases that are not as sophisticated as you might think. One of the largest recruiters in the country said that there are more than 20,000 resumes and names on file. When the recruiter gets a mission, the first step is to look in the data base and, after winnowing possible candidates from there, go out on the market. There are three problems with this practice:

   a. Under what heading is a candidate listed in the data base? Does it reflect the true potential of the candidate? This usually is out of the candidate's control. Which resume the recruiters receive can determine how you are classified.

   b. How current is the data base, and how many candidates are listed in the files with the same qualifications you have? How often is the data base updated? Some recruiters take their data base and research seriously and have a person or department responsible solely for records. Even so, there must be problems in the sorting and criteria applied when they receive so many resumes every day.

   Recruiters who specialize in a specific sector of industry—microcomputers for example—retain a list of people they know and whose careers they have tracked for a number of years. This type of personalized data base is much more useful to a recruiter and will have fewer names. It also supports the argument that you should keep recruiters advised of your accomplishments while you have a job—not just when you are looking. Remember, they want to search you, not vice versa.

   c. When sending your resume to a recruiter, what certainty is there that you will be placed in their data base at all?

   If you are out of work, is it worthwhile to approach recruiters? The answer definitely is yes. If you get into their data bank, someone just might have a current job search that matches your profile. A mail campaign (letter plus resume) will let recruiters know of your interest and give them an overview of your capability.

   Recruiters are busy people. If they are interested in you, you can be sure you will be contacted. However, if you do not hear from them, they are not being rude; they just have nothing to report.

There is little sense in pestering recruiters for progress reports. But suppose that, like any other networking prospect, you have a referral (bridge) to that recruiter. In that case, they will be interested in you for two reasons:

- You represent a potential candidate.

- If they are supportive now, you can later become part of their network for missions when you do get settled.

For a listing of recruiters in the U.S., you can write for the *Directory of Executive Recruiters* compiled and published by

> *Consultants News*
> Templeton Road,
> Fitzwilliam, NH 03447

The directory lists retainer and contingency recruiting firms alphabetically, by industry, by function and by geographic area in a highly readable format. Since this book is published only once a year and recruiters move around, it will become progressively obsolete, so work with a current edition.

Candidates who are open to relocation should do a mass mailing of a cover letter plus resume to as much of the list as possible.

But suppose your geographic preference is Los Angeles. Why send a resume to New York or Atlanta? Many recruiters work the country rather than just their home town. Several Los Angeles recruiters divide their time between the East Coast and California. Since you never know where an opportunity may originate, sending out a resume is an inexpensive method of covering all the bases.

You can also buy from *Consultants News* self-stick address labels for all the recruiters in their listing, the retainer section only or the contingency group only. Buy a set of all their labels unless you have reason to limit your search to a very tight geographic area.

Print both your resume and a brief cover letter and do a mailing covering the entire country using the labels. If you want to address envelopes yourself, the directory will be adequate.

Remember to add a personal touch by signing your letters with a blue felt-tip pen.

Your cover letter should be very simple. Example:

YOUR NAME
YOUR ADDRESS
YOUR CITY, STATE ZIP

YOUR TELEPHONE
YOUR FAX (IF YOU HAVE ONE)
YOUR E-MAIL ADDRESS (IF YOU HAVE ONE)

(Date)

Name of recruiter
Company
Address
City, State ZIP

Dear *<Specific Name>*:

On the chance that you may be working on an assignment for a chief financial officer (*Or any other specific functions like* marketing manager, personnel manager, programmer, *but AVOID president, vice president... ambiguous titles*), I am sending you my resume.

My most recent experience has been in microcomputers, but I also have excellent knowledge of the electronics, wholesale hardware and toy industries.

My geographic preference is Los Angeles (*better if you do NOT have a preference and keep your options open*). (*Preferred no statement or*) I am open to any area where there could be an excellent opportunity.

I am seeking a challenge where I can use my skills in

- (*One of your most important skills... that should be of interest to your reader*), Diversified accounting knowledge—led accounting departments with up to 34 professionals

- (*Another important skill*), Communications—represented the company in dealing with banks obtaining favorable lines of credit

- (*Another important skill*), Training—personally trained more than 50 employees in all aspects of accounting and bookkeeping

- (*Another important skill*), Operations—provided daily management of the Accounting Department including preparation of annual, quarterly and monthly reports.

I would welcome hearing from you.

Sincerely,

Your full name (*signed with a pen with blue ink*)

Enclosure (*your resume*)

Note: To increase your chances, whenever possible, always write to a specific person.

While the *Consultants News* listings are excellent, they are not complete. Check the *Business to Business Yellow Pages* in your county, and any other geographic areas of interest, and you will find additional addresses of both types of recruiters, generally without differentiation. Also, ask some recruiters for the address of a local Executive Recruiters Association in your state and write for its listing. Your mailing will then be as complete as it can be.

Once the mailing is done, forget about it and react only to opportunities that come your way. Do not chase after recruiters. They will not appreciate it, nor will it help your cause.

When recruiters do call, they will want to know how much you made in your last position. Tell them both salary and the package, but also tell them what range you will accept for a good opportunity. Do not indicate your salary in the mailing; it serves no useful purpose and may spread a possible disqualifying figure to many people. Suppose your resume is in their file and you subsequently get a job at a significantly higher salary. Based on their information, the recruiter will peg you in the wrong job level. There always is time to talk salary when an opportunity is at hand.

The important thing to remember is to get your resume in recruiters' hands as early as possible in your campaign so that you will be covered should there be an open position in their file. If your search is confidential, omit the name of your current employer and merely list the industry. Example:

Eastman Kodak Company   1992 - Present
Rochester, New York

could be

Leading Photographic Materials   1992 - Present
Manufacturer & Supplier

Employment Agencies

Employment agencies differ from recruiters in several ways:

1. They work within specific regions, although they may be linked together by computer to furnish candidates from other geographic areas.

2. Employment agencies move more quickly than recruiters. When they have an assignment, they either advertise or pull candidates from their data base, but they begin immediately to present candidates to the prospective employer.

3. Most bona fide agencies have their fees paid by the employer. Some will insist that you sign an agreement giving them up to 15 percent of your starting annual salary, with the promise that they will try to recover this from the company. Do not sign any agreements without reading them thoroughly and be wary of anyone promising you a job for a fee.

   Ask for a list of satisfied references and carefully check it out. Know which counselor will be working with you and check that person out.

4. Agencies work on all types of jobs, from entry level to middle management. Many are specialists in certain industries, functional areas and types of positions. They cover factory workers, office workers, computer personnel, truckers, through to supervisory positions.

Employment agencies only make money when they place people, and sometimes you may be routed to a job that really is not for you. You must be careful that they stick to your agenda—not the agency's.

Some agencies may send your resume to a large number of companies, just to test the water. Some of these companies may be on your target list of planned approaches, so be careful to limit the information you give an agency. You want to control your program. Try to insist that they let you know beforehand which companies they are contacting so you can avoid any conflicts.

Many companies will pay agency fees. But the agency may present candidates who have agreed to pay the placement fee, which could bias the company's selection since it would prefer not to pay.

Agencies guarantee most placements, so if a candidate does not work out in one or two months, the agency either will refund the fee and/or find a replacement. If you decide to pay the fee, find out in advance what happens if you are terminated during your probationary period.

Agencies are on a fast track and you should be on your toes. Keep to yourself information that you do not want compromised and try to get them to keep your resume circulation within your objectives.

To get a quick handle on what agencies are active in your area, look in your Sunday classified section and your Yellow Pages. You can call a few to see if they handle positions of interest to you. If they do, visit them and see how they operate. Since they are very busy people, you will find most agency personnel frank and to the point. Many can give you useful tips on the market you are approaching.

Placing an Advertisement

Almost every day, job searchers place advertisements in *The Wall Street Journal*, local newspapers or trade publications. In general, these ads go unread by those to whom they are directed. However, if you have a rare specialty that is not of general interest, a trial ad may be worthwhile. You would be better off putting the ad in a trade publication rather than a regular newspaper.

Some recruiters do watch these listings, and small companies with limited search budgets might be attracted by this kind of ad. Another possible result could be a short-term consulting job.

Unfortunately, personal ads usually are expensive. If you do not meet any of the above criteria, think twice before investing the money.

Registering with a Computer Service

There are data base firms throughout the U.S. that boast that certain companies turn first to their files before commencing a general search. If the data base is financed by the searching companies, and there is no fee to the candidate, it costs you nothing to register. But if they request a fee, do not bother without a lot more information on their success rate in placing candidates. Someday this will be a powerful means of placement, but at the moment it is only beginning. Do not lose sight of a very important point—resumes do not get jobs; people do. Networking, meeting people, is the preferred method for finding your next position.

Applying in Person

For middle-management-and-above jobs, you cannot just pop in and hope for an interview. People who hire—the decision-makers—make appointments.

If you feel the job you are seeking would most likely be handled by the personnel department, there is nothing wrong in stopping by to ask what is available and leaving your resume and/or application. Generally, you should find out in advance if the company is hiring, and that information may come through your network of contacts, telemarketing calls or even watching the classifieds.

In areas where there is a high demand for specialized talent, you should watch the ads for "hiring fairs." These are open houses hosted by several companies. Fairs are a good source of information and a good way for you to shop a company. Most fairs are aimed at high-tech candidates with special skills or knowledge. Even so, plan to attend if there is one in your area, if only for the chance to meet people on the inside of these companies. They are there to encour-

age your prospecting and, while they may not be recruiting your particular skills, they may be a source for referrals.

School Placement Bureaus

For new entries into the labor market, school placement bureaus are excellent. They arrange times and places for recruiters to visit and meet with interested candidates. You should investigate your school's policy and how to avail yourself of its services. This does not mean, however, that you can put aside preparing a top-notch resume and perfecting interviewing and negotiating techniques.

If you are in the job market and are seeking a change, or if you are unemployed, you will find that school placement bureaus may help, but only very passively. They will be happy to list your resume and pass it along to any inquiry that might come in. Some schools, like Harvard Business School, regularly publish all inquiries and send them to interested alumni. The school cannot, however, assume responsibility for the quality of the opening. If you are out of work, be sure your resume is on file with your alma mater, but do not count on anything coming from that quarter. If it does, it will be the exception. You are better off contacting former professors and schoolmates on a personal basis as part of your networking process.

THE MAIL CAMPAIGN TO TARGET COMPANIES

From your exercises in Chapter 2, you have defined the kind of environment, position, working conditions and location your next job should have. You have reviewed your skills and accomplishments and know what you have to offer a potential employer. It is now time to select a list of target companies. Your target list could include competitors, suppliers, former employers, new companies you have discovered or companies from related industries.

Like the executive recruiter, you have to research companies and their management. Factors such as size, products and/or services, position in their industry, corporate policies, opportunity for advancement, attitude with respect to hiring your age group (including entry level), location, position in the economy, sales and profits are easy to research and will help you know better what you want and where to find it. One of the most important parts of your research will be to identify the people you would be working for and the decision-makers regarding your hiring. These people should be part of your research, and your approach to them, whether by mail or through personal contacts, is essential.

This part of the job search campaign is one of the most important, yet also one of the most neglected. Candidates often are in such a rush to "get their program rolling" that they do not realize this kind of research (homework) will assure better utilization of their energy.

There is a chance factor in encountering opportunity. But equally important is hunting with a purpose. The time invested in research will make you a better networker because you will know more about the companies and people you will be seeing. There is no substitute for knowledge.

Visit your local business library and create your target list of companies. Try to select at least 10 to 20 that you can actively pursue. The library has directories that can provide you with names of executives, their biographies, products, locations and key information about each firm (see Appendix C). Any publicly owned company (i.e., listed on a stock exchange or over-the-counter) will be glad to send you its annual and 10-Q and/or 10-K reports, which furnish a wealth of information about the company, its management, how it performed and what general problems it may be experiencing.

To help you gather information about your target company, use the sample check list on page 138.

Once you have a list of target companies, the next step is to find the person most likely to respond to your skills and potential. It may be anyone from the president on down. Finding your contact requires effort, and this is where research pays off. Networking is the surest method, but a good reference book can help. When your information comes from a directory or other reference, call the company to verify that the person still is in that job. Make this call to the switchboard, where the operator can quickly check your information. If asked why you want this information, reply that you intend to write that person and want to be sure you have a correct title/spelling/address.

Reaching Your Target Companies

Try a limited mail campaign consisting of a dozen companies at a time from your target list, with carefully researched contacts. The reason for a limited mailing is that you must follow-up each mailing with a phone call (instead of waiting for a reply) and try to complete the contact with a personal interview. Your letters should conclude with a statement such as, "I will be calling your office in a few days to set a mutually convenient time for an appointment." This process becomes unwieldy if you take on too many companies at a time.

What kind of mailing should you do?

1. If your salary is less than $50,000 per year and you are addressing a large company, your letter should be sent to the senior vice president or division manager of your specific interest, not the personnel department. You should send a good cover letter and a resume.

2. If your salary is more than $50,000 and you are addressing a large company, your letter approach should be either to the president or chief

DATE October 19

TARGET COMPANY INFORMATION FORM

Company ABC Company

Address 16000 Wilshire Blvd., Suite 2345, LA, CA 90024

Telephone (310) 555-8989   FAX (310) 555-8990

SIC Code* 3679   E-mail ABC@link.com   Internet www.abc-net.com

Prospective contacts (with title) John Stevens, President, Frank I. Long, V.P. Finance,

Jack Barker, Director of Manufacturing

GENERAL DATA: number of employees 1400

Sales $321 million   Reported earnings $4.2 million

Number of facilities/offices 3 in CA, 1 in HI, 2 in Europe

Products Electrical switches, circuit boards, computer accessories, distributor of

imported products

Expansion programs Maybe into Asia??? Article in LA Times on Feb. 20th

Anticipated needs Director of international sales???

News (problems, current events) Recent changes on board of directors

John Stevens appointed President in January. Came from G.E.

Potential position International sales

Pertinent accomplishments 10 yrs. direct European sales, work with

Westinghouse Electric, experience with COMPAQ

APPROACH: Bridge (referral) Jim Conners at Union Bank
or

Mail & Call (see telemarketing) Last resort
or

Reply to an ad (mail or in person) Not effective

Source _____

Information still needed More information on their banking - plus other

bridges into company. Goal to have a referral into the company in 4 weeks!!!

Set appointment: Date/Time End of November latest

NEW referral ???? Pending

* = Standard Industrial Classification Code

DATE_____

TARGET COMPANY INFORMATION FORM

Company _____

Address _____

Telephone _____ FAX _____

SIC Code* _____ E-mail _____ Internet _____

Prospective contacts (with titles) _____

_____

_____

GENERAL DATA: number of employees _____

Sales _____ Reported earnings _____

Number of facilities/offices _____

Products _____

_____

Expansion programs _____

_____

Anticipated needs _____

News (problems, current events) _____

_____

Potential position _____

Pertinent accomplishments _____

_____

APPROACH: Bridge (referral) _____
or

Mail & Call (see telemarketing) _____
or

Reply to an ad (mail or in person) _____

Source _____

Information still needed _____

_____

Set appointment: Date/Time _____

NEW referral _____

* = Standard Industrial Classification Code

executive officer. Do not send your resume but a well-constructed broad-cast letter.

3. If you are addressing a small or medium-size company, write to the president regardless of your salary level. In this case, use a broadcast letter without a resume if your salary is in excess of $50,000. If your salary is less than $50,000, use a cover letter and resume.

How to Compose a Cover Letter with a Resume

1. Write to a specific person, never a title.

2. Tailor your resume for the company you are targeting. Do not date your resume.

3. The first paragraph should state the purpose of the letter, using one of the opening statements or accomplishments from your resume to get started.

4. Your second paragraph should make a general statement incorporating another of your accomplishments or some of your skills.

5. Your third paragraph should explain what you think you can contribute to the company and why you would like to work there.

6. Your closing statement should convey that you would like to meet with this person at his earliest convenience and will be calling for an appointment.

The resume that accompanies these letters will be arranged to suit the job sought. The objective is an interview.

The Broadcast Letter to a Target Company

The difference between a broadcast letter in reply to an ad and one to a target company is that the former is designed to meet the specific criteria of the ad while the letter to a target company gives your general strengths (unless you know beforehand that your target company has a specific need that you are addressing).

Taking Apart Your Broadcast Letter.

Either through networking or research, you have identified the person who would be hiring you. This is the person you want to impress to provoke an interview.

Joyce Sato
37 Villa Street
New York, New York 10021
(212) 555-2222

(DATE)

«Data SATOMM-TargetCompanies.DOC»

«title» «fname» «IF mi»«mi» «ENDIF»«lname»
«IF pos»«pos»
«ENDIF»«IF co»«co»
«ENDIF»«address1»
«IF address2»«address2»
«ENDIF»«city», «state» «zip»

Dear «title» «lname»:

I am in the process of seeking a new healthcare human resources management position where I can use my skills in:

- Employee and labor relations - resolved grievances without a single judgment for companies with up to 1,600 employees

- Workers' compensation - saved more than $10 million through effective claims management and administrator selection

- Recruitment - personally recruited more than 1,500 employees

- Compensation and benefits - developed and implemented cafeteria, paid time off and employee assistance programs

- Training and development - initiated and delivered programs in cultural diversity, sexual harassment, interviewing skills and violence in the workplace with more than 1,000 participants.

On the chance that we may have areas of mutual interest, I will be calling you in a few days with the hope of setting a convenient time to meet.

Sincerely,

Joyce Sato

Joyce Sato

enc.: resume

Jack Armstrong
123 Olympic Avenue
San Diego, California 92345-9876
(619)555-6666
e-mail: jarmstrong@link.com

(DATE)

Ms. Jeanne Wilson
Wilson Real Estate Management Corporation
6578 Vermont Avenue
Los Angeles, California 90033

Dear Ms. Wilson:

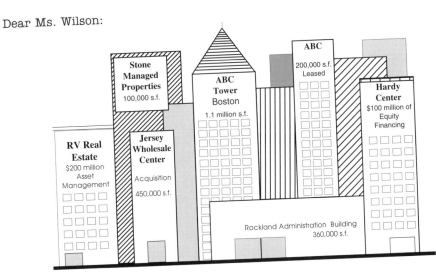

I am seeking my next real estate challenge and thought of your company.

On the chance that we may have areas of mutual interest, I will be calling you in a few days.

Sincerely,

Jack Armstrong

enc.: resume

Your first paragraph must catch your reader's attention. Using one of your most significant accomplishments (one that would appeal to your reader), it must show, "Here's someone different."

Your second paragraph should address your interest in this company. It should show why you have singled out this firm and how this ties into your interest (which should be his when you are through).

Then you list accomplishments that prove your point. The accomplishments should be your answer to his anticipated needs. Of course, if you can learn his problems beforehand, you will be in a much better position to select and refine your accomplishments from your 20-Second Resume.

Your closing paragraph winds up your letter by suggesting that further conversation would be beneficial for all, and you will be calling for an appointment.

Look at the example on page 143.

Hazards of a Mail Campaign

Many times your broadcast letter (or cover letter and resume) will not reach the person you address and will, by means of secretarial efficiency, be sent to the personnel manager or vice president of human resources.

If they are not looking for someone with your exact experience, you will get a computer letter thanking you for your inquiry, saying you have a most interesting background but they have nothing at the moment. And, with your permission, they would like to retain your resume in their files in case something comes up.

This does not mean you should drop your target company. It means you must find a better way of reaching your key person there. This brings you back to networking and finding a bridge to that person.

How much better to call that person and say, "Mr. Scott, during a discussion with Charles Beene [your bridge], he suggested I call you, as he felt that you would be interested in my accomplishments in magazine sales. Do you suppose we might have a brief chat on Thursday or Friday of this week?" What makes this conversation possible is that you have used your contacts to locate a bridge, Charles Beene—someone known to Mr. Scott. This immediately places you in a different light with Scott. Though he may still ask for a resume, chances are he will actually read it. Imagine further, if Beene calls before you do to let Scott know that you sold $35 million worth of magazines last year!

YOUR NAME
YOUR ADDRESS
YOUR CITY, STATE ZIP

YOUR TELEPHONE

(DATE)

Mr. John Scott
President
Blott Book Publishing Company
34 Arrow Street
Los Angeles, CA 00000

Dear Mr. Scott:

Last year I was responsible for distributing $35 million in magazines throughout the Southwest. This represented a 5 percent increase over the previous year and a margin improvement of 2 percent.

I began as a junior salesman 15 years ago and through a series of promotions have risen to the position of sales manager. I have heard of your expansion, and I am very interested in moving into the book industry, where I could apply my sales and marketing skills.

If we had a chance to talk, you would discover that the publishing industry is my passion. My accomplishments include:

* Launching five new magazines and, in a period of 18 months, generating sales of 200,000 units per month.

* Increasing sales by 456 percent over a period of seven years.

* Recruiting, hiring and training a sales team of top performers.

* As Production Manager, increasing efficiency of operations by 250 percent in three years.

I graduated from Columbia University with a B.A. in fine arts and served in the USAF as a 1st Lieutenant.

Mr. Scott, I feel confident that a short conversation about my experience and your growth plans would be mutually beneficial. I will be calling you early next week so that we can choose a convenient time.

Sincerely,

Your Name

The challenge at this point is to find a bridge. If you have the company's annual report, you can approach their auditors who may know the person you want to meet. Or, you might contact a branch of the company and try for an information interview with its manager. Lawyers, bankers, members of a professional association, customers or suppliers, may serve as bridges. In other words, you must work around your problem until you find someone who knows the person you want to contact. This is why you must carry your target company and network lists with you all the time: You never know when you will run into someone who can help you.

Strategically, it is only by personal contact that you find out useful information. The mail approach cannot provide this detail.

Suppose you are interested in the TFR Company. You decide to send them either a cover letter and resume or a well-written broadcast letter. You decided to orient your letter toward the marketing side of your career.

Alternatively, suppose you take a different approach and, through a bridge, meet someone in the company (who is not necessarily the person who will be hiring). This contact informs you that the company desperately needs sales managers, not marketing people. With this new information, you can revise your entire campaign. Now your resume will be oriented to your sales accomplishments, not marketing.

CHAPTER 6

Networking

hat is networking? Networking is getting out and meeting people either formally or informally in groups or one-on-one. It is a chance to get to know other people and letting them know something about you. In the process, you obtain information (about careers, companies and people) and build personal contacts that eventually will make you known to potential employers. Your contacts become your team of supporters, leading toward your objective. Networking will expose you to the maximum number of opportunities in the shortest time. Can talking to just one person be as effective as advertising to thousands? You bet it can!

Mail campaigns are very much linked to networking. They are an important part of the total cycle designed to get you interviews. But smart job searchers will spend up to 75 or 80 percent of their time meeting people and working the informal route for a job opportunity. Networking is meeting people you have selected to get you into your target companies or referrals you get from research and advice interviews that can introduce you to opportunities in the hidden job market.

The term hidden job market refers to jobs that have not yet been advertised in the press, or to recruiters or agencies. They are uncovered primarily by word of mouth.

OBJECTIVES

The measure of a network is how it helps you meet new people and discover job opportunities. What kinds of people are able to help you?

1. **Decision-makers:** people who have the potential to employ you in their own company. They may not have a job opening when you arrive but, after learning about your accomplishments, they can create a position. Remember, Granovetter found this occurred in **43.8 percent** of the cases studied. In addition, while you may be approaching a decision-maker for referrals, the interview can quickly shift into a specific need in his company. It can happen, provided you network!

2. **Referrals to decision-makers:** people who can lead you directly to a job opportunity through their immediate contacts.

3. **Referrals to other contacts:** people who can provide you with a bridge to your target company or to another person.

4. **Advisors on your search:** people in a position to inform you about a new profession or career change. You can learn details about new companies and industries and even add to your target list.

5. **Referrals from people with wide connections:** suppliers or providers of service to your targeted job market. They know people in your industry or your target group and may be willing to make inquiries on your behalf.

ADVANTAGES

1. **Networking means meeting people on a referral basis; you are no longer a complete stranger**. You have the rapport of your contact leading the way. How you approach your networking list and conduct interviews will be discussed in detail in Chapters 7 and 8. Networking is infinitely better (and easier) than a cold call—and will provide the expertise you will need for making the unavoidable cold call.

2. **You can plot your own course of action.**

3. **You can set your own pace**. You can mix research interviews with advice and direct interviews and add variety to your search. You should mix different kinds of interviews in your schedule to vary your routine and give yourself some "breathers."

4. **You can be original**. You are not competing for an "open" position. Without competition, attention is focused on your accomplishments and skills rather than on specific criteria, and you have a better chance of getting results!

   Another encouraging fact about the hidden job market is that there are seldom many candidates competing for the job. In some cases you may be the only candidate!

5. **You can be flexible**. Suppose you are on an advice interview and yet succeed in interesting your contact regarding a position he had been thinking about. At that point, your advice interview becomes direct. You are free to guide your interviewer's attention to whatever accomplishments are appropriate for his needs.

6. **In presenting your accomplishments (benefits), you can actually create a position for yourself**. You can precipitate a job by consolidating responsibilities never before examined and organized by your prospect.

   For instance, suppose you are seeking a financial position. You previously have solved problems in inventory and accounts payable and have demonstrated an ability to computerize these arduous tasks. If you encounter a company with similar problems, you stand a good chance of being asked to look into its activities right on the spot: a short-term consulting position leading perhaps to a permanent job.

7. **Your referrals will help you get meetings with people they know**. It is much easier and effective to have a third party call and recommend you than doing it yourself. Which would you prefer? "Hello, John, I ran into a very sharp person the other day and I think the two of you should get together…" or your call alone: "Hello, Mr. Smith, I'd like to introduce myself. We haven't met, but I'm sure we have many areas of mutual interest in…."

8. **With proper networking, a candidate will run into at least one job opportunity every 12 to 16 meetings**. This is just an average, and not all opportunities will be the job you want. But, it shows the hidden job market is loaded with job possibilities for the taking.

9. A by-product of networking is that acquaintances often turn into friends. This has been reported by a number of candidates. A good network is an ongoing process. You will continue to meet new and interesting people. It offers the opportunity to expand your world and enhance the quality of your life.

   The hidden job market deserves your attention. How do you get started?

THE TOOLS

Network List

The first thing you must do is develop a network list. This list includes everyone (yes, everyone) you know. Who are these people? This list will be made up of:

FRIENDS

▶ Relatives	▶ Schoolmates
▶ Professors	▶ Doctors
▶ Dentist	▶ Neighbors
▶ Friends of Other Family Members	▶ School Alumni
▶ People on Your Christmas/Holiday Card List	

SOCIAL CLUBS & ASSOCIATIONS

▶ Community Associations
▶ Religious Communities
▶ Hobby Clubs

▶ PTA
▶ Sporting Clubs/Groups

BUSINESS CONTACTS

▶ Business Associates—Past & Present
▶ Former Company Service Groups
▶ Previous Employers
▶ Accountants
▶ Consultants
▶ Political Contacts

▶ Former Company Suppliers
▶ Friends in Former Companies
▶ Attorneys
▶ Bankers
▶ Independent Business Owners
▶ Recruiters—You Know Personally

SERVICE ORGANIZATIONS

▶ Insurance Agents
▶ Stock Brokers
▶ Ad/Public Relations People

▶ Sales Professionals
▶ Real Estate Brokers

Most candidates have not had much experience in calling people for interviews. In breaking into networking, begin your calls with people you know well. Make your first calls to people you feel will respond to your request to get together for a brief chat about your resume and accomplishments. As you develop experience, you can add people you know only as acquaintances and, later, people to whom you have been referred. With practice, anyone can become a good networker.

You should use the following criteria in selecting people to approach:

- People easy to approach and talk with—most likely good friends and former associates.

- People who are knowledgeable within your field of interest.

- People with wide connections of their own by virtue of their jobs or associations.

- People who have had a reasonable success pattern in their work and who are accustomed to dealing with the public.

- People who are able to help you with new career information.

- Other job searchers who can exchange their networks with yours.

Your network and target company lists should be carried in your briefcase at all times, because you will be adding to them continually.

Your Computer

Your networking and target company lists are the primary resources of your program and, if you put them in your computer, they can be updated with ease. You will want to (and need to) communicate with the people you meet. A PC will make that communication less of a chore.

A PC also will permit you to add new names and addresses, and sort them and reprint them in various ways—for example by last name, company, city, activity and Zip code. You then will be able to identify which contacts you wish to pursue and what additional feedback you need from your network.

Your Telephone

Sooner or later, you will have to use the telephone to make appointments. Even with mail campaigns, you must call for an interview date. If you wait for someone to call you, it may never happen. People are just too busy.

People today are more accustomed to being approached by telephone than they were only a few years ago. Consequently, techniques have rapidly developed in telemarketing (see Chapter 7). But tougher measures of defense have also evolved, especially by secretaries screening calls. This brings us back to our network.

In making calls, it is much easier to get through with an introduction. In telemarketing, this is called a *bridge*. Unless you like cold-calling, developing bridges into companies and to people of interest will become a priority for you.

Using the form on page 152, you can create a directory of your network.

SOME WORDS OF ADVICE

When you were purchasing agent or vice president of the XYZ bank, or whatever post you held, many people appeared to be your friends and were solicitous of your advice and perhaps even depended on you for their business. You probably thought of these people immediately and put them high on your list for networking.

You will find, as practically all candidates do, that this list can be divided in two. There are the fair-weather friends, who would do anything for you when you were vice president and who will now be suddenly very hard to reach. You cannot depend much on their help.

On the positive side, there are the people who will rally to help you in whatever way they can. These are your real friends, the ones who will be remembered long after you are resettled in your new position. You can expect some

Network Directory Worksheet

22

Name John Smith

Job title Vice President, Business Development

Company Bankers Trust   Tel. (office) (212) 555-0904

Business address 275 Park Avenue, NY, NY 10022

FAX (212) 555-0944   E-mail JS43@aol.com   Internet www.bankers.com

Relationship New Contact   Tel. (home)

Home address

Admin. Assistant Mary Stone   Tel. (office) (212) 555-0905

Date called May 2

Referred by Tom Ferry   Referral's tel. (212) 555-4444

RESULTS Had to call twice, got him on the second call.

Nice, easy-going fellow, lived in LA for 6 years. Knows lots of people in the banking world.

Good friends with Bob Frank who is V.P. of Business Development at BOA and Larry

Green, private investor turned broker.

- New referrals Larry Green (212) 555-7700 of Merrill Lynch, also Jack Barry of

Capital Investors, (213) 555-8888

- Other appointment He will be out on the West Coast in June, arrange meeting.

- Other info (about companies/industries) No time for an interview

FOLLOW-UP Call him on May 10th to set up Los Angeles meeting.

- Letter
- Call Next week
- E-mail Thank you sent May 4th

Using this format, you should research every name you can think of.

Network Directory Worksheet

\# _____

Name _____

Job title _____

Company _____ Tel. (office) _____

Business address _____

FAX _____ E-mail _____ Internet _____

Relationship_____ Tel. (home) _____

Home address_____

Admin. Assistant _____ Tel. (office) _____

Date called _____

Referred by _____ Referral's tel. _____

RESULTS _____

_____

_____

_____

_____

_____

- New referrals _____

  _____

  _____

- Other appointment _____

- Other info (about companies/industries) _____

  _____

FOLLOW-UP _____

- Letter_____

- Call _____

- E-mail _____

Using this format, you should research every name you can think of.

disappointments in your network list and it is just as well to know it now, before you get started.

DYNAMICS OF NETWORKING
Where to Find the Needs

In the hidden job market, almost every job is discussed in some way with friends or associates before it is advertised in the press or circulated to recruiters. When someone is promoted, discharged, transferred or retired, there is a period when this news is known only to a small circle.

The opening is analyzed first at the department level, then passed to upper management for approval. Next, a review of existing personnel is made for possible promotion from within. After all these processes, the need is presented to the personnel department as a requisition for a search, and an ad is placed or a recruitment assignment is given out.

This informal process of job creation happens every day around the world. A new order is quoted on; there will be a need for more people to handle the load. The company is informed it has the winning bid; all departments are asked to review their personnel needs. Jobs are created before anyone on the outside knows they exist.

Your task as a networker is to discover and penetrate one or more of these small circles of information and present your profile and accomplishments before the job requirement is announced outside the company.

This is accomplished by meeting people from all professions who ultimately can place you in contact with someone who knows of a specific need. Once inside the circle of information, you will have the advantage over anyone else. One part of your networking will be meeting people you have targeted. Another segment will consist of adding people you meet along the way to your network. Since the path of information is a chance factor, *everyone* you meet is important to discovering the need as it develops.

Some companies encourage their employees to bring in candidates. Your network might lead you to an employee who may not be connected in any way with your particular skills but is aware of needs that have to be filled in his own firm. Some companies offer a bonus to any employee who brings in another employee who lasts six months.

You will also be reading the news. People get promoted, die, retire; there are acquisitions, mergers, reorganizations and expansion. Many of these news events mean valuable jobs. It is only by keeping in contact with people, who in turn know people, that you can tap this market.

For example, you may have been in contact with a company that had no specific position for you. But in the news, another division in the same corporation may announce an expansion in your area of expertise. How do you make the approach? You go back to the person you met initially and ask for an introduction. Since one of life's basic laws is that nothing remains constant, a real network is continually in motion. You can use these contacts to keep in tune with the changing job market.

Professional Organizations and Associations,

Here is a gold mine of contacts, yours for the asking. You should be networking as many organizations and associations connected with your profession as you can, even if you are not a member.

If you do not know where to begin, try your local library for the *Encyclopedia of Associations* to find local groups near you. Call and ask to talk to the president. If you can arouse interest, you could be invited to a meeting. It is a fertile area to network.

Try to get a list of the membership. Then follow networking principles, keeping in mind that everyone is important in developing contacts. Begin with the secretary who will be your initial contact with the association's president.

Trade shows provide another means of locating employment needs. Here, a large segment of an industry exhibits its products and services. Key executives of the company often are in attendance. If you can meet one or two people in companies of interest to you, you might discover a need that has yet to be announced. The obvious advantage is that the companies are there and supplying the information you need rather than responding to your approach. Listening to what each executive says about the company or its competition (expansion, new products, investments, etc.) will give you ideas about where you can apply your accomplishments.

The Pyramid Process

Here are some networks that led to jobs:

Case 1. (Candidate's job objective: general manager)

First contact (advice interview*): A friend (contact made by telephone) who is vice president of corporate development in a high-tech company, who suggested the...

Second contact (advice interview): Business broker who suggested the...

For descriptions of the three kinds of interviews, see Chapter 8

Third contact (advice interview): Division manager in large company who suggested the...

Fourth contact (advice interview): Plant manager (new in his job) who suggested the...

Fifth contact (advice interview): Small, struggling business entrepreneur who suggested the...

Sixth contact (advice interview): Partner in Big Eight accounting firm who suggested the...

Seventh contact (advice interview): Another small business broker who suggested the...

Eighth contact (direct interview): A business consultant who was looking for a chief executive officer for a firm he was advising, which led to a job offer.

Case 2. (Candidate's job objective: operations manager)

First contact: (a telephone call without a bridge, i.e., a cold call). A research interview with the general manager of a small company in a town 100 miles to the north. His company and name were researched from a state manufacturers directory. This meeting led to a...

Second contact: A financial advisor in a nearby city (advice interview) who suggested the...

Third contact: The president of a small, developing, but very successful high-tech company situated 200 miles south, who had no job in mind at that moment. Impressed by the initial encounter, the president arranged additional meetings. Three interviews later, he recognized a need for an operations manager and made a job offer (initially an advice interview that changed to a direct interview). This case demonstrates Granovetter's statistics that 43.8 percent of jobs are created on the spot.

Note: All the above appointments were first made by a telephone call.

Why were these candidates successful?

- In each case the job was never published or turned over to a recruiter. The candidate was not after a job vacancy—he was seeking people with problems or needs he could solve. Using the techniques that you will discover in Chapter 8, he was able to identify the problems of his prospect, either before the meeting through research or during the interview. Once this was done, he was able to draw upon selected accomplishments from his personal work history that demonstrated his potential skills as a problem solver to his prospect.

- The companies in the above examples were small or medium size. In small companies, you can reach top managers (and decision-makers) easier, there are fewer formalities in the hiring process, you stand out more because there may not be someone in the company with your skills, and, because of needs, hiring decisions are usually faster.

- From the initial contact to the final job offer, each candidate was using referrals, except for the initial research contact of Case 2, where it was a cold call for information. The candidates never asked for a job—only for information or advice.

- From the employer's point of view, the scenario was: In the midst of any number of problems (production, sales, administrative or financial), in walked a person having the demonstrated skills to solve one or more of the company's problems. The employer was equally impressed by the manner of the candidate's job search, thinking, "If he does that for himself, he'll do it for me!" Without a defined job vacancy, the job was created on the spot around the skills of the candidate. What interested the prospect was a solution to his problems.

- When the job was exposed, each candidate showed not only talent to solve problems but enthusiasm to get involved. This spontaneous availability for immediate help is extremely appealing to someone in trouble.

It was absolutely impossible to predict that any one of these network contacts would have led to a job.

Aside from the initial contact that started the chain of meetings, each interview produced other contacts to expand the candidate's networking in other directions (new pyramids).

LOCATING A  INTO A TARGET COMPANY

TARGET COMPANY People you want to meet in your target company.	**EXAMPLES OF** **NETWORK BRIDGES** Professionals & Tradespeople
Chairman of the Board	Auditors Attorneys
President, C.E.O.	Suppliers Trade Associations
Executive V.P., C.O.O.	Professional Clubs Bankers (local branches)
Vice Presidents	Customers Advertising Agency
Division Managers	Chamber of Commerce Consultants
Plant Managers	Recruiters Retired Executives
Director of Operations	Real Estate Brokers Business Brokers
Department Managers	Stock Brokers Collection Agencies
Supervisors	Asset Base Lenders

◄ ◄ ◄ ◄

Techniques for making the bridge connection:

1. Complete your target list of companies and people you want to meet. Target companies can come from your current, prior or a new industry of interest.
2. If the company is public, get their annual and 10-Q and/or 10-K reports. The company will furnish this, if requested. Find out who they use as auditors, bankers, advertising agency, attorneys and other professionals.
3. If the company is private, ask them directly by phone who they use or question local businesses in their area (bankers, Chamber of Commerce and suppliers) until you find someone who knows people in the company.
4. Watch newspapers and trade magazines for news and information as to what your target company is doing and with whom.
5. Your first networking contacts will lead you to other business contacts who can get you started networking in your target companies.
6. To help you with all of the above, check with the reference books cited in Appendix C.

CHAPTER 7

Telemarketing Yourself

 ou have seen that networking will be your most powerful tool for getting yourself placed in the job you want in the shortest period of time. To do this effectively, you need to develop telephone skills.

Most executives spend a large portion of their day on the telephone. But representing a company on the phone and marketing yourself over the phone are two entirely different things. Executives who routinely closed million-dollar deals over the phone have behaved as if they had never seen one in their lives when it came time to call someone about a job interview.

Because there has been so little written on using the telephone for job search, candidates have tended to rely on mail campaigns to obtain interviews. Mail campaigns are neither efficient nor productive unless linked to the telephone ("I will be calling you early next week…"). When your letter arrived, your executive may not even have seen it before it was rerouted by his secretary to the personnel department. Multiply your letter by the 100 or more regularly received and you can watch your chances diminish before your eyes.

On the other hand, an aggressive candidate can cut right through this wall of uncertainties by calling. Given the right skills, you can communicate directly with any business executive in the country. These telephone skills will serve you well, not only during your job search but for the rest of your career.

The following exercises are designed to provide a nuts-and-bolts approach to the art—and it is an art—of getting through to your party. They require both practice and preparation. While some of the statements are intended to make you reach for openings, you must still feel comfortable during the conversation.

What will make things easier for you is that many of the principles of telemarketing come from the interview process itself. It is only logical when you think of it; an interview actually begins on the telephone.

Interviews have different uses. Initially, you will be asking for ADVICE INTERVIEWS, in which you will get recommendations from friends and associates. Later you will want to arrange for RESEARCH INTERVIEWS, which are designed to provide you with an information base that will help you reach your goal: the DIRECT INTERVIEW, which is your opportunity to sell yourself face to face with a prospective employer.

APPROACH

People You Know Well

The easiest phone calls to make are to friends. Starting with these calls, you will begin to get your message organized and, with practice, become more comfortable. When calling friends, try to focus on what you need: an interview. Your discussion will be more casual. Begin with your interest in their world and come back around to what is new in yours. Do not ask for a job, even if they have the possibility of hiring you. What you want is advice, referrals and a chance to get together.

Your friends have networks that they can share with you, and they may know of situations that you might investigate further. Focus on your accomplishments, job objective(s) and target list.

Interviews with friends are a great way to begin your search in the hidden job market. The temptation will be to do everything by phone, but I recommend that you see them in person. Moving from friends to business associates you know well will be more comfortable after your initial contacts.

GETTING THROUGH

A business phone call for an appointment most of the time follows a path:

The Switchboard

The Secretary

Your Target Person

The Switchboard

The switchboard operator usually does not screen calls unless asked to do so, and your call will be put through directly to the office nine times out of ten.

However, the switchboard operator also can provide information important to your search. When speaking, use a tone of voice that encourages help. Avoid sounding authoritative or demanding. Make the operator feel that you value the assistance given. The switchboard can:

- Confirm that a person is still in the job. People move. If you are working from a reference book, verify the title, spelling and mailing address. All this can be done very routinely by merely saying, "I have correspondence for Mr. Smith and need to verify his exact title." If Smith is no longer the vice president of marketing, you can say: "So I can update my records, can you please give me the full name and spelling of Mr. Smith's replacement?"

With a busy board, your questions must be brief! But if you have the opportunity, you also should ask, "Does Mr. Smith have a direct line?" You may not always get this number, but if you do, you have a good chance of reaching Smith directly around six p.m., bypassing completely his absent secretary.

- Get the name and extension number of Mr. Smith's secretary. It is nicer to address someone by name instead of "Miss...er...what's your name?"

- The switchboard operator often knows who is in and who is out. If you ask, "Is Bob Smith in today?" it might get you one of several replies: "Yes, he's in but his line is busy," or "Yes, but he's been in meetings all morning," or "No, he's visiting our New York Office today," or even "Yes he is. May I tell him who's calling?"

You want to keep the ball in your court. When someone is not in, the natural response is, "May I take your name and number?" Once this information is passed along to a secretary or receptionist, you have lost control. If you are put on the spot, leave the information but indicate that you will be calling back.

Warm Up

Switchboard/Receptionist

This exercise is useful to most candidates, but imperative for those who are not yet at ease on the telephone. Arrange to role-play with a friend various situations involving a call to the switchboard. After you have agreed on the procedure, you should actually call from one location to another. Leave your answering machine on "record" and play back conversations later.

The following are some typical questions. Have your friend mix them up so that you will learn to adapt your script.

Possible Questions from the Switchboard.

Operator	Responses
1. "Who's calling, please?"	
	(Give your name.)
2. "What is the name of your company?"	
	(If you are still employed or have recently left a company, you can say you are "from" your prior company. Remember, this is a true statement.)
3. "Who are you calling?"	
	("Mr. Smith," assuming you have verified that Smith is still in the position and is located at this address.)
4. "May I tell him what this is regarding?"	
	(To the switchboard operator, you can say, "It's a personal matter" or "He will know what this is regarding.")
5. "Is this regarding employment?"	
	(Your answer is "I'm working on a marketing project and would like to discuss it with Mr. Smith." What you are saying is absolutely true; you are working on a marketing project—and you are the product.)

Possible Questions/Statements from You.

1. "May I have Mr. Smith, please?" (Be assertive, your voice should reflect that you *are* going to get through to him.)

2. "Could you please tell me who is head of the sales department (or any other activity in the company)?" (When you are not sure to whom you should speak, the switchboard operator has your answer. In this case, your tone of voice should be questioning and enlist aid.)

3. "How do you spell his (her) name?" (Be patient; there will probably be other calls to answer. Courtesy will get you everywhere!)

4. "I want to verify your exact mailing address."

5. "Is Mr. Smith still at this address?" (Verification)

6. "Is Mr. Smith still vice president of sales?" (Verification of a reference from a book.)

7. "Who has replaced Mr. Smith? May I have that spelling?"

8. "Could I confirm your address?"

9. "How do I get to your office from _____? I would be taking the _____ Freeway."

10. "What are your office hours?"

11. "May I please have Mr. Smith's direct line? I may be calling after hours."

The Secretary

Most secretaries of successful executives are well trained in keeping their boss separated from the unwanted world. A chief executive officer receives calls from a wide variety of people, and the more successful and well-known he is, the greater the number of callers (fame has its disadvantages): stock brokers, real estate agents, loan companies, seminar sales people, consultants, accounting service organizations, charities, job seekers, suppliers, dissatisfied customers, recruiters, outplacement counselors. All are trying to catch the attention of your target.

Secretaries are quite different from switchboard operators. They know, perhaps more than anyone in the company, what is going on in their boss' world. They know his friends, associates, boss, customers, suppliers and family, and are in position to screen his calls. You need their cooperation if you are going to get in to see Mr. Smith.

If your target person is in middle management, there is usually less resistance in getting through. However, someone who is over-solicited may ask to have calls screened. The following discussion is oriented to the worst situations; you will find many instances in which your calls breeze through. For the few times you want to get through and cannot—read on.

The key to getting past a diligent secretary is a good bridge. More than likely, the bridge you use as a referral is already known to Mr. Smith's secretary who, not wanting to offend, will communicate your message to Mr. Smith, "Paul Jones is calling, referred by Jack Dole." The chances are that Smith will take the call, not because you are Paul Jones, but out of courtesy and friendship for Jack Dole.

But secretaries may be tough or may not know your referral. A lot depends on your voice and your approach. Consider these two examples:

You	Secretary
"Good morning, I would like to speak to Mr. Smith."	
	"Whom shall I say is calling?"
"Paul Jones, Mr. Jack Dole suggested I call."	
	"Could I let Mr. Smith know what this call is regarding?"
"It's a personal matter."	
	"Mr. Jones, is this regarding employment?"
"Yes, I'm interested in working for your company and Mr. Dole indicated that Mr. Smith would be interested in my resume."	
	"I'm sure he would be. Could you please send us a copy so I can pass it along to Mr. Smith? He will then get back to you."

The candidate has lost control of the conversation.

Or,

You	Secretary

"Good morning, Miss Moran, my name is Paul Jones. I would like to speak with Bob Smith, please. I'm calling at the suggestion of our mutual friend Jack Dole. It's about a marketing project I'm working on."

"Can I have the name of your company?"

"I'm from the Jones company."

"One moment, please."

It is no secret which of the above conversations got Paul in to speak with Mr. Smith. There are several things to be learned before speaking to secretaries:

- Be friendly and firm in asking to speak to your target person. Do not hesitate. If your voice communicates that you do not expect to get through, more than likely you will not.

- Use names. Not Miss…but, "Miss Moran, I would like to speak to Bob Smith," not Mr. Smith. This implies that you know Bob Smith or, if you do not, using his first name implies that you should know him. Exceptions would be people who hold very high positions and people who are much older than you. In those cases, a little respect goes a long way. When in doubt, use "Mr."

- Indicate straight out that you are working on a marketing project. This is true. You are marketing yourself. If Miss Moran wants to know more about the project, you can indicate it concerns "medical products" or "financial controls" or "personnel relations" or whatever specialty you are pursuing. By mentioning a project, you immediately draw attention away from the unspoken question: "Are you looking for a job?"

- The moment you indicate it is a personal matter, you imply that it has to do with employment, unless your bridge is also involved with Smith on something personal. However, that is a longshot. You can refuse to give details about your project by saying it is a "personal project." Even with your bridge, if she has been instructed really to keep people at a distance, she might ask you to write a letter to Mr. Smith outlining what you want to talk about.

A lot of your success will come from your voice and your ability to project that what you have to discuss with Smith is important.

- Most secretaries, if they do not feel you are seeking employment, will want to know the name of your company. If you are still employed, that is no problem. Give the name. If you are unemployed but are still on the payroll, you can say, "I'm *from* the XYZ Company." You can still be considered from a company even though you are no longer active with them. However, if you feel uncomfortable about saying you are from a past employer, create a company of your own: "I'm Paul Jones, from the Jones Company." This follows the tradition that everyone who calls should be from somewhere! Play the game.

- If you are fortunate enough to hold a Ph.D. degree, then by all means indicate, "Dr. Jones for Bob Smith, please." The "Dr." implies any number of possibilities and your ease in getting through will be greatly enhanced. In this case, if you indicate that it is a personal matter, the secretary will not think you are calling about a job-related interview.

- If you are from out of town you can use a different approach. "Good morning, Miss Moran, I'm Paul Jones, calling from New York (or wherever) for Bob Smith." Long-distance calls are usually given priority in any office. Or, if you have recently moved to the area in which you are networking you can say, "Good morning, Miss Moran, I'm Paul Jones, in from New York and I'd like to talk with Bob Smith." She may ask if Mr. Smith knows you and you can say, "I'm calling at the suggestion of Jack Dole." This type of call implies that you are only available for a short time and perhaps it is important that you get through while you are still in town.

  If you encounter a secretary who just will not let you through, try calling early in the morning, late in the evening, or even at lunch when there is a stand-in. If all else fails, go back to your bridge and let him know you are having trouble. He can help by putting in a call to Smith, or just a call from Dole to Miss Moran may be enough.

- If your bridge is a member of an association or club of which Mr. Smith is a member, then you can proceed as follows:

  "Good morning, Miss Moran, I'm Paul Jones calling at the suggestion of Jack Dole. It's in connection with the Association of Financial Advisors." Miss Moran will immediately think your call will have meaning to her boss and will most likely pass you through. You do not have to be a member of the Association of Financial Advisors to mention that it is in connection with their organization.

- When you do not have any bridge or associations: How do you get through? In this case the less said, the better. Your voice must be as if you speak to Bob Smith every day. An example:

(Secretary) "Good morning, Mr. Smith's office." Or she might say, "Good morning, Miss Moran speaking."

(You) "Bob Smith, please" (Nothing else, no explanations, your voice must imply you are going to get through.)

Keep in mind that switchboard operators and secretaries are people. They are often overlooked by the caller in his rush to get to his party. Being nice and asking a favor when all else has failed can work miracles. Returning to the above conversation, Miss Moran is not convinced that you should speak to her boss.

You	Secretary
	"Can I please know who is calling Mr. Smith?"
"Paul Jones, I believe Bob Smith is head of production for your company?" (Something you already know is true, but you are going for a "yes" answer to set the mood.)	
	"Yes, he is. What is your call regarding?"
"I've been working on production problems of a similar nature and wanted to have a brief discussion with Mr. Smith. When would be a good time to call so we may chat a moment?" (You are going for a telephone appointment assuming you will get through.)	
	"Mr. Smith is usually in his office early and the phone is less active then. I suggest you call around 7:30 in the morning."
"Thank you, Miss Moran, you've been very helpful and I look forward to talking with Mr. Smith."	

Your approach in this conversation is to enlist Miss Moran in helping you find the most convenient time to get through.

In a few instances, you will not get through. The block is 100 percent effective—perhaps too good. In that case, do not insist, but keep Smith on your target list. Work on finding a bridge or try to "bump into" your target at one of his club meetings or places he may frequent. If all else fails, write to Mr. Smith about your interest in meeting him and the fact that you will be calling in a few days for an interview.

Then, when you call the next time, you can say:

You	Secretary
"Paul Jones for Bob Smith, please."	
	"Does Mr. Smith know you?"
"He's expecting my call."	
This might get you through, or another question:	
	"What is this about?"
"It concerns my letter of April 3rd to Mr. Smith."	
	"One moment, please."

Your letter will have explained that you are in the process of making a job change and would like the advice of Mr. Smith concerning your campaign. You will have sent your letter marked "Personal and Confidential," which might mean that Miss Moran has not seen it.

At this point, you may at last get to speak to Mr. Smith since he will know something about you.

Obviously, the more times you call with a bridge, the easier your entry.

Most secretaries are only following instructions, and once they feel comfortable will do all they can to arrange the conversation. But be aware that they are expected to protect their overworked boss.

Warm Up

Questions You Might Get from Secretaries.

You	Secretary
1.	*"Your name, please?"*
"I'm Paul Jones."	
2.	*"Does Mr. Smith know you?"*
"I'm calling Mr. Smith at the recommendation of Charles Beene." Or, "Charles Beene referred me to Mr. Smith." Or, "Mr. Smith is expecting my call." Or, "Charles Beene told me he has spoken to Mr. Smith and I should call." Practice other possible replies.	
3.	*"What company are you with?"*
"I'm from the _____ Company." Or, "I'm with the Jones Company."	
4.	*"Does Mr. Smith know your company?"*
Reply, "He may."	
5.	*"What is it you wish to discuss with Mr. Smith? He's very busy."*
"I'm working on a marketing project and would like to get some advice from Mr. Smith."	
6.	*"Please give me your number and we will call back."*
"I'm out all the time. My number is _____, but I'd prefer to call you back, what time would be best to call and reach Mr. Smith?"	

7.

"I appreciate that it's personal, but Mr. Smith has asked me to inquire about all incoming calls."

"I understand that and only require a few minutes of Mr. Smith's time. Charles Beene said that Mr. Smith would be interested in what I have to discuss."

8.

"Would you like me to transfer you to personnel?"

"No, thank you, I was hoping to speak with Mr. Smith about my project."

You will want to practice in replying to the above questions (mix them up). The name of the game is "Getting through to Mr. Smith."

While working on the approach, your voice and phrasing must have conviction: You *will* get through to Mr. Smith. If you are wishy-washy in your request, a professional secretary will try to block your call, feeling you are not important to the boss.

The Target Person

You have reached your target person. Your objective is to get an interview. If that becomes impossible, your fallback objective is to get *referrals*. What do you say?

Have your data sheet in front of you. You know about the company or have notes about the person from your bridge, or both. There may be some newsworthy item about an accomplishment your target person was connected with, which you picked up in a trade magazine or newspaper. Before calling, you have PREPARED your back-up information.

A Call with a Bridge

Look at the structure of this conversation:

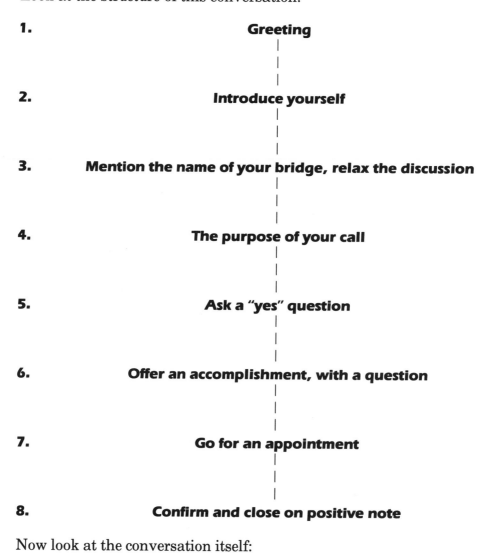

1.   **Greeting**

2.   **Introduce yourself**

3.   **Mention the name of your bridge, relax the discussion**

4.   **The purpose of your call**

5.   **Ask a "yes" question**

6.   **Offer an accomplishment, with a question**

7.   **Go for an appointment**

8.   **Confirm and close on positive note**

Now look at the conversation itself:

Caller	Mr. Smith

Steps 1 & 2

"Good morning, Mr. Smith, I'm Paul Jones."

"Good morning, what can I do for you?"

Steps 3 & 4

"In talking with Jack Dole last week he suggested that I give you a call. I'm in the process of making a career change and would like your advice. I'm not going to ask you for a job. But I would appreciate your ideas since I've been working in your industry."

"I don't know if I can help you."

Step 5

"Your company has had a problem in marketing tamper-proof containers for the consumer market?"

"We sure have."

Steps 6 & 7

"In my last company that was also a big concern and I was researching alternative packaging. Does our research interest you?"

"Very much."

"I would like to discuss this with you; would next Tuesday or Wednesday be better?"

"Let me see, Tuesday is a little busy. You said Wednesday?"

"Sure, Wednesday would be fine. Do you prefer the morning or afternoon?"

"How about 5 p.m.? It should be quiet here. We can talk."

Step 8

"That's fine, Mr. Smith.
Wednesday, May 14th at 5 p.m. at
your office. I'm sure that you'll be
interested in some of the techniques
we were exploring."

Here is what happened in the example.

Greeting & Introduction: Paul greeted Mr. Smith with a friendly and positive tone. Mr. Smith could almost see the smile on Paul's face as he introduced himself.

It is important that you open the conversation in a manner that makes people want to listen to what you have to say. You must project a natural friendliness that is neither familiar nor stilted.

Bridge, Relax Conversation: Paul immediately mentioned his bridge, Jack Dole, and at the same time relaxed the conversation by stating that he would not "ask" for a job. This is not to say that if a job is proposed or suggested, he would not be open to discussing it. He simply is not going to embarrass Jack Dole, Mr. Smith or himself by asking for a job. This is important so that Smith is not on guard or feels he must forestall any discussion regarding employment— which neither party knows about at this point.

Purpose: Now Paul does mention what he wants from Smith. He wants his advice on a career change, his opinion of Paul's accomplishments and resume, and suggestions regarding other people who could be interested in meeting with Paul.

Since Paul has done some research on Smith's company, he mentions a problem that ties into Paul's work.

Ask a Yes Question: "Your company has had a problem in marketing tamper-proof containers to the consumer market?"

"We sure have."

Another form of question could be less direct and more subtle: "I believe the packaging of consumer home medications has also been of concern to your company?"

Or,

"Making tamper-proof containers for consumer medical product distribution has become a problem for most companies in the industry. Has this affected you?"

What is important here is to get a "yes" reply. Paul wants agreement early in the conversation because it will make his agreement to make an appointment easier.

In telemarketing, the goal is to get the conversation going in a positive direction. Probe just a little to find what could be a need, and then present an idea or accomplishment that fills that need, opening the way for an interview.

Your Accomplishment/Question: Paul describes one of his key accomplishments in a way that makes Smith want to hear more.

"It so happens that in my last company that was also a big problem and I was team leader of the group assigned to come up with alternative packaging. We developed a number of solutions and I'd like to meet other people concerned with this problem. Would you be interested in what we discovered?"

"Very much."

Suppose Paul was not in the pharmaceutical business but was a manufacturing engineer. He might say, "In my last job, I was able to reduce manufacturing costs by more than 35 percent while sales were rising at the rate of 14 percent a year. Would that kind of performance interest you?"

Smith might reply, "It sounds very good."

Of course, the quality of the accomplishment and how it relates to Smith's business is important. If Smith feels that he is going to learn from the caller, he selfishly will want to meet him to pick his brains. This achieves the call's objective, an interview. Each party is following his own agenda, and both can be realized in an interview.

Most executives are takers. They do not give easily, but are quick to seize an opportunity. For these individuals all you want to do is make your conversion: Accomplishments become potential benefits that match one of their needs.

Appointment: "I would like to discuss this with you; would next Tuesday or Wednesday be better?"

"Let me see, Tuesday is a little busy, you said Wednesday?"

"Sure, Wednesday would be fine. Do you prefer the morning or afternoon?"

"How about five p.m.? It should be quiet here. We can talk."

The caller assumes that *he is going to get an interview, so he does not even ask for one.* He skips right over that unwritten question to go for a date. Rule: If you do not want a "no," do not ask a "no" question. If you raise a doubt, others will join you.

Confirmation/Post Close: "That's fine, Mr. Smith. Wednesday, May 14th at five p.m. at your office. I'm sure you'll be interested in some of the techniques we were exploring."

The meeting is confirmed and, to avoid "buyer's remorse," the target is assured that what he agreed to (an interview) will not be a waste of time but, to the contrary, a very positive meeting.

"Mr. Smith, I look forward to our meeting and discussing with you how I was able to reduce costs in our company while sales were on a continual rise."

A Cold Call Without a Bridge

This call can best be made after you have had practice with people you know and have successfully made appointments using a referral.

There is not much difference in these calls except that you do not have a third person to lean on going in. However, not having a bridge does not excuse you from doing proper research about the company and the people you want to meet.

Look at an example:

You	Other Person
In a questioning voice to the switchboard operator: "I'd like to confirm that Mr. Bob Smith is still president of your company."	
	"Yes, Mr. Smith is president."
"Fine, I'd like to speak with him. And what is the name of his secretary?"	
	"Mary White. One moment, please."
	"Mr. Smith's office. Mary speaking."

In a voice with authority but friendly: "Ms. White, Bob Smith, please."

"Mr. Smith is in a meeting. Who's calling, please?"

"Paul Jones. We've been working on the same marketing problems and I'd like to discuss a current project."

"What's the name of your company?"

"The Jones Company."

"One moment, please."

"Hello, Bob Smith here."

In a friendly voice: "Mr. Smith, my name is Paul Jones. We've been friendly competitors for a number of years and having just completed work at the XYZ Company, I wanted to get your advice. I'm not calling to ask you for a job. I've heard some reports that your company is about to expand in the Los Angeles area. Is that true?"

(Cautious) "Why yes. What kind of advice do you want?"

"I've been selling medical products and in my last year at XYZ Company, sales went up by 22 percent. I'm considering a career change and am looking to meet people who could be interested in that kind of performance. Could we get together briefly for a chat next week some time, say around Wednesday or Thursday?"

"I'd be pleased to meet you but I'm still not sure that I can help you. Perhaps a few minutes' time will be all right. Can you be at my office Wednesday around 11:45 a.m.?"

"11:45 a.m. next Wednesday would be just fine."

"Before you hang up, give me your telephone number just in case."

"My number is (213) 555-6789. I'm sure that we will have an interesting discussion. Good-bye."

This is telemarketing! You preplanned the outcome of your conversation using proven sales and marketing techniques.

But suppose Smith replied, "I'm sorry but I don't have time to see you."

You have a few replies to work from (second objective, get referrals):

1. "I understand that you don't have much free time. Could you suggest some people in your organization I might talk with concerning my marketing accomplishments?" Here, you must remind Smith that he has on the line a super salesperson who just might be worth meeting.

2. Another possible reply: "I'll be very brief and would like to tell you a little about some of the things I've been doing...or, when do you suggest I call back?" Here, you are going to have a short interview on the telephone with the goal of getting some names from Smith, either in his company or elsewhere.

If you do not get your interview, you should send a letter with your resume indicating your specific interests and that you will be calling back to set an appointment.

APPROACHING RESEARCH INTERVIEWS

The discussion up to now has been aimed at getting you in to see people who can give you advice (referrals), as well as getting into a target company without using a bridge. You have seen that you do not have to *ask* for a job. If they have one, you will be considered for it as you talk.

But sometimes you want a pure research or information interview. Here you must reaffirm that you are not going to ask for a job. You genuinely need information that may lead you to other people to meet.

For the research telephone appointment, the same principle of calling for an advice (to obtain referrals) or a direct (to investigate a job opportunity) interview applies. Look at the structure of this conversation:

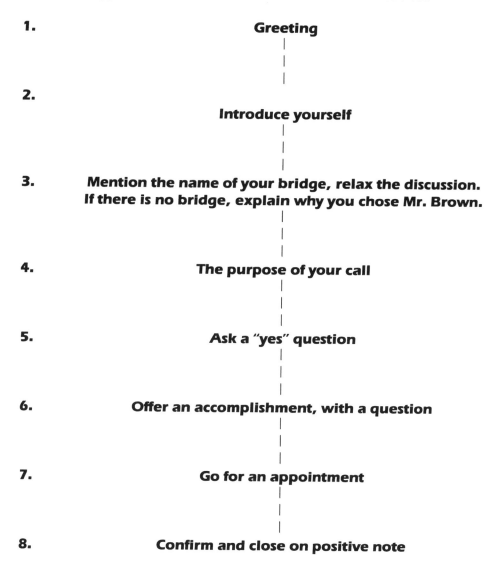

1.   **Greeting**

2.   **Introduce yourself**

3.   **Mention the name of your bridge, relax the discussion.**
         If there is no bridge, explain why you chose Mr. Brown.

4.   **The purpose of your call**

5.   **Ask a "yes" question**

6.   **Offer an accomplishment, with a question**

7.   **Go for an appointment**

8.   **Confirm and close on positive note**

You	Mr. Smith
(Introduction) "Hello, Mr. Smith, my name is Paul Jones and I'm very much interested in having a chat with you about real estate."	
	"Hello, I don't believe I know you. How did you get my name?"
(Cold call explanation, relax the conversation) "I've asked around for someone who has had a lot of experience in real estate and several people have mentioned your name. I'm not going to ask you for a job."	
	A laugh, "I didn't expect you to! What can I do for you?"
(Purpose of call, yes question) "My goal is to see if I'm suited for a sales position in real estate, and, from what I understand you've been involved with sales for a number of years?"	
	"Yes, for about 20 years. I don't know of any job situations but I would be happy to help you. What have you been doing?"
(Accomplishment, question) "I've been sales manager for a medical supply company and have always had a very successful career. Last year, I sold more than two million dollars' worth of patient care materials. However, I've been traveling up to 70 percent of the time and this has prompted me to think about making a career switch. I have a few questions about real estate in general and understand that at least it would solve my travel problem?"	

"That it would. Do you have a resume?" (People will fall back on a resume.)

(Appointment) "Certainly, and I'd like to drop by next Tuesday afternoon or Wednesday morning and bring it along so we might chat a few moments?"

"Tuesday afternoon around five would be fine. Do you have our address? Give me your telephone number just in case."

(Confirmation, post close) "Excellent, yes, I have your address and look forward to our discussion. See you next Tuesday, May 6th at five p.m. My telephone number is 555-4545. Thanks, Mr. Smith."

The above call for a research interview was made without a bridge. As you can see, you must have some point of reference to make the call. People will want to know, "Why did you call me?"

Another example of a cold call for a research interview:

You receive a letter in the mail from a large stock brokerage firm. It is a solicitation for IRA accounts. The letter is signed: Jane Black, Account Executive.

You	Other Person
In a friendly voice: "Hello, is Jane Black there?"	
	"Yes, who's calling?"
"Paul Jones."	
	"Hello, this is Jane Black. Paul Jones, are you over (pause, while there is a flutter of papers on the end of the line) on 15th Street?"

Smiling voice: "That's pretty good, Jane. Yes, we live at 14440 15th. Your letter prompted me to call."

"You're interested in the IRA literature that I sent you?"

"Yes, but not in the way you think. I wonder if you could recommend the best salesperson in your office?"

A laugh: "You're speaking to her!"

"Jane, I've been in sales for quite a number of years and am thinking about making a switch to selling stocks and bonds and wanted to learn more about it. Do you suppose you would have time to have lunch one day next week so I might ask you some questions about your work?"

"Why not. How about next Wednesday?"

"Fine, I'll come down to your office. I look forward to meeting you, next Wednesday, around noon."

"Fine, see you then, Paul."

This research cold call for an interview was easy because Paul took advantage of an opportunity from an outgoing salesperson.

Since this is a pure research conversation, you can be a little more relaxed in your structure. It is like one neighbor talking to another over the fence. If you have research interviews to arrange, try a few of these calls early in your search.

Not every cold call will be this easy. You may be asked to send in a resume first or you may be routed to someone else. You may be passed over to their personnel department anyway, since they could best explain opportunities at that firm. If they will see you, meet with them. Lots of things can and will

happen when you call. Be flexible and ready for a variety of possibilities. You can prepare yourself with

Practice, Practice, Practice ... and Practice.

Helpful Hints

Script Training: For each type of conversation you are apt to have, be it with a switchboard operator, secretary or an executive, you should prepare a series of short scripts following the different scenarios as illustrated in this chapter.

Scripts should be:

Natural. Do not act as if you are reading something even though you have worked out beforehand what you are saying. Rehearsal will help you forget the script while sticking to your ideas. Listen to playbacks of your recorded conversations.

Brief. Keep your phrases short and simple. Let the other person have a chance to reply.

Concise. Be precise in what you want to say. Avoid vagueness by getting to your point.

Conversational. Never forget you are not alone on the line. Use the concept of SAY IT—ASK IT: You make a statement and turn that statement around into a question related to your objective. "While I was at DFC company sales rose by 24 percent last year; would that kind of performance interest you?" Or, "Is an increase of sales important to your plans?" Or, "Would you like to know how I did it?" Structure your questions to make "yes" replies easy for your target early in the conversation.

Scripts should take into account all the various things you can imagine will go wrong for you in a conversation. Learn to plan answers to difficult questions before you begin talking. Prepare a short one- to two-minute commercial about yourself that you can use when you need to give some background. Memorize it so it becomes natural: Who you are, what you do, where you did it, one or two major accomplishments, a request for an advice or research interview.

What are the most difficult points for you in calling someone? Work on those.

Sit down with your tape recorder and try to duplicate an actual telephone conversation. With a partner, try calls where you each take a different role. Vary the situations.

Listen to recordings of your own voice. How do you sound? Are you cheerful, friendly, sure, negative, aggressive, insecure? You will be very surprised at how you sound to yourself. Your first reaction will be: "It's not me!"

In correcting any shortcomings, hold on to naturalness.

Candidates trained in telemarketing dramatically shorten the time needed for generating interviews. Telemarketing techniques, coupled with your natural personality and practice, will help you become a more persuasive communicator.

Voice Mail

Voice mail systems create problems for job-seekers. While there is no hard-and-fast rule for getting past these electronic barriers, here are some suggestions that can improve your chances of making contacts with the right people:

- If you obtain someone's voice mail on your first call, try transferring to the operator. Usually this is done by pressing either 0 or # and then 0 or just waiting for instructions. When you reach the operator, ask if your party is in today. If the person is there, ask the operator to assist you to locate the person. If the operator comes back and says that your target person is in a meeting, then you should indicate that you will call back. Do not necessarily leave a voice mail message at this time.

- Try calling back at different times. Your goal is to find your target person by the phone.

- If the message you get indicates that someone is taking calls for your target person, you might try speaking with that person to find out the best time to call. Do not leave a message on the assistant's voice mail.

- If you continually get a voice mail message and the operator is not any help, then you can leave a very short message. "Hello, this is Mary Stevens, I would appreciate talking with you at your earliest convenience. I have an important question. I can be reached at 310-555-7777." Or, "Hello, this is Mary Stevens, I am calling at the suggestion of our mutual friend, Jack Armstrong. My telephone number is 310-555-7777. Thank you for getting back to me." Or, "Hello, this is Mary Stevens, Jack Armstrong suggested that I give you a call concerning a project I am working on. He thought that we had areas of mutual interest. My phone is...." Keep your communications short, positive, friendly and courteous. Practice with your answering machine. Do not leave other messages on this person's voice mail. If you call again and reach a voice mail recording, hang up or try to go through the operator or assistant. Leaving frequent messages becomes annoying and makes you sound like you are trying to sell something. Sometimes it is better to call the company switchboard rather than calling your target person's direct line. You can at least reach the operator this way.

- If all else fails and you do not get any call back, write an interesting letter following the samples in this manual.

GETTING READY—OVERVIEW

- You have prepared the networking list of people you want to meet for the three types of interviews: advice, research and direct.

    Who do you call first?

    Your old friends.
    Business associates you know well.
    Recent business acquaintances.
    All the people you will be referred to.
    Follow-ups to your mail campaign.
    Cold call prospects.

- You have prepared your target company list and back-up information tied to names on your network list. (Research.)

- You have collected classified ads in a spiral notebook. Some you will write to, others will be approached via networking. You have tracked down the name, number and address of the person you want to reach.

- You have various scripts devised for a range of possible conversations so you will be comfortable in introducing yourself and arranging an interview.

- You have your resume in front of you in case you need to fall back on it for information.

- You have your calendar in front of you and are ready to make appointments—and write down immediately the time, place and date.

- If you are calling for an appointment regarding information (research interview), have your list of questions handy. You may not be able to get your interview, but your contact may be willing to talk to you then and there.

STRATEGY OF A PHONE CALL

> **1. Objective**
> **2. Who are you calling?**
> **3. Approach**
> **4. Presentation**
> **5. Close**
> **6. Post Close**

Objective

Know in advance what you want. In your job search, it is an interview. Later, other calls can be:

Follow-up after a meeting to get or give information and/or another interview.

Confirmation of appointments.

Going after an interview as follow-up to a mail campaign.

Contacting old friends and acquaintances—near and far.

Obtaining new referrals (if an interview is not possible).

Discussion about an actual job.

Feedback to and from your network.

Know Who You Are Calling

Learn as much background as you can about the person before you call. This is easiest at the time you get your referral.

1. Professional Considerations

Title.

Activity (i.e., line manager, administrator, staff, sales—what does this person do?).

Level of activity. (Is this a superbusy person? Hard to get to? Easy-going and relaxed?)

History. (What school did he attend? What company was he with previously? Is there anything in his past to tie you together?)

Clubs/Associations. (What organizations is he affiliated with? What places does he frequent? Do you know anyone in any of them?)

How does this person fit in with other information you have gained about the company?

2. Personal Considerations

Is this person a peer or on an entirely different level?

Have you had any information concerning his attitude toward helping people?

Has this person been in the news? If so, could that relate to you and your discussion?

How long has this person lived in the community? The longer the period, the more people he will know.

Is this person working in one of your target companies?

3. Getting Information

The above questions are posed to help you get a mind set before getting on the phone. Too many people network without purpose. "Give Herb a call; I'm sure he'll help you. Tell him I said to call. His number is...." A lot of networkers stop at that, say thanks and are on their way. What a wasted opportunity!

When a person recommends someone to you, ask questions about the professional and personal considerations mentioned above. You do not have to get all the answers to the questions indicated. This is only a checklist. For example, you are in an interview and about to get a referral: "Paul, you indicated that you want to meet someone in the TXW Company. As a matter of fact, I know Jack Dole, vice president of research and development. Would you like to meet him?"

"That would be an excellent introduction, John. Could you tell me a little about Mr. Dole?" From the ensuing conversation, Paul learns that Jack Dole has known John for more than 15 years; they used to work together at the REX Company. Dole plays golf, travels a great deal, has had a very successful career at TXW and is widely respected in the company and his industry. He is a workaholic and the best time to catch him in is early morning or late in the evenings. He often skips lunches.

Part of this information is very useful for your telephone call; the remainder will be helpful when you get to see him. Your strategy regarding Dole is fairly clear now: If you want to catch him directly, try early in the morning, at lunch or late in the day. Your call stands a good chance of going directly through, since his secretary probably will not keep the same schedule. Maybe John has Dole's direct-line number, which is even better.

When you are doing your research on target companies and you identify an executive you want to approach, make notes. Later, if you get a chance to call or meet him, you will be prepared.

When You Call

- Be prepared to be rejected. No one bats 1,000 in this game. But a score of .500 is excellent!

- Make calls for appointments every day. Start off gradually with an hour's worth of calls. Work your way up to two to three hours. Try for at least 10-20 interviews per week.

- Always ask for directions on how to get there. If in doubt, call the switchboard operator back and ask.

- Always write in your calendar: the person's name, telephone, street address, city, name of your bridge and any special instructions.

- When you get your interview and confirm the time, date and place, end the conversation as quickly as possible.

DYNAMICS OF A CALL

The first seconds of any call are critical to the overall success of your communication. The party who hears your voice for the first time never will have a neutral reaction. How you sound will immediately register an impression.

Let us look at some of the variables that affect that impression:

- **Rate of Speech**

Try to match the rate (speed) of your party, i.e., speaking either more quickly or slowly. Speaking quickly to a slow talker makes you sound like a hustler, just as speaking slowly to a fast talker makes you come off as someone dragging your feet.

- **Tone of Voice**

Your voice should project. Enunciate clearly and be conscious of your diction. Practice modulating your voice by changing both the speed and volume. This will help you emphasize key points and keep the other party interested. Examples: Listen to newscasters and announcers. When you present a question, let your voice rise slightly at the end.

Your voice should be warm in order to establish a friendly contact. Examine successful calls and what you did to make them happen.

While you may not be face to face with your party, your voice should bridge the gap.

• The Mood

Never attempt networking calls if you are in a bad humor. Impatience, frustration and irritability will be communicated instantly to your listener. Smile when you call and mean it!

• Importance of Being a Good Listener

A conversation is not an exchange unless each side listens and acknowledges what the other is saying. In listening to someone, you must learn enough to help you reach your objective—an interview. What are some of these critical factors?

- You must learn how to interpret voice nuances, pauses and hesitations in the replies of your prospect. Being sensitive to his mood will permit you to adjust your approach in conversation and achieve your goal.

- It is important to communicate that you are listening to his comments. If you do not listen—and show it—he will stop listening to you. During the conversation, acknowledge some of his statements even if you do not agree.

- Never ignore an objection. Confirm it by repeating the objection, then go on and find an objective that you can offer as a solution.

Example:

You	**Other Person**
	"We have too many people as it is in our company."
"I can appreciate that you have too many people. Does that include top-performing salesmen?"	
	"Well, we never have enough good sales people."
"In my last company I increased sales for the San Francisco area by 22 percent last year. Would that be worth ten minutes' discussion? I could drop by Tuesday of next week. Would that be convenient?"	

In this exchange, you are not denying that they have too many people; rather you are changing the focus of the conversation to an objective that you can satisfy. This may not always work. If his answer was, "We're well staffed on salespeople, too," your reply might be, "In my last position I increased sales for the San Francisco area by 22 percent and would like your ideas on people I might meet who would be interested in a top sales performer. Do you suppose we might chat for a few moments next Tuesday, or is Wednesday better?" Your objective is an interview that can go either of two directions: toward a possible job or, at minimum, referrals to people who might know of a need for your skills. Networking begins on the telephone.

In a good conversation, you will ask a few questions related to what the other person is saying. While he may not be ready to see you as a candidate, he should be interested in meeting a top performer. After all, his circumstances can change too.

In listening to his answers, you will get a general idea of the person's personality, his mood, how busy he may be, what his interests really are and what you will have to overcome as you progress toward your objective. This will come through in his voice, inflection, tone and manner of speech.

A good conversation consists of letting the other person talk. While you have your message to get across, it is wise to get continual feedback. Without it, your presentation risks being merely acknowledged, and you may never progress to an interview.

The goal of a good listener is to determine what kind of person is on the line and how to adjust your approach using that knowledge. This comes with practice and experience.

On the other hand, you also will be listened to and there are some rules you should observe:

> Never lie.
> No false promises.
> No complaints.
> Be careful not to oversell or get overly involved with your own history.
> Do not be negative.
> Avoid hesitation, especially in reply to an objection.
> Do not be too aggressive or pushy.
> Your replies should reflect the nice person you really are.

Key Words

A good telemarketing approach is to use key words or phrases that you have worked out beforehand to lead his reply in the direction you want to go. This is

why getting "yes" answers is important in the beginning to set the mood for a positive conversation.

People sometimes have favorite ways of expressing themselves. When you encounter such expressions, you can reply in kind to be in harmony:

"I see what you mean." "Yes, that looks good." "It's clear to me."

Or,

"It sounds good." "I hear you." "You come across loud and clear."

Or,

"I'm comfortable with that." "Feels good to me." "Before deciding, I'd like to weigh that in my mind."

As you will see in Chapter 8, The Interview, the SAY IT—ASK IT concept is a perfect way for carrying out an interview, on the telephone or in person. SAY IT—ASK IT is very much like two people playing tennis, only the rule of the game is neither side drops the ball. You want the volley to go on and on—until you reach your objective.

When presenting accomplishments over the telephone (as in the interview), follow with a question.

For example:

"I've helped companies increase their sales by 25 percent. Would a 25 percent sales increase be exciting to you?"

"In my last position I increased profits by 12 percent. Would that kind of performance be helpful here?"

"I've just completed a market research study for the XYZ Company along with suggestions that show how it can move from number two position to number one in the Philadelphia area. Do you require any background information that could help increase your sales?"

"Last year I designed a new software program that saved our company $350,000 in data processing. Would that kind of performance interest you?"

Action Questions

These questions take a general idea from your listener and turn it around to focus it on a possible need.

(Question to you) "Have you worked in the computer industry before?"

(Your reply) "Do you want someone with computer experience?"

Or,

(Question to you) "Have you been involved in international sales?"

(Your reply) "Do you need an international sales professional?"

Turning Around Objections

You must listen to what your prospect is saying. In the following examples, the prospect is being defensive without showing his true needs. Your replies first acknowledge his statements, but with a good question you turn the objection into an objective. See how this works:

You	Other Person
	"We already have too many people on our staff."
"Are you saying that you have too many people at this time?"	
	"That's right!"
"Do you also have too many programmers with Pascal experience?"	
	"No, we never have enough of them. Do you know of anyone?"
"That's my specialty. I have been doing Pascal programming for three years. If I could cut down on your overload would it be worth investing twenty minutes of your time?"	
Or,	
	"Look, Steve, we have nothing now. Call me in six weeks."
"Sure, by the way, do you still have problems in your computer department?"	

"Actually I do. That's why I can't see you."

"Well, I'll bet you didn't know this, but I've been working on computer problems at the ABC Company for the last six months and they are now running on time with three fewer people. I feel confident that a short discussion might show you how I can help you with your problems. Can we get together on Thursday, or is Friday better?"

Or,

"Look Steve, I told you that we have no openings at all."

"I understand that you have no openings at all, but if you ran into someone who increased his company's sales in a declining market by 26 percent, would you want to meet him? Wouldn't that be worth ten minutes of your time?"

"Yes."

Then let's get together next Tuesday for a brief discussion and I'm sure you'll find our time will be well spent."

• Other Forms of Questions

Asking open-ended questions will encourage conversation. Use these kinds of questions if you perceive that your prospect wants to talk in general before getting specific.

You: "How do you find the consumer pharmaceutical industry today?"

Using closed questions will focus and direct your conversation in a very specific fashion. These questions are aimed at directing your prospect to a subject you want to focus on.

You: "Do you have enough sales people for Southern California?"

SUMMARY ON GETTING THROUGH TO YOUR PARTY

1. **Referral/Bridge:** You can be extremely successful in your telemarketing efforts if you have a bridge. Your conversation with a prospect is immediately on a more personal and trusting level. Advantages of a referral are: easier to make contact, a better reception, and there is already a relationship between you and the bridge that makes your call more meaningful.

    During one job change, a candidate was told that there was one person he had to see (Mr. X). Mr. X was running a $4 billion company and was in the process of completing a very large turnaround. Our candidate could not imagine talking his way in. Yet, many people told him that this person would be able at the very least to provide many good referrals.

    So, the candidate added X's name to his target list. One day one of his networking contacts suggested he meet an attorney who had just completed a big assignment that happened to be part of X's operations. They spoke for a long time and the attorney asked the magic question: "How can I help you?" At that point, having heard that the attorney knew Mr. X, the candidate asked: "Do you think I could get in to see Mr. X?" "Is that all you want? Just call Maggie, his secretary, and tell her I suggested she book an appointment for you. I'll be speaking to X this afternoon and I'll mention that you'll be calling." And, before leaving the attorney's office, the candidate learned quite a bit about Mr. X.

    He was now well equipped for his telephone call and visit. The candidate not only met with X, but spent about two hours with him in his office reviewing his accomplishments. His resume was circulated among several people by Mr. X. One of these people later suggested a large company in need of the candidate's services and a match was made. Without an introduction to Mr. X, this chain of events would have been next to impossible.

    Reminder: Once you have had your interview, let your referral know either by phone or letter what happened. It is very important to keep contact with your network, especially since they will come back to you with more ideas when they see appreciation and action on your part. It is satisfying for your bridge to see you succeed as a result of his help. He becomes part of your "team."

2. **The professional organization:** If you have a list of names from an organization, and your career has some relationship to their overall activity, you can tie your call to the organization's activity.

A candidate wanted to network in a suburb of Los Angeles. In his interviews, he ran across an attorney who happened to be a member of the local Rotary Club. Their conversation went well and the attorney suggested that the candidate look over the roster of Rotary Members in his area. The attorney was prepared to open the door for whomever the candidate wanted to meet on the list. With the attorney's reference, he was free to call names. This instantly expanded the network by 20 people and gave him broad access to the business community in that area.

3. **Clubs:** Watch for guest speakers at various clubs in your target area. It is a wonderful way to hear new ideas and later you can make an appointment by telephone, indicating that you were in the audience. A little (honest) flattery can go far.

4. **News events:** Local newspapers furnish a lot of information about business people. If you are only looking at the classifieds, you are making a mistake. Watch for news about people in business as well as your community. A news article is a good reason to call.

   Collect news about your referrals as well as possible contacts at your target companies. If it is a local paper and the story has a byline, give the reporter a call. Mention your interest in the article and ask for a meeting. When you are face to face, discuss his impressions of the company and/ or the people interviewed.

5. **Market research:** People enjoy being asked for their opinions; it appeals to their ego. You can get through to people when you are working on a marketing project that could interest them. If you have a subject you wish to study and, at the same time, someone of interest to approach, you can combine your objective for an interview with a market research call.

INCOMING CALLS

You have been networking, sending out letters, answering ads and spreading the word about your availability. It is only natural that you will get calls.

- **The person who makes the call has the advantage.** They are prepared to talk with you about a subject. On the other hand, you may not have your notes at hand, which can put you in weak position. What to do? A classic solution would be: "Hello John, I'm on another line. Can I call you right back?" (Be sure to get his telephone number [again] before hanging up.) This gives you a chance to check your records and prepare yourself for a strong and positive conversation.

THE COMPLETE MANUAL FOR CAREER-CHANGERS

- **You may get a call from someone you do not know.** They may have heard about you from one of your network, be calling from a blind ad you answered, from a recruiter's office or an employment agency. In these cases, it would be wise to have on hand your files of advertisements, the date you replied, your book of call reports, your Target Company List and back-up information, as well as your chronological correspondence file. You can locate your materials during the conversation. This is the reason you have been keeping all those meticulous records! Keep them organized and handy.

During this call, LISTEN CAREFULLY for the purpose of their call: interview, information, your availability. If someone wants to conduct an interview over the phone, first make every effort to try to set up a personal meeting. However, if you cannot get a meeting, or the person is calling long distance, you will have to settle for a telephone interview. All the advice in Chapter 8 will apply even though you are on the phone. Your replies should be natural and prompt. Try to avoid hesitation. Finally, be sure to ask appropriate questions (SAY IT—ASK IT).

TELEMARKETING YOURSELF

The Switchboard

1. Confirm names, positions, addresses.
2. Learn secretary's name.
3. Try for direct telephone number of your target person.
4. Is your target person there?
5. Obtain instructions on how to get there.

Your Approach

1. Patient.
2. Appreciative.

The Secretary

1. Address by name.
2. Introduce yourself.
3. State purpose of the call—to speak to Mr. Smith about your project or…
4. State your company.
5. Be prepared to call back if your target person is not available.

Your Approach

1. Polite.
2. Affirmative—you are going to get through.
3. Appreciative.

Your Target

1. Introduce yourself.
2. Mention the purpose of your call.
3. Relax the conversation.
4. Indicate your bridge—if you have one.
5. Ask a "yes" question.
6. State an appropriate accomplishment.
7. Confirm and close for an appointment.

Your Approach

1. Friendly.
2. Sincere.
3. Listen for reaction.
4. Respond to objections—do not argue.
5. Be prepared to change your plan (e.g., send a letter and resume, if requested, and then call again).
6. Go for an appointment.

Techniques

1. If you do not want a "no" answer, do not ask a "no" question.
2. Listen to his tone and follow.
3. Listen to his speed of conversation and follow.
4. Overcome objections with objectives.
5. When you get your appointment—get off the phone.
6. Script out as many examples as you can.
7. Practice conversations with a friend.
8. Record your practice sessions, replay and note where you can improve.
9. Never call for appointments in a bad mood.

CHAPTER 8

The Interview/ Negotiations/Action Plan

T HE INTERVIEW

Your efforts thus far have been designed to prepare you for the most powerful medium of communication: the face-to-face meeting.

There are three types of interviews you should expect: Advice Interview, Research Interview and Direct Interview. We will take a look at each.

Advice Interview

This interview is actuated by a broadcast letter, cover letter with a resume, a phone call (with or without a bridge) or a letter of introduction.

The advice interview gives you the opportunity to perfect your presentation of your career, accomplishments and personality. It will give you practice in asking questions and obtaining information. With practice, you soon will feel more comfortable and will be able to control the conversation to obtain the specific information you need.

Primary objective: referrals (bridges to a target company or person or for new contacts). Secondary objective: possible job opportunities.

Pointers for the Advice Interview:

1. **Be remembered.**

    *   Establish rapport.

        Be sensitive to your interviewer's office. It reflects his interests (photos, trophies, books, computer, decor, etc.). Any of these items could be the ice breaker you need to relax your first contact. "You're a golfer? Where do you play...?"

        A good interview is characterized by an exchange of information. Learn about the interviewer by taking a genuine interest in him: "Before I talk about me, I'm interested in what you do and your company's activity."

If there is not much time to chat, you must get into your approach but, above all, avoid pressuring your host.

Provide a clear understanding of your objectives with a brief overview of your career to date. You will have prepared a short commercial on yourself (duration about one-and-one-half to three minutes), giving a broad sweep of who you are professionally (leave out the personal). Repeat this script (from memory) now. In your introduction, state that you are in the midst of making a career change and are delighted to have the chance to review your qualifications with him. Questions from both sides are the controlling factors.

- Relax the conversation.

  Make it clear that you are not there to ask for a job but are seeking advice. You will immediately take any pressure off your meeting. Example: "John, I want to thank you for seeing me today. As I mentioned, I'm not here to ask you for a job, but could really use your advice."

  Note: You are not going to ask for a job; however, when John gets to know you, he may suggest a job. Be alert.

  It is important to thank the person on the spot for seeing you and spending time with you.

- Get feedback on your resume.

  You would like his opinion of your resume and job campaign. In this manner, focus is directed to your accomplishments. Go through your background in as much detail as the conversation will permit, but do not make long speeches. Instead discuss each accomplishment and encourage questions and suggestions. The best test of your presentation in any interview will be when someone asks you, "How did you do that?"

- Obtain specific information about the overall job market.

  Show him your target list. You might say: "You know a little about me now. How do you see me fitting into one of these companies?"

2. Get what you came for: his professional contacts (either to reach a target company or person or to increase your network list).

- You must communicate to your listener that you need his help in obtaining professional contacts who could understand and appreciate your expe-

YOUR ONE-AND-ONE-HALF-MINUTE COMMERCIAL

Or
"Tell me about yourself."

Key Conversation Point	Your Script Prompt
Introduction.	Name: _____
Thank him for his time.	Thank you: _____
Relax the conversation (advice & research interviews).	Not asking for a job: _____
Mention your bridge.	Referral contact: _____
Your education.	Schooling: _____
Your specialty.	Activity: _____
Work history review.	Most pertinent jobs: _____
Responsibilities.	What did you do: _____
One or two major accomplishments.	Benefits: _____
Your present availability.	Why you are looking: _____
Your goal.	Your objective: _____

Application

1. Who are you talking to? Knowledge of the person you are addressing determines the scope and direction of your presentation.
2. How much time do you feel you have to discuss your background?
3. Does this person make hiring decisions? Can he make referrals? Does he know of job situations in or out of his company?
4. Is this someone in your profession? You can use buzz words. Otherwise, do not plunge into detail that may cause you to lose control of the conversation.
5. This format will vary with advice, research and direct interviews.
6. Do not forget to ask a question at the end of your commercial to learn what your host does. (SAY IT—ASK IT)

Do Not Forget to Be

1. Natural.
2. Friendly.
3. Genuinely interested.
4. Observant.
5. Interesting.
6. Well rehearsed.

rience, whether or not they know of a job. Reassure your listener that you are not going to ask his contacts for a job. This is important.

Ask your question: "John, I'd like to meet other professionals and executives who might be able to offer ideas on my career change. Can you suggest anyone I might meet?"

Do not stop here. If you do, John will only think of people who may have a job for you, and chances are he will not know anyone. So, you must continue: "It's not my intention to ask these people for a job, but I would like their comments and ideas." Put this in your own words and say what is natural for you.

Sometimes the question comes from the other side: "How can I help you?" If so, use your target list of companies and people you would like to meet. If John recognizes any of the people or companies on your list, one of his referrals may be a bridge for you.

He also may know other people to call for further meetings. Encourage John to give you those names, even though his contacts may not be in a position to hire you. For example, if John is an attorney, he can suggest other attorneys who have different contacts.

- Always ask permission to use the person's name as an introduction bridge. It is only common courtesy. Some candidates have had people give them a name, only to be told in the same breath, "But please don't mention my name; it won't help." The referral may be a competitor, or maybe John does not want to mix your search in with his affairs. You may decide to keep these names on your network list but develop other bridges to them. Regardless, you must respect all confidences.

- Ask for introductions. Referrals are great, but not enough. Try to get John to call or write to his referral on your behalf. In this interview, maximum success will come when John picks up the phone and tries to set an appointment with someone else right on the spot. He also may offer to write his contacts and perhaps even enclose your resume with his recommendation. Ask for copies of any letters so you can follow up each with a call. Next best is the number of someone to call, using his name. He also might suggest some organizations, recruiters or other situations you should explore. Take good notes.

- Plan what to say if he starts talking about a specific job opportunity. You should be prepared so that your accomplishments match up with an immediate need within John's company.

"John, that opportunity sounds interesting. I didn't come here to ask you for a job, but I would like to pursue your suggestion further. Can you introduce me to the people who will be directly concerned?" Or, if John has a need himself, "What did you have in mind?"

At this point your advice interview is a success and you are converting it to a direct interview.

An advice interview can occur almost anywhere, but you are better off away from distractions and noise. Meeting people over lunch or at breakfast is great. If you are in an office, the meeting may be more productive in a conference room, away from telephones. Even if your interviewer merely comes from behind his desk to join you, the stage is set for a more casual and comfortable conversation for both of you. It is a good idea now to give John a copy of your resume; it becomes a topic for discussion.

Networking is personal. Think in terms of people rather than companies. If you know one partner in an accounting firm, meeting other partners can be just as beneficial to your objective. Each of us has our own world of people, even though at some points they overlap. Therefore, each person you meet contributes to your network.

3. The follow-up/post close.

- Before you leave, ask if you can be of help to him. In meeting sales people, for example, routing a customer their way is a nice way of saying thank you. Since you are networking continuously, chances are good that you can run into this kind of situation.

- Ask permission to keep him informed of your progress with the people to whom he has referred you. This will automatically open the way for continuous contact—and new ideas.

- Always write a thank-you letter.

4. Problems. There are some common problems candidates run into when getting started with networking:

- New to the area: You do not know anyone.

If you move to a new area, you need to locate people who will see you even if they do not know you. One good way to establish connections is to have your present contacts refer you to branch offices or colleagues in your new territory. Example: An executive moved from Chicago to Los Angeles and wanted to start his informal (advice) network. Before leaving Chicago, he approached his network of friends to give him names and addresses of other company executives located in Los Angeles. From this list he was able to rapidly build a good and productive network list. Being new in the area made him an interesting person for people to meet.

- They never return your calls.

  The error here is asking Mr. Smith to call. The candidate should find out from Smith's secretary the best times to call back and take appropriate action. Keeping the ball in your court also keeps you in control.

- For candidates who are still employed, finding free time is a problem.

  A creative candidate will make appointments for breakfast, lunch or a drink after work. Many executives work on Saturday and this can be a good time for interviews.

- "I don't have anyone in mind for you."

  Smith is not yet comfortable sharing his personal network with you and introducing a relative stranger to his immediate circle of contacts.

  If this happens, there is little you can accomplish by forcing the situation. To the contrary, you should relax the conversation by saying, "May I call you in a few days so you have some time to think it over?" and restating that you are not asking for a job! Normally, your statements will be well received. Later, when you write to Mr. Smith thanking him for your meeting, remind him of your desire to meet people who can advise you, and that you will call in a few days for some names.

- People are too busy to see you.

  The candidate is too obviously searching for a job rather than seeking to meet people. You must make it perfectly clear that you are not going to ask for a job but want advice, which means only a "few minutes of your time." Your mail campaign should stress that you would like to meet that person for information and/or advice, not a job.

- What happens if you are refused an interview?

  No one bats 1,000. It can happen, and you should be prepared. Mr. Smith may say, "I'm sorry but I have no time to get together with you and I'm not sure that I'm the person you should see." At this point, switch the focus of the call from arranging a meeting to a telephone interview concentrating on getting some names of other people. Your reply could be, "I perfectly understand your time constraints. My goal is to meet executives like yourself in ... (your field of interest). I've been told that you know a lot of people.

Could you perhaps suggest people who are involved with sales of...?" This request will usually produce results. If the answer still is "No," politely excuse yourself and go on to the next name on your list.

Write to Mr. Smith, anyway, restating your research goal and including a resume. He just might think of someone and recontact you, or give your resume to someone else.

- They ask for a resume first and do not want to see you.

Here you have a few options. You can suggest that you would like to drop the resume off and shake hands with him personally. If that does not work, write a letter, enclosing your resume and affirming that you would still like to get together to have that person's advice. Follow the letter with another call.

- Some people will insist on having your "meeting" right on the spot over the telephone.

In this case you will miss the person-to-person contact. While it is not ideal, you can present enough of an outline of yourself—including a few accomplishments—to get the person interested in a short meeting.

For example: "In my last position, I was able to increase sales by 25 percent. Would you be interested in learning how I did it?" SAY IT—ASK IT. Do not lose sight of your goal to get a personal meeting. You should have a script for this kind of situation, worked out in your practice sessions.

You soon will learn that rejection and selling go hand in hand. Professionals learn how to discard rejection and move quickly to another prospect. A very successful executive whose sole job is selling second mortgages for investment purposes confided that for every success, she has 100 negative replies. She says every "no" makes her happy because it gets her closer to the one "yes." That salesperson is a success because she has the right attitude.

You are only trying to get advice, and usually it is flattering to someone that you want his counsel. If you make the right presentation, the refusal to get together will be the exception, not the rule.

ADVICE INTERVIEW

Your Objective	Primary: Get referrals—your target companies & others. Secondary: Identify a job situation. Change to a direct interview.
Preparation	Know about the person you are approaching (if possible). Know about the company (if possible). Know your accomplishments. Have a list of people and target companies ready.
Approach	Your one-and-one-half-minute commercial (version adapted to an advice interview; could include people in and out of your immediate profession). Your lead question: "Please tell me a little about what you do and about your company."
Presentation	Review part or all of your resume (depending on time permitting and interest of your host). Encourage questions about you. Provide short answers.
Close	Obtain your objective: referrals, a job lead and/or another interview. Be prepared for his question: "How can I help you?" Use your target list.
Post Close	Thank your host in person and later in writing. If he proposed any referrals and/or a job lead, assure him that it will be a positive meeting. Eliminate buyer's remorse. If he did not propose any new contacts, ask to call back at a later date. Always get permission to use your referral's name. Ask if you can keep your host up to date with a call if he suggests a referral. Do not lose contact; he may have other suggestions. Never forget to try to help this person as your networking continues. "What goes around comes around."

Research (Information) Interview

Primary objective: Information. Secondary objective: Other people to see (bridges). Third objective: To discover potential job opportunities, anywhere.

The same principles discussed in the advice interview section (establish rapport, relax the conversation, talk about your resume), apply here. The only difference is that you are asking for information that will help you evaluate a career move, a new industry or profession, background on buying or starting a business, or a relocation.

The research interview is the easiest to conduct of the three types of interviews since you are talking about an activity and not just people. Your host should be happy to discuss the subject he knows best, and, if you select wisely, you should be able to learn quite a bit.

Where do you get names of people to approach for research interviews? Your initial networking list will provide enough names to get you started. You will also find people just by picking key firms and calling, asking to speak with someone in sales (or marketing, or production, or...). Your list of prepared career questions will dictate whom you should contact.

You will also be able to initiate interviews by mail, though beginning networks operate best through telephone contacts.

In the research interview, you are there to ask and to learn. Most of the people you contact will be without a bridge; therefore, all the telemarketing techniques you learned in Chapter 7 will come into play.

Assuming you get your appointment, your purpose is to get answers to the questions you have prepared beforehand. In the research interview, you first need to build confidence. Explain why you are there:

"Mr. Smith, I'm grateful for the chance to meet you and want to learn about your activities in real estate. My business experience has been a little different, but real estate has always been a big interest of mine. How did you get started?" Smith may begin to explain about his work or may come back to you with some questions to verify who you are. In that case, give a brief overview of your career so Smith has a feel for your potential and some comfort level in going further with you. You must create interest for someone to want to help you. Friendliness goes a long way.

An example of an abbreviated overview might be:

"I've been in marketing for the last seven years, particularly in the medical-

RESEARCH INTERVIEW

Your Objective

Primary: Get information.
Secondary: Get referrals. Identify a job situation. Change to a direct interview.

Preparation

Know about the person you are approaching (if possible).
Know about the company (if possible).
Know your accomplishments.
Know the questions you want answered.

Approach

Your one-and-one-half-minute commercial (version adapted to a research interview; most likely someone out of your immediate profession).
Your lead question: "Please tell me a little about what you do and about your company."

Presentation

Review part or all of your resume (depending on available time and interest of your host).
Encourage questions about you. Provide short answers.

Close

Obtain your objective: information, referrals, a job lead and/or another interview.

Post Close

Thank your host in person and later in writing. If he proposed any referrals and/or a job lead, assure him that it will be a positive meeting. Eliminate buyer's remorse.
Always get permission to use your referral's name. Ask if you can keep your host up to date with a call if he suggests a referral. Do not lose contact; he may have other suggestions.
Never forget to try to help this person as your networking continues. "What goes around comes around."

care industry. I've been responsible for a number of sales increases for my company, but while I like the health-care industry, I'd like to explore other sales activities where I could use my skills. You've been in real estate for some time. Could we chat about how I might fit into your profession?" This should be scripted and practiced.

Smith may ask for your resume, which you should have ready. It becomes a means to review accomplishments. But be sure you get to your preplanned list of questions.

Although you are after information about a particular profession or activity, be alert to the possibility that this type of interview can change. It may turn into an advice interview, where you will be introduced to people in your own field who might have a need or know of one. You must be flexible and become a good listener. You never know how a conversation may turn.

Direct Interview

This is the most important moment in your job search. Through your networking, you are finally face to face with someone who may have a job for you in his company. You may be the sole candidate or one of many, depending on the circumstances of your introduction. How you conduct yourself in the direct interview can mean the difference between a job offer and just another meeting.

You have to convince the other party to buy your product: You! What techniques will you use?

Six Magic Steps:

1. Preparation

Part of good interview preparation is finding out all you can about your interviewer and his company. You have several excellent sources of information in Appendix C. Check with your librarian, the college placement office or the company's public relations department for additional materials if necessary.

If you are presented by a recruiter, he will furnish background to help make your interview a success.

If the company is listed on a stock exchange, you can get its annual, 10-Q and 10-K reports, which show much more detail on the company and its internal operations. Check your phone book for the nearest Securities and Exchange Commission office. A local brokerage firm can supply you with a copy of a listed company's *Standard & Poor's* report.

You may also learn about the company from the local press. Reading *The Wall Street Journal* or trade publications will give you additional background useful in your discussion. Keep a scrapbook of articles about companies of interest. Your interviewers cannot help but be impressed that you cared enough to do research on their companies.

Preplan the outcome of the interview. For a first encounter, your bottom line is to generate enough interest to be invited back to meet other people. It is rare that a serious offer is made during the first interview for other than entry-level positions.

Once you have been back, and are interested in the position and the company, your objective then becomes an offer. We will address this phase under Negotiations.

2. Approach

You want to control the interview. How is this done? There are several ways of looking at the interview dialogue. The secret of success will be the harmony achieved by both sides.

- Establish a rapport as an equal with your interviewer. He should not be considered an adversary but rather a partner. Do not be overly impressed by his position or authority. Your common bond is that you each have something to contribute to the other. He has a problem and you are his solution.

He has the choice of many, while you have mobility to look at several opportunities. You are not bound to one another.

He must be competitive in his offer to you, and you must be content that you will be properly rewarded.

A good beginning approach is a short but complete statement about yourself. It might be a brief rundown of what you have been doing in the last few jobs, citing one or two major accomplishments. It should be scripted and practiced. Then stop!

The concept of SAY IT—ASK IT is never more important than at this moment. It will permit you to control the conversation. Each time you make a statement or answer a question, finish by including a well-positioned question of your own: "Mr. Jones, so I can better relate to you and the ABC Company, could you tell me a little about what you are currently doing?"

Or,

"John (if you are on a first-name basis), I read about the recent acquisition your company made in Chicago and how you expect it to add to your sales. Could you tell me a little more about your present operations so I can better understand your company?"

You have now let the interviewer know that you have done some homework on his company, and you are giving him a chance to tell you what is going on in his world. This is the beginning of a dialogue that you will be controlling with well-placed questions.

Adapt your questions to your circumstances; i.e., if you are an attorney, your question would be:

"John, could you tell me about your legal operations (not problems) so I might better relate to you and the company?" By using this kind of question you are very much in control of the interview, because John is about to educate you on how he sees his company, his work and other factors that could affect you.

John most likely will reply with a very positive overview of his company or department. People do not want to expose weaknesses on the first review. Record John's analysis in your notes.

3. Probe

Find out what John needs. Reinforce these needs in John's mind as the conversation progresses. To continue:

He has just given a five- or ten-minute recital of his company's and/or department's operations. He is fairly satisfied with all the positive things he has been talking to you about. Your next question is:

"John, that's some agenda you've outlined, and you've done some pretty exciting things [you must acknowledge what John has been telling you]. But tell me, is there anything you would like to change or add or improve?" A very innocent question on the surface; however, you have just invited John to tell you what is wrong with his company and where he needs help.

John may reply: "Well, we need to improve our sales now that we've added a Chicago office. As you know, overhead has gone up and unless I get at least 25 percent more sales than last year, our new acquisition can bring down the group's total profits." Here at last you begin to know what is bothering John. He needs sales. Not just sales...profitable sales.

At this point the interview is going better than you may have imagined. You know one major area where there is a need. Continue with your probe by summarizing what John has just told you:

"You mean that if your sales increased by 25 percent, that would also increase your profits by, how much do you estimate?" John might reply: "The contribution would be on the order of 10 percent."

You now have all the information about the need and its bottom line. Your question has brought out that with a 25 percent sales increase, John could add as much as 10 percent incremental profit to his operations.

You now have seen the two phases of the probe:

a. Invite discussion of where it hurts.

b. Carry through the idea to show just how important the problem (hurt) is.

4. Presentation

You now know John's problem. You also know very well ALL your accomplishments. You do not need to dilute your effectiveness by dumping all you have done on John; he does not need it all. You only need to say what you have done that could be a value to him. This is the **ABC Principle.**

Accomplishment = **B**enefit (John's need), with the **C**onversion being made by the candidate.

It might work this way:

"So if I understand you right, John, a sales increase of 25 percent would add upwards of 10 percent in profits. That sounds mighty familiar. In my work for the ABC Company, sales increased more than 35 percent each year in the last three years and margins improved as well. Is that the kind of performance you are seeking?" (SAY IT—ASK IT)

Try to imagine John hearing this music to his ears. In front of him he has someone who not only understands his problem but has been doing what he needs for the last three years and then some. Is John interested? You bet he is.

There are, of course, other situations that can come up during the presentation phases. For example:

Suppose John asks you something that you have never done. You just might say, "No, I haven't done so and so." A better reply would be: "No, I haven't done that but I did do (another accomplishment that shows you took a new idea and, without previous experience, made it work)."For each question, you cannot answer merely yes or no, but instead you must use the question to bring out an accomplishment.

During your entire conversation you must focus on the interviewer and listen carefully to what interests him. Keep your accomplishments in line with his interests.

If you perceive that the interviewer is not interested in what you are discussing, switch back to his interests. Never lose your sensitivity to the reactions of your interviewer.

5. Close

The interview is going well and you want to continue your discussion; however, you still have not gotten what you came for: another interview. If John does not volunteer that he would like you to meet other people on his staff, you can gently move the conversation in that direction.

"John, your sales problems sound interesting and challenging! I'd like to learn more about them. Do you suppose I might be able to meet some people on your team and exchange ideas?" We are following the principle of SAY IT— ASK IT: A positive statement followed by a question that should provoke a positive answer. John's reply could be:

"Why yes, that's a good idea. Let me phone Joe Brown now and set up a meeting; he might even be free this afternoon." Objective is in sight: another interview.

Suppose John does not react favorably to your idea to meet with other people in the company at this time. This means one of a few things:

- John has other candidates to meet; it is too soon for a decision.

- John is less impressed than you anticipated.

- John already has decided in favor of another candidate.

If any one of the above is true, there is no sense in forcing your way further. What you can and should do is follow up your meeting with a letter in which you repeat your key advantages and express your enthusiasm for the position. After one or two weeks go by without a reply from John, you should call to find out where the company is in its recruitment. Your call should be one of interest and enthusiasm. Even if an offer has been made to another candidate, it may not work out and your enthusiasm could mean a reevaluation.

DIRECT INTERVIEW

Your Objective
Primary: Get another interview; later, an offer.
Secondary: If an offer does not develop, go for referrals.

Preparation
Know about the person you are approaching (if possible).
Know about the company (if possible).
Know your accomplishments.
Know who the decision-makers are.
Know where your skills fit in.
Be up to date on news about the company.

Approach
Your one-and-one-half-minute commercial (version adapted to a direct interview; people who will understand your prior work experiences).
Your lead question: "So I can better relate to you and the XYZ Company, can you tell me a little about your department, division, company or…?"
Take notes. Acknowledge what you hear.

Probe (two part)
1. Your next question: "Is there anything that you would like to add, change or improve?"
2. Summarize the importance/impact of solving the problem(s) you hear by placing a bottom-line on the solution(s).

Presentation
Select an accomplishment that shows you have solved a similar type of problem for someone else. Then ask: "Would that kind of result help your situation?"
Use the ABC Principle and SAY IT—ASK IT.

Close
Go for your next interview or an offer.

Post Close
Leave with a positive statement. "I'm sure our next meeting will be as productive as this was."
Always follow up with a thank-you letter and introduce new supporting information or an idea. Summarize the next step (yours or his).
Remember, you do not need to ask for a job. Everyone knows why you are there. The important thing is to be enthusiastic about the company and your possible role in it. The rest will follow.

6. Post Close

Things have gone well. The next interview is in sight. Arrangements are being made. You do not want to have John regretting his decision to go forward with you. The post close eliminates buyer's remorse. The post close is very much like the restaurant that serves you a fabulous meal: When presenting the equally fabulous bill, they include some mints. The post close leaves a sweet taste in the mouth.

After your next interview has been set, you might say: "Thanks, John. I'm sure Joe and I will get on well and have a very productive meeting." Now politely *get out*. You cannot do any more by hanging around.

To review what has happened:

- You arrived in John's office well prepared about him and his company.

- You gave a brief (rehearsed) rundown of your business career with one or two accomplishments (not more than a few minutes).

- You followed the principle of SAY IT—ASK IT by returning the conversation to John with your question on what he and his department are doing.

- You acknowledged this and began the probe by asking what he would like to improve or change or add. (Again, SAY IT—ASK IT.) He gave you more information.

- You summarized what he said, bringing home the importance of his need.

- You presented your one or two accomplishments that could satisfy his need (ABC Principle) followed by the question, "Is that the kind of performance you need in your next sales manager?"

- You went for the close, getting your next interview lined up.

- And on to the post close to eliminate buyer's remorse.

Before you leave the first interview, make sure you have enough information about the job and the company to make a good presentation on your next interview.

This formula, with a thousand and one variations, will permit you to control interviews successfully.

One of the main variations will occur when your conversation jumps from your accomplishments to discussion of a possible offer. Then you will get into more difficult questions and answers, which will be discussed later in this chapter, along with some possible responses.

Do not let an interview run longer than one-and-a-half to two hours. If it is running long and you feel you are rehashing material already discussed, try to wind it up with a question that will get you invited back.

"John, I know how busy you are and I can see our interview has been running a long time. I'm very interested in the job. Can we set a time now for our next get-together?"

FOLLOW-UP

When the interview is over, organize your notes. Send a follow-up letter acknowledging what was discussed, introducing a new idea and/or indicating further action. Each interview follow-up requires its own kind of letter. See Appendix B for examples.

If you do not have a reply to an open position within two weeks after your follow-up letter, call to restate your interest and find out what stage the recruitment process is in.

If you find that you have been turned down, leave the door open for future discussions (with a letter). You may have been second choice and the first one may not work out. Grace in defeat makes a powerful impression.

HELPFUL HINTS FOR A BETTER INTERVIEW

There are some basics you should have fully digested before going to any interview.

En Route

- Have maps in your car. Before you leave in the morning for your networking calls, write out directions and daily agenda on an 8-1/2" x 11" sheet (hour, person to see, address, telephone number, your bridge [referral person], any special directions). Having this in advance will make your day a lot easier. Save your directions for any return visits.

- Take your answering machine's remote control with you to field calls from wherever you are. Make sure the machine is working properly and has an intelligent outgoing message.

- Carry your master telephone list with you. You may receive calls during the day that you will have to return from the field.

- Practice speaking with a tape recorder so you are aware of how you sound. If you do not have a tape recorder, you can leave your answering machine on and record yourself. Learn to project your voice in a clear, positive manner.

- Always carry change for metered parking.

- Use your telephone credit card to make calls away from home. You will then have a record of all calls for tax purposes.

- Be organized before and during the interview. Have a clean briefcase, pen or pencil handy, a spiral notebook to take notes, copies of your resume, your reference list and any other information you think you might need.

- Even though you may be out of work, people may still ask for a business card. For as little as ten dollars, you can have your own business cards printed with name, address and telephone number. It will be handy to have one when you arrive at the reception desk, and it is something else you can leave behind.

- Be five to ten minutes early, but no more. If you are running late, or even think you might be, call ahead. Do not ask for the person you are going to see, but rather his or her secretary. Simply say, "This is…(your name). I want to let Mr. Smith know I may be a few minutes late. Would you please tell him that I am on my way for our meeting?" Full stop. Get acknowledgment that your message will be delivered right away and get off the phone. If you are routed to Mr. Smith, you risk having your meeting canceled. But if your message is delivered, he will not be disturbed if you are a little late because you thought enough to call. Never be late without a phone call.

    The most critical moment of an interview is its beginning. The seconds that follow your arrival have a big impact on the impression you make. Your gestures, your handshake, the tone of your voice and your expression are messages received by the interviewer and immediately initiate the judgment process. How can you present yourself in a favorable light?

- External Factors

    You do not need a Mercedes to impress people. But do have a clean car. Imagine that you might be asked to give someone a lift. Be prepared.

Look like the job you are going after. Dress correctly, be properly groomed, avoid flashy clothes, heavy cologne, do not smoke. Be alert to what is going on around you. No flashy jewelry or hairstyles. Men should wear calf-length socks that stay up. Watch out for dandruff on a dark suit. Are your nails clean?

In the Waiting Room

- Do not get too familiar with secretaries or receptionists. Your conversation may be reported back up the line.

- Be polite with EVERYONE, from the parking attendant (if there is one) right through to the boss's secretary. While you may not be remembered for politeness, you absolutely will be for rudeness.

- If you are kept waiting, do not show your annoyance. If it makes you late for another appointment, reschedule whichever appears more important.

  During the wait, you might ask the receptionist for an annual report or any other company literature.

- Parking can be expensive. Some companies validate parking, so ask the receptionist about company policy.

- Even if you are running late, freshen up in a restroom to assure you will be at your best.

- Leave your umbrella or overcoat in the reception area.

- When sitting in the waiting room, sit comfortably and fully in a chair. Perching on the edge of a chair or wringing your hands show signs of anxiety and stress. Try to relax.

- Do not use your host's office to make telephone calls unless it is absolutely necessary.

During the Interview

- Make sure your palm is dry before a handshake. Grab the other person's hand firmly and look him in the eye.

- Do not sit down until invited to do so.

- Maintain good eye contact. If you let your eyes wander, the interviewer will think you are trying to hide something.

- Be relaxed but pay attention to what is going on.

- Do not chew gum or smoke.

- Watch out for your special personal habits: Avoid touching hair or your nose if you tend to do this, do not pick at or bite your nails, do not play with things during an interview. Relax and focus on the person(s) before you. If you find yourself tensing up, try an old salesman's trick: Flex your toes in your shoes (out of sight, of course).

- Smile when appropriate. Be natural and sincere.

- Watch how the interviewer is seated. Try to be in harmony as you talk. If his legs are crossed, you might do the same. Body language is subtle but can put you on an even keel with your interviewer. You do not have to copy movements, but try to take your cues from your interviewer's signals.

The Discussion

- Manner of speech is important. If the other person talks slowly, it might be difficult for him if you speak quickly, and vice versa. Try to be in harmony with your rate of speech and tone of voice.

- Do not be a name-dropper unless you really think it will help you, and then be sure you are telling the truth, because other people may know that person even better.

- Never be negative about a former employer or employee. If you have nothing nice to say, keep quiet.

- Avoid answering too quickly. Think out your replies.

- Do not bring up salary.

- Learn the real job behind the written specification.

- Try to find out the interviewer's priorities.

- Do not discuss personal problems or politics.

- Do not use flattery.

- Do not be a yes man and do not argue.

- Watch expressions that devalue what you are saying, such as "in spite of" or "nevertheless" or "my problem was …"

- Never show documents from a previous employer that could be considered confidential.

- Do not volunteer your resume, but if asked, do not delay giving it. There is no sense in frustrating someone you are trying to impress. But stick to your presentation. If possible, hand over the resume and ask if it can be reviewed a little later. (This applies only to the direct interview. The resume can be used as an ice-breaker and discussion item in the research and advice interviews.)

- There will be periods of silence. Use them to think and organize your replies.

- If you do not hear the question, ask to have it repeated.

- Be patient; never interrupt.

- Remember, the interview is a conversation. Listen at least 51 percent of the time.

- Keep your replies short and answer the questions. Do not open other subjects—unless you feel it necessary to redirect the interview.

POTENTIALLY TRICKY QUESTIONS

During the interview, you may be asked a variety of questions. There are no perfect answers, yet some thought and discussion about potentially tricky subjects can help you avoid disaster.

1. Tell me about yourself.

This is the classic opener and gives the interviewer time to size you up—if you let him. Give a brief overview of your career (prepared and rehearsed in advance), beginning with your education and taking him through key job changes. Add one or two major accomplishments and then turn the interview back to him with, "So I can better relate to you, could you please tell me a little about your (company, department, etc.)?"

2. What is your opinion of the last company you worked for?

Stay neutral or positive, no negatives. Try to focus on situations in which you learned and/or contributed something.

3. Have you changed jobs frequently? Are you a job hopper?

Work out in advance a good rationale for your moves. People do change jobs, and if your reasons are sound, say so. Do not be defensive.

Some acceptable reasons: Reorganization (a new manager arrives and brings in his team), the company was in difficulty and had a massive layoff, a major contract or customer was lost resulting in loss of sales, the company was sold, you were offered a relocation that would have meant no apparent opportunity, or....

Reasons to avoid: Did not get along with employer or other people, did not like the management policies, passed over for a raise, too much pressure, too much work, too much overtime, too many arguments, problems of health, personal problems interfering with work, or.... Avoid long stories and negatives.

4. What salary are you looking for?

(See Negotiations.) Stress opportunity and potential. A return question: "It's hard to discuss salary without knowing more about the job or responsibilities." Or, if you are discussing a specific job: "What is your range?" Then relate your experience to the range without being necessarily precise: "I think my experience would put me near the high end of your range, don't you?" (SAY IT—ASK IT). Do not volunteer information about your past salary.

5. What were you making in your last job?

(See Negotiations.) If you are in front of a recruiter, tell him your salary package. If you are in an interview, try to put the salary question aside. A good reply is, "I was well compensated in my previous company but really do not wish to prejudice myself here by being too high or low. Can we delay this until after we've looked at all the aspects of your current need? What is your range for this job?"

6. Have you ever been fired?

If yes, have a good explanation worked out and tested with friends. "We had a change in general managers and although I had been doing a great job as you can see from my accomplishments, I was let go for one of his former associates."

Or,

"The company decided to close down its California operation and offered me a job in Chicago. We would like to stay in this area so that's why I'm looking around."

7. Can you work under pressure?

Indicate that you can, then counter: "How much pressure is involved in this position?" Learn what he means by pressure. If you are a pro at pressure jobs, give him a few accomplishments.

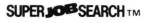

8. What did you think of your supervisor?

Whatever your true feelings, be positive. "He was the kind of person I could learn from."

Or,

"We were able to communicate well and things got done quickly."

9. What is your greatest strength?

Go to your list of strengths and then tie each of them to an accomplishment. "Is that the kind of quality that would help your company?"

10. What is your greatest weakness?

Look at your list of weaknesses (from Chapter 2) and relate the weakness (excess) back to your strength. "I like to get things done. Sometimes I get impatient, but I'm getting a handle on it."

11. How much do you know about our company?

You better have done your homework! Have you uncovered information about their products, sales, profits (or losses), news or personnel? See preparation.

12. Are you willing to relocate?

Do not pause—have your answer ready. "Yes, for a super opportunity. What did you have in mind?"

13. You've moved around. How long would you stay with us?

Again, this needs preparation. "I'm seeking a long-term opportunity where I can learn and grow. Does this come with the position we are discussing?"

14. What were your reasons for leaving each former job?

Think this out clearly. Be positive about discussing former companies. See Question 3 for additional ideas.

15. Do you have a drinking problem?

Believe it or not, some candidates have had this question. A possible answer might be: "No, is that a problem you've encountered previously?" If you have had a drinking problem in the past and are on the road to recovery, there is no sense in bringing it up, especially as the question referred to the present. Had the question been stated: Have you *ever had* a drinking problem—and you once had one—you could say, "I once was concerned about having too many Manhattan lunches, so on my own, I stopped all drinking during working hours." (If you still have a problem, help is available. Get it!)

16. What kind of manager are you?

Have a few key examples tied to accomplishments that show your management capabilities. Then say, "Is that the kind of performance you are looking for?"

17. What motivates you?

Money, opportunity, growth, a chance to learn, nice people, fair play…any others?

18. What do you not like to do?

A loaded question. A positive reply might be, "I'm the kind of person who does whatever is necessary to get the job done. When I do run into something disagreeable, I try to do it first and get it behind me. I have no particular dislikes."

19. Would you compete against me for my job?

Take this one easy. "I'd like to think that when you are promoted I could be a candidate for your position."

20. Why have you left your present job?

You know you are going to get this one, so here's your cue. Be positive. See Question 3.

21. Did you increase sales/profits in your last job?

Here is your chance to elaborate on your best accomplishments. "Is that the kind of salesperson you seek?"

22. How did your boss, co-workers and subordinates get on with you?

Have some examples of the kind of team player you are. This is a good time to bring up that you are a nonpolitical person.

23. Do you know how to motivate people?

This is a leadership question. Know what it takes to be a quality leader. In preparation, think of the best people you have worked for and list their attributes in leadership. Recognition and helping the people who depend on you often weigh as heavily in motivation as monetary reward.

One important key to being a great manager is to be able to delegate while maintaining control. If you can show some accomplishments demonstrating this ability, you are top management material.

24. What are your short-, medium- and long-term goals?

Tie your answer to goals that could conceivably be realized in the interviewing company. Limit your goals to just the short and medium range. Be realistic. A good reply is oriented toward growth in one's job through learning, experience and accomplishments.

25. Do you prefer working in small, medium or large companies?

Remember where you are when you answer!

26. Have you helped your company reduce costs?

Again, try to tie to your accomplishments. Then add a question, "Are those kinds of savings of interest to you?"

27. What is the toughest job of being a manager?

A good reply is, "To surround myself with people who are better than I am in their individual specialties."

28. Why do you want to work for our company?

Your reply could be based on their reputation for product, management, international scope, technology, as a nice place to work and grow. Know their products, policies and potential for you.

29. Why should we hire you?

If you know the job requirements, and match up some accomplishments, say, "...If there are opportunities to do that and more here, then this is a great fit. What do you think?"

30. What do you look for in a new job?

Be careful! Better know a little about the company and the job you are after.

If not, push in the direction of excellence based on former accomplishments (benefits).

31. How many people have you hired?

If you have hired a number of people, pick one or two who have done well thanks to your help. This question naturally relates to your ability to evaluate people.

32. How many people have you fired?

Watch out—another loaded question. "Letting people go is partly the company's responsibility as well as the individual's. Something did not work and it is good to analyze why. I did have to let people go in my last job. It made me realize how important it is to make the right selections the first time around."

33. What was your greatest success?

Pick one of your most significant accomplishments tied to their needs.

34. What has been your biggest failure?

Discuss this one with friends before the interview. If it can be something you were later able to correct, it becomes a learning experience.

35. What kind of day-to-day schedule did you have in your last job?

Stress action, performance and results rather than administrative work.

36. How do you feel about the progress you made in your last position?

(Accomplishment=Benefit[Need]; Do the Conversion [ABC].) "When I started with the Blake Company, I was given responsibility for their operations in France and Holland. After I turned them around, they made me general manager—Europe. With the strong dollar today, how are your international operations performing?"

37. What were the most important problems you encountered in your past job?

Use the ABC principles and you will have some good answers.

38. Did you have any frustrations in your past job?

Catch-22 question. Frustrations are a normal part of any job. Relate some of

the bottlenecks you experienced, but more importantly, indicate what you did to overcome them.

39. Why do you feel that you are ready to take on greater responsibilities?

Work from your accomplishments (ABC).

40. Tell me some of the creative work you have done.

Creativity means how you developed an idea, a new product, a new theme or a new program and how it improved the operation.

41. Are you a leader?

Give examples of how you followed leaders and how you successfully led other people. To be a good leader, you first must be a good follower.

42. Do you like to compete?

Competition is great as long as it does not sacrifice the rest of the team. If you are competitive, relate it to the total company effort and not your personal ambitions.

43. Do you consider yourself successful? Why?

If you have been doing the kind of work you enjoy and have accumulated some accomplishments, this could be the basis for your answer. "When I started out at the ABC Company, I was one of five salespeople. In five years, I have more than doubled my salary and am now sales manager. I feel good about what I've accomplished. Does that kind of performance match your needs?"

44. What can you do for our company that someone else cannot?

By now you should know the requirements of the job. Match your accomplishments against needs and mix with an interest in what you have seen/heard so far. As for the other candidates, you really cannot answer, nor would you want to. Answer from what you feel you can do.

45. What do you like best and least about the position we are trying to fill?

You can choose the best. As for the least: "At this point I see no important negatives, that's why I'm so interested!"

46. How long do you think it would be before you could make a contribution to our company?

Do not be in a hurry on this one. There normally is a period of transition to learn the ropes. "If the transition goes to plan, I would guess relatively soon. What would you expect?"

47. How high do you aspire to rise in our company?

"One step at a time. Let me do a good job where I am. If I move up the ladder that's fine. I'm open and ambitious."

48. Are you considering any other jobs at this time?

If you are, say so—but without detail. If not, "I have some irons in the fire." is enough.

49. What was the last book you read?

You do read. Be careful. He or she may have read the same one.

50. What magazines/newspapers do you read?

A good time to mention trade journals that would reinforce your interest.

51. How long have you been looking for a job?

If it has been a long time, you might mention if you have been doing any consulting or other part-time work.

52. Describe your ideal job.

Refer to your list of preferences in Chapter 2. Do not forget the requirements of the job at hand. Mix the two well. Do not be unrealistic.

53. How much money do you expect from this position?

No fast answers here. See negotiations. Try to find out the range they have in mind and then figure where you are. A good answer is, "I would like to make as much as I can as a measure of my contribution. What is the range for this job?"

54. What do you think your references will say about you?

Good things, you hope, especially since by now you have discussed your resume with each.

55. How many people did you supervise in your last position?

Do not exaggerate; this can be verified. "I supervised five people in our department and was later promoted to manager, which increased the number to 35. Our department placed second in cost reduction for the entire company last year. Does cost saving count high in your requirements?"

56. How would you describe yourself?

Think of your professional and personal management style statements on your 20-Second Resume. Review Chapter 4.

57. How would your spouse describe you?

Something to think about.

58. What things do you feel most confident doing?

Stick to accomplishments. Think of their job requirements.

59. What would you like to improve upon?

Pick something that will not be a deterrent for this position. Better computer skills, speak better Spanish, or…?

60. How do you spend your free time?

Be reasonable. This is not the time to mention that you like jumping out of planes, even if it is true.

61. What are your major accomplishments and how did you do them?

Here is your dream question! Pick the ones that pertain to the job in view. You know you have struck pay dirt when someone asks, "How did you do that?"

62. How many hours should a person devote to his job?

As many as needed to get it done and then some.

63. What things would you like to avoid in your next job?

Be on your toes. If there were politics in your past position, you might indicate that. Be careful.

64. How old are you?

This is an illegal question—yet can you imagine not answering it?

65. Don't you feel that you're over qualified for the position?

Ouch! If you have a lot of experience and they are thinking of a younger person, you may get this kind of response. A good answer is, "I imagine my experience would make me more valuable sooner!"

66. You have not been in this part of the country very long, do you think that would make a difference?

If you adapt quickly, this is the time to say it...and back it up with an example. Flexibility is usually valued highly by employers.

67. Do you mind working for someone of the opposite sex or someone younger(!!) than you?

It is the job that counts. Stick to the job specification and do not get side-tracked on implications.

68. You have never done this type of job before. How do you expect to succeed?

Bring up some accomplishments that show how you tackled new things and did well.

69. Do you mind travel?

By now you should know how much travel the job will require; otherwise, it is a good time to ask. This could be a trick question if you have a family. Think it out.

70. What are the most important factors in...(type of job you are going after)?

If you do not have a job description, you should ask for one so that you can reply item by item.

71. Do you mind taking some psychological tests?

If this is company policy, you have no choice. Try, though, to arrange beforehand to see and review the results. This way you will learn something about yourself.

72. Are you aggressive?

"If you mean am I a go-getter, yes, I am. If there's an opportunity, I like going after it." Defuse the tough implications.

73. How many days were you out ill last year?

If you have been out a lot, this could be damaging, unless you can impress upon the person that it was a one-time illness. "Unfortunately, I was out three weeks because of an auto accident. Even though I wasn't at fault, it was costly in time. But I maintained daily contact with my office and made sure the work got done. Everything's okay now."

74. Why were you not successful in your own business?

If you were in a business that had to be closed or sold, your answer could be, "I wanted to try my own company and discovered that I was happier in a larger organization. I was able to (sell or close) so that everyone was satisfied. I know what it takes to succeed. Will entrepreneurial skills help in this job?"

75. Does your present company know you are planning to make a change?

Be careful. Your answer could come back to haunt you. "I've grown just about as far as I can and see no further opportunities. At the appropriate time I expect to let my company know and, of course, when I'm ready to move, will do everything to make the transition as smooth as possible."

76. Why have you decided to change careers?

Your answer could be based on growth, interest, opportunity, increased responsibilities or greater product knowledge. Tie this into the job at hand.

77. Why did you get divorced?

This is an illegal question. However, a mature answer could be, "I was married young. People grow up and change. Unfortunately, our changes were in different directions."

78. How do you take criticism?

Most people have problems taking criticism. If the criticism is part of a formal evaluation program where you can learn and improve, that is fine. "I would welcome the opportunity to learn how to do my job better. Do you have a formal program for employee evaluation?"

79. Do you have any questions?

You sure do…!

QUESTIONS YOU MIGHT WANT TO ASK

A good interview is an exchange of information. Listening is critical for the candidate. The interviewer will give you more information than any written job specification. You will want to ask pertinent questions as the interview progresses. Before going into the interview, your outside research should be complete. Your questions should be focused on the job, rather than general information. The following list of questions will help. However, use them selectively and only when appropriate for the conversation at hand. Be polite, thoughtful and careful when asking questions. They may border on subjects that the interviewer is not prepared to talk about.

Initial Questions

Questions About the Job and the Company.

1. Is there a job description I can look at?

2. What will my responsibilities be?

3. How long has this position been open?

4. Where does this position fit in the overall organization?

5. What are the most important qualifications for this position?

6. What is the growth plan of the company?

7. Does the department have a budget?

8. Who are the company's major competitors?

9. Which markets do you regard as most important?

10. Who are your major customers? Are they mostly local, national or international?

11. What will my priorities be?

Questions About Your Future Supervisors, Collaborators and Subordinates.

1. Who held this position before?

2. What was his background and why is he being replaced?

3. To whom would I be reporting?

4. What is his background?

5. How many people will be reporting to me?

6. Are they all located in one place?

7. What is their experience level?

8. Does management have regular meetings?

Questions to Be Answered Later (and Only When Appropriate).

1. What are the prospects for advancement?

2. Could you explain what employee benefits you offer?

3. When would health coverage begin?

4. How much travel would be involved?

5. Would relocation be necessary now or at some future date?

6. When do you expect to decide on this position?

7. What is the next step in the procedure?

There are other things you will want to know, such as the profitability of the company (if you do not know already), its plans for growth in your area, how long it has been in business, is it important among its competition, is this a dead-end job or can one really grow with it and the company, how many bosses will you really have, what is the reputation of the company, have they had labor problems, who owns the company, what has its growth been over the last several years, is it located in a desirable area, will the company pay relocation expenses, is a job contract possible, what is the company's policy on vacations and sick leave and how are promotions and salary increases decided.

But, be careful. A wrong question can be misinterpreted and can screen you right out of the running. Try to learn as much of this information as possible outside the interview. Discretion is the rule of the day in presenting questions. When in doubt, keep your question in reserve. Focus your questions about the job and never bring up salary at the beginning. First, sell them that you are their candidate.

MORE ABOUT THE INTERVIEW PROCESS

1. Stress

Anyone faced with an interview is bound to have a little anxiety before getting into the actual discussion. How to deal with stress:

- Eat properly and avoid caffeinated beverages, tranquilizers and alcohol. Sleepiness or over-stimulation will work against your best efforts.

- Get enough sleep and exercise regularly.

- Release your tension by discussing your search with someone else. Be frank about your feelings and problems.

- The more you prepare yourself and the more experience you gain in meeting people, the better you will become as an interviewee. Remember, you are also interviewing the company to see how it would be as a home for your skills and future.

- Do not put all your hopes into one interview. You must keep your search going until you are on the job, and then some.

2. What to Do When the Conversation Bogs Down

If you see the interviewer looking at his watch or becoming distracted from the conversation, you may be taking too much time to reply, the interview is running too long, he already has decided that you are not his candidate (direct interview) or simply that you will not be getting the referral information you want (advice interview). Be sensitive to these signals and politely try to wind up the interview while still trying for some referral names.

You may get into situations that will be hard to control if the interviewer wants to discuss lots of irrelevant matters. You will have to go along until you can get back on your program. Be alert for your opening and bring the conversation back on track with a pertinent question.

The above situations illustrate that communication between you and the interviewer is at a standstill even though conversation continues. When you begin to recognize these situations, you are in a position to avoid them:

- Are you so anxious to move ahead that you talk too much? If this is happening, you need practice with another job searcher.

- Because of your frustration, have you become too aggressive? Get rid of tension before going into the interview.

- Are you bored with your own story? Listen more. Offer only those accomplishments that fit your discussion, not your whole history.

- Can you detect that your listener is not really interested in your presentation? This is something to work on in a group—how to make it more interesting.

- Are you feeling sorry for yourself and letting it show? Sure, it is frustrating looking for a job. But realize you will succeed! Stay enthusiastic about your program. Look forward, not backward.

- Have you become bitter because your search is taking too long? There is no sense in becoming angry at the world because of your situation. Millions of people right this minute are looking for work just like you are. If you want to find a good job, you will!

- You are in an interview and suddenly you burn out. If this happens, ask if you can be excused and go to the restroom. Throw cold water on your face and take deep breaths. Moving about will help get you back on track.

If you are convinced of your strong points and believe in yourself, you will be able to communicate these feelings to other people.

3. After Any Interview

After each interview, write down your comments on what happened, what went well, what could have been improved and what you still need to research. Plan your next step. Did you listen to everything the interviewer was saying? Did you pinpoint your replies to his needs? What do you need to stress further?

UNUSUAL INTERVIEW SITUATIONS

Groups

Sometimes interviews are conducted with more than one person from the company in attendance. In this situation, focus on the person talking and listen carefully to his questions. Reply as if you were in a one-on-one interview and only address your comments to one person at a time. You do this by turning your head and moving eye contact to each person, but returning to the person who presented the question. As you make your contact, you can sense reactions— who is with you and who might have further questions.

Concentrate on using a group interview to increase your information. You also have additional exposure to members of the company who can support your candidacy. Most hiring is done by consensus. Pace yourself, take one question at a time and give short, direct answers.

Direct your questions to different persons in the group to draw them into the discussion. By doing this, you will sense who your supporters are and who still has to be "sold." Let them get their doubts out on the table so you can at least have a chance to reply.

A typical group for a production manager's job might be: vice president of human resources, director of engineering, director of manufacturing and purchasing manager. All these people are concerned that the chosen candidate will help, not hinder, their efforts. A support group is the ideal way to practice this type of role playing, and candidates report that it really helps.

Screening Interview

The interviewer is looking for negatives about each candidate to eliminate as many as possible. Such interviewers are usually professionals who are skilled at drawing out details that could trip you. To succeed in this type of interview, probe for company needs and stick to your accomplishments. Do not stray from your agenda.

Second Meeting, In-Depth Interview

You have been invited back. Great. This time you want to receive a job offer. Your conversation must continue with accomplishments (benefits) and what you can do for the company. Most likely, you are being interviewed by the person you will be working for. Concentrate on your skills and knowledge of your job. Keep in mind the employer's requirements. Use SAY IT—ASK IT expressions to learn more about their needs. Recalling the first interview and the qualities that were specified for the job, keep within the framework of the position. Avoid discussion about salary until you get an offer.

Third Meeting

Depending on the level and/or importance of the job, it might take more than two meetings before an offer is made. Obviously, you are being very seriously considered at this point. If salary has not come up, it will now. This is the time to apply the techniques under The Negotiation, which follow. Keep in mind that each person you meet, either in group or individually, will be discussing his or her reaction to your candidacy. This is why you must focus on the job and stick to facts so that any subjective evaluation brings people back to your accomplishments (benefits).

Restaurant Interview

When people eat, they relax. Many interviews are conducted over a breakfast, lunch or even dinner. Be on guard. Remain focused on what you want to say. Listen carefully to the casual conversation but limit your personal "war stories"

to accomplishments. Do not let your defenses down too far with chummy conversation. A good drink at lunch is iced tea. For dinner, no more than one glass of wine. Keep control of the conversation with good questions. Be interested in the other people present, including wives. Remember, the sign of a good conversationalist is being a good listener. Note and remember names.

The Trip

Some companies may invite you on a trip to visit one or more of their facilities. You may travel alone or with other people. Though you may not be aware of it, you are being observed in a semi-work situation, a trial run. Be polite with everyone you meet and remember that whatever you say probably will be discussed later among the staff.

If you see something wrong and think you could improve things, resist giving off-the-cuff solutions. Without in-depth knowledge regarding the circumstances, it is better to hold these observations for the right place and time.

With Your Spouse

After the first few interviews, you may be asked to bring along your spouse. This is particularly likely when relocation is necessary. The company wants to be sure that the family is okay on the move.

It is a good idea to rehearse difficult questions with your spouse, such as your feelings about making a move or what your spouse thinks of the area, company or job. Sharing your answers to the questions in Chapter 2 will help.

In some positions, entertaining customers may be necessary, and the company will be "interviewing" your spouse to be sure that together you make a nice impression. Your image must be unified.

WHY INTERVIEWS GO WRONG

The more interviews you have, the more you will discover that your success depends on saying the right things, feeling the part and avoiding delicate subjects. However, there sometimes are other factors that can mean an unsuccessful interview:

Physical Characteristics

1. Poor personal appearance.

2. Lack of eye contact.

3. Weak and humid handshake.

4. Trouble in communicating (voice, grammar, diction, mannerisms).

5. Lack of energy.

Protocol

1. Arriving late without calling ahead.

2. Being rude.

3. Neglecting to recognize and thank the interviewer for his time.

4. Being ironic.

5. Being too familiar.

Objectives

1. Unclear purpose.

2. Too much emphasis on money.

3. Only interested in what the company can do for you.

4. Indecisive.

5. Unprepared.

Prior Employment

1. Critical of past employer.

2. Unexplained, numerous job changes or gap in work history.

3. Poor references.

4. Name-dropping.

5. Deficient experience and education.

Attitude Concerning the Job

1. Too many excuses.

2. Too aggressive.

3. Reluctant to relocate.

4. Lack of confidence.

5. Lack of questions and interest about the job.

Knowing in advance what can go wrong will help your networking, mail campaigns and interviewing techniques stay on track. When you get up to speed with two to four interviews (direct, research or advice) per day, you will be doing fine.

THE NEGOTIATION

You now have been networking and meeting people. You have had a good interview and are about to get an offer. Do not relax and let go—yet!

The final interview phase is the salary negotiation. You have to develop a strategy that is simple but effective.

Before the Salary Negotiations

1. The Range.

What is the job really worth? Keep in mind that this is totally independent of what you were making previously, although your interviewer will try to relate one to the other.

- Finding out what a job is worth takes research. If you know some recruiters, call them. A recruiter will ask for information about the company that you may want to keep confidential. Stick to information about its industry, sales, number of employees, profitability, number of people you will be supervising and your overall responsibility. A recruiter can give a pretty accurate appraisal of what the job is worth and, more importantly, give you a range for reference.

- Another way to evaluate a job's worth is to call a few employment agencies, indicating that you are considering hiring for a similar position. What kind of a salary package do they think would be appropriate? Keep in mind that most employment agencies work within a limited salary range, and many are specialized within certain industries.

- Friends in the industry can give you some ideas on the salary question. You may have contacts within the company who can help you.

After enough investigation, you will have a pretty good idea of the market value of the position. Take the time to do this properly—it will make all the difference in the negotiation.

2. The Salary Package.

The salary package is made up of all or parts of the following:

Base salary

Benefits:

> Bonus (by project, discretionary, individual, company)
> Car Allowance
> Health Insurance
> Life Insurance
> Dental Insurance
> Educational Allowance
> Stock Options
> Profit Sharing
> Pension Plan
> Deferred Income
> Paid Vacation
> Disability Insurance
> Severance Pay (negotiated in advance)
> Salary Review—how often
> Expense Account—how liberal
> Relocation Allowance
> Cost-of-Living Adjustment
> Employment Contract

Before getting into strategy, examine the benefits and what they can mean to you.

Bonuses: Bonuses are best when they are tied to a specific deed or accomplishment rather than a discretionary factor. Bonuses can be for an entire department, the whole company or an individual. You need to know the company's policy on the bonus question and what has been done in the past. If the bonus is based on your performance, you will have to be sure it is realistic.

Car Allowance: Depending on company policy, a car allowance can be worth $10,000 or more per year. The ideal situation is for the company to lease or give you a car and a credit card for gas, and pay for maintenance and insurance. With today's high automobile expenses, this can be an important addition to a salary package. Check with your accountant to find out how much of this allowance will be judged as taxable income.

Health, Life & Dental Insurance: How generous are the company's plans? What amount does the employee have to contribute? How do their plans compare to your previous health plan? If you have a large family, this is especially important.

Educational Allowance: Can you have time off from work to go for an advanced degree? How much of this expense will the company pay? How does this add financially to your overall package? Will promotions or pay increases follow your new degree?

Stock Options: Are they available to employees? Can you get incentive stock options that are sheltered from taxes? Project some growth in the company stock and see if this will be an important factor. Stock options are usually only interesting in companies that trade their stock on an exchange or intend to do so.

Profit Sharing: What has this yielded in the past? How would this affect your first year's salary and beyond? Did you have similar benefits in your previous position? How do the plans compare?

Pension Plan: How long will it take to become vested? What will it mean to you at retirement?

Deferred Income: Has the company done this in the past? What does your accountant say about it?

Paid Vacations: Can vacation time be accrued from year to year? What is the vacation policy? How does this measure up against your former employer?

Disability Insurance: What plans are available and what are the benefits?

Severance Pay: In some situations, mostly at senior levels, executives negotiate their exit salary in advance. For example: "It's all wonderful today, but suppose there's a change in top management and they want to bring in their own team. I've been doing a good job; what happens if they want to let me go?" Severance pay packages vary from a few months to (in rare cases) several years. If your position warrants such discussion, this can be a very important factor to negotiate before the fact. Have a knowledgeable attorney look over the conditions while you are in the discussion stage.

Salary Review: How often? Are reviews for merit only or do they cover cost of living as well? What has been the company's policy? Sometimes you can accept a lower initial salary provided there is an earlier review.

Expense Account: Some companies are rather liberal with credit cards for business entertainment. Watch out, though. Just because the company allows certain expenses, does not mean the IRS will. Rules change constantly. Discuss this with your accountant.

Relocation Expense: Will they pay for only a portion of your move or cover all expenses in selling your home, moving personal effects and the expense involved in buying a new home? It is something to think about if you will be required to relocate. Depending on how badly you are needed, some companies will even buy your home and take on the job of reselling it just to free you for the move.

Cost-of-Living Adjustment: If you are moving from a small town in up-state New York to the Los Angeles area, watch out! Your new home can cost three times the price of the house you just sold! While you are examining all the factors of moving into a new area, look at what this will do to your personal expenses. You will have to do some trial budgets. Talk with a number of real estate people and your accountant to see what the real difference is in cost of living. Use the forms in Chapter 1 to evaluate these changes versus your present lifestyle.

Another expensive move is from the U.S. to Europe. There are big differences in the cost of living. What are the income tax considerations? What are the inheritance tax problems? For any major move, be sure to speak with experts in the field (real estate brokers, accountants, attorneys and, if you can, some local people in the same social/income bracket as yourself).

Where public schools might have been satisfactory at your old address, you may now require private schooling for your children. These are just some of the things to take into account. A generous cost-of-living adjustment can make a significant addition to your salary package.

Employment contracts are rare in relation to the total work force, but for top positions they still exist and you should be aware of what goes into them. Do not press for a contract. You might make the company feel that the contract status is more important to you than the job itself. Emphasis on a contract can also mean that you feel insecure. Your investigation of the job should reveal if the company has a contract in mind. If a contract is proposed, be sure to consult a knowledgeable attorney to help you understand all its ramifications.

3. Your Needs.

There is yet another number you should have in mind: What is your rock-bottom, monthly financial need? To arrive at this figure, divide your last year's total expenditures by 12 for an average monthly requirement.

Use the income and disbursement analysis forms in Chapter 1 to save time in your financial review and help you keep control over your search.

Here is an example:

Suppose your basic monthly requirement has been $2,500, including taxes. Your monthly salary before deductions in your past job was $3,000. In making a

change, you hope to increase your salary. How much? Assume you would like a 20 percent increase. This means that your objective would be at least $3,600 per month. However, if you could do even better, say with another 20 percent increase over your last salary, your perfect salary would be $4,200 per month (before deductions).

Your goal in negotiating should be between your *salary objective* of $3,600 per month and *perfect salary* of $4,200 per month. You should try hard not to settle for less than your last salary, or in this case, $3,000 per month, keeping in mind your absolute minimum requirement of $2,500 (which will grow with inflation).

To review:

Minimum Requirement	$2,500 per month = $30,000 per year
Last Salary	$3,000 per month = $36,000 per year
Salary Objective*	$3,600 per month = $43,200 per year
Perfect Salary**	$4,200 per month = $50,400 per year

  * = 20 percent over your last monthly salary
** = 40 percent over your last monthly salary
Note: To be consistent, the minimum requirement has taxes included, and salary is before tax deductions.

Assume inflation has been running around five percent per year. To see how your salary would have to advance yearly, you can project whatever level you finally negotiate by a five percent increase each year just to maintain your current purchasing power.

Suppose you negotiate your salary of $3,600 per month. Assuming a five percent inflation factor and no merit increases, your salary would have to grow as follows to make sure you still have the same purchasing power in the next five years as year one.

Today	$3,600 per month
1 Year Later	$3,780 per month
2 Years Later	$3,969 per month
3 Years Later	$4,167 per month
4 Years Later	$4,375 per month
5 Years Later	$4,594 per month

In considering any job, you must look at how your salary can grow just to cover inflation, which you can estimate before and during the discussion. Review the example above, substituting your figures. Do not think only of today's salary.

During the Salary Negotiations

1. Positioning Your Salary

You come to the salary negotiation with some information. You know: a) The range that outsiders have given. b) Where you fit in that range. c) Perhaps the reputation of the company with respect to salaries in general. d) Maybe, by luck, the salary of the person before you. e) Your last salary package. f) Your minimum requirement. g) Your objectives.

2. Measuring Your Potential Salary Against Company Needs

In any negotiation, there are two sides to every issue: what you want and what they want to give. A good negotiator concerns himself with the requirements of the other side. Have you determined what the company really needs with respect to this position?

Items to look at:

What are the responsibilities of the job?

Authority over how many people, size of budget?

What is the degree of technical competence required?

How much experience is needed?

Where is the company with respect to its life cycle?

How soon does this job have to be filled—i.e., urgency?

Is this a staff or line position?

Does this position contribute directly to profits?

How does this position tie in with future expansion?

How long do they expect to wait for results?

These items must be weighted in importance based on what you have learned in your interviews. For example, if they require someone immediately and you

are available, you then have extra negotiating power for a higher salary. Do you have a specific talent that is not easily found in the area? Would it be more expensive for the company to relocate someone else when you are already there? These factors are the basis for a good negotiation.

3. The Strategy

• Never bring up your past salary.

In your discussion, they will already have asked what you were making before. While it is best not to answer, it is hard to refuse, and you are not looking to create arguments. Remember, the job of the interviewer is to try to find out what you were making before. Here are some answers:

"I really would like to concentrate on the position we're talking about with your firm. The salary I had with my other company was based on different work and responsibilities. What is the salary range for this job?"

Or,

"I don't wish to prejudice my position with you by mentioning an old salary that really is unrelated to the opportunity at hand. Could you indicate what range you have in mind?"

Or,

"I was well paid at ABC Company, but my work was different. I am enthusiastic about working with your company and feel that if we agree I am your person, there won't be any problems on salary. What is the range for this position?"

You can see the direction to move: In your own words, indicate that your old salary and job belonged to a different world. You first want to be sure that you qualify for the job in view, and your previous salary—higher or lower—may jeopardize that. At the same time, however, probe for the range they have in mind.

When the interviewer continues to insist, and you feel that you cannot avoid any further, be sure to mention the MAXIMUM for the package you had at your old job. That is, if you were making $3,000 per month but had a car and other perks, then add all that together. That will put you in the top end of your own spectrum. Have this worked out beforehand.

• When the interviewer wants to know how much you want.

If you can find out the range that the company has in mind, then you can fix your objective more intelligently. It does not hurt to use some accomplishments along the way to support your position on the high end of any stated range. Look at some possible replies:

"With my qualifications for the position, what compensation level do you feel is appropriate?"

Or,

"Please keep in mind that I already have seven years' experience in doing…, which means I would be productive practically from day one. Is that the kind of professional you are seeking?"

Another way to answer this question is to focus on the company's needs and plans (see above list). Example: "Can we talk about your needs and my experience? When you think of the fact that I increased sales by 35 percent each year for the same type of products, and that I introduced two new lines, which tie directly into what you want me to do for you, how much is that worth to your company?"

- Getting an offer.

The key here is not to ask but rather to get an offer—which may be substantially more than you thought you would get in the first place. Whatever you do, do not come out with a strong statement like, "I need at least $3,500 per month!"

When asking your salary question, your tone of voice should be one of examining the matter rather than asking for a total commitment. You are also making the other person come to grips with the fact that they need you.

With the proper tone (and some confidence) you can then ask: "By now, John, you have a pretty good feel for my qualifications and the potential my accomplishments represent for the XYZ Company. What remuneration would you consider fair for the job we have been discussing?" John may reply, "Well, I was thinking of $4,000 a month. How does that sound to you?"

Here is a negotiating technique that could be worth several thousands of dollars to you! It all depends on your reply.

Suppose you were to look up at the ceiling, pause a few seconds, frown just a little and say, "Hmmmmmm, $4,000." And STOP. Silence. Let the next words come from John no matter how long you have to wait.

If John is really bent on having you on his team, the pause that follows will be upsetting. After all, you did not jump out of your chair saying, "That's just fine!" You acted concerned and hesitant. So in the pause that follows, John may

say, "Well, suppose we up that $4,000 to $4,500. Would that be better?" Or, "We didn't discuss a car allowance. Suppose I were to add $300.00 per month more for that?" There could be a lot more variations on this theme, or John could say, "Sorry, that's the best I can do...." If you feel that you want to accept the $4,000 but are not sure, you can ask to have some time to think it over and make an appointment then and there to have a final discussion.

- Know how to make concessions.

Sometimes it is okay to step back in salary to move up faster in a different environment or situation. Do not be attracted by salary alone; you risk making a serious career mistake.

If you really want this job but you still are apart on the salary, what compromise can be made that will give you room for growth? How can you make this a win-win proposition? This is the real art of negotiating.

Suppose you wanted a monthly base of $3,500. Their offer is $3,000. The benefits are about the same as those provided by your former job. There is a chance for a bonus, but you cannot count on it. What can you do to satisfy everyone's needs? Some form of compromise is needed.

At this point, you can take a different approach with the interviewer. Suppose you say, "John, I really want this job, and I feel I can do well for the company, but I'm concerned that the starting salary is too low. I guess you want me to prove my worth to you, and I'm willing to do that. The year-end bonus shows me that you're willing to reward performance. But one year is too long. Can I make a suggestion?"

John is all ears; he nods agreement. "John, if I accept the job at $3,000 per month, can we agree that I will have a job review in three months and, if my performance is good, I can have the $3,500 that I feel I am worth? You get a chance to see what I'm capable of doing and I'll have the opportunity of meeting my needs. How about it?" If you were John, would you take such an offer?

Putting the monthly base pay aside, you now can address the benefits. Here is an opportunity to make up any loss you had on the base itself. Again, some research on typical benefits for the industry and the company will strengthen your position.

The End of the Negotiations

If you can get more than you have been earning at your previous job, so much the better. If you can only duplicate your last salary but it is 15-25 percent over your minimum need, that is not bad. But if you must drop below your last salary, and the salary offered does not cover your basic needs, something is wrong and you will have to rethink the entire matter. As a rule, it is good to ask to have a few days to reflect on any offer.

A recent study on the subject of salaries for people making job changes indicates the following:

Two groups were studied. One took jobs at a significantly higher salary than their previous jobs. Another group took promising positions, but at lower salaries than their previous employment. Five years later the group that took the lower salaries had a higher average salary than the group that took the higher initial pay.

In any event, the next line from you can be, "I appreciate your offer, John. Can I have some time to think about it?" If the offer is really very acceptable, you might say, "Can you give me some detail about the benefits that would go with it?" Save your discussion of benefits until after you have more or less settled that the base salary offer will not be subject to further negotiation.

Always ask and fix a time for another meeting to conclude the salary discussion. Your discussions should end on a pleasant and agreeable note.

More Than One Offer

It is not uncommon for one offer to arrive close to another. This is a good time to use the criteria that you filled out in Chapter 2 regarding your likes and dislikes. You may have some additional questions based on your preferences for each offer. When completed, your evaluation should help in making your final decisions.

If you want to delay one offer while waiting for another, or speed up one that is dragging, there are some helpful guidelines.

- If the first offer is made without a job description, you can suggest putting one together, which will buy you time for the other company to come to a decision. At the same time, you can mention to your preferred company that you have an offer and would like to entertain theirs if they genuinely feel that a decision is imminent. Never say this unless it is true, since they might suggest that you go ahead and take the other offer.

- If you have more than one offer and are waiting for another, and there is no chance to delay it with the above technique, you should ask for a little time to think over their offer, indicating that you have a few offers and want to really study them all. You run the risk that the offering company may withdraw and go to another candidate. Only you can measure how strong their negotiators have been in trying to recruit you.

You will have to weigh all of your alternatives and judge the risk in dealing with a present offer, waiting for another that may not come when you want it or just continuing to look. No one can decide this for you.

After the Negotiations...But Before Your Decision

When you have the base plus the benefits, you can look at the PACKAGE and see how this measures up against:

- Your prior situation.
- Your present needs.
- Your expectations for the job.

Are you the answer to their need? Have you compared the job description and qualifications with your education and experience? Is this position as important as they make it out to be? How urgent is their situation?

With answers to the above questions, you should now refer to your list of preferences in Chapter 2. How does this job and company stack up to your personal feelings and goals?

Negotiation is a give-and-take affair. It is trying to meet the other person's needs while filling your own. Admittedly, this cannot always be done. If someone pegs a job way below what you feel it is worth, or what your research says it is worth, then they get the better of the bargain.

When jobs are hard to come by, an interviewer can get away with this. But when the market reverses, watch the exodus. All that good training and experience will go to a competitor. Personnel managers today have more savvy and understand that pushing too far can cost them losses later in good recruits.

You can get a lot of advice on negotiation, but at the end of the day, a fair arrangement will last the longest. Holding back on what you were making in your previous job will give you the advantage, since their salary range may be higher than what you were making. It is an important point to keep in mind.

Reviewing the Negotiation

- Determine the salary range.

- Know your needs—to the penny.

- Concentrate on the needs and plans of the company.

- Know what you are prepared to trade.

- Take time to review their offer.

Conclusion

You have accepted the job and are ready to begin. Make sure the offer is a firm one, and preferably in writing. Now you must demonstrate all the fine qualities that contributed to your list of accomplishments. Remember, getting an offer and winning a good salary places a responsibility on you to deliver. You have two loyalties: the company and your supervisor. Support both and you will be on the road to success. In positions of responsibility, never forget or lose faith in the people who work for you. They depend on your leadership, fairness and example for their success. Make this your best job ever! And do not stop networking!

Practice

In outplacement training, part of the last phase is to interview candidates using a video recorder so they can see and hear how they perform while a counselor conducts typical advice and direct interviews. If you have access to this equipment, by all means practice.

You have the Tricky Interview Questions listed in this manual. Let someone ask you questions from the list at random in a practice session, with or without a video recorder.

You also can use a tape recorder for practice. If you do not have one, but do have an answering machine, you can leave the machine on and record a day's worth of outgoing calls, then listen to how you fielded the conversations. What can you do to improve your techniques?

Practice with other candidates can be of tremendous value. By sending in the Registration Form in the back of this book, you have an opportunity to be matched up with another job searcher. Based on the information you provide, we will try to put together practice groups in your area so that you can perfect your techniques in telemarketing, interviewing and negotiation. You also can share experiences in finding bridges and meeting people on your target list. There is no cost to you if you register as indicated.

WIN-WIN NEGOTIATIONS

What You Need to Know

1. Your total prior salary package (salary plus benefits).
2. Your absolute financial need.
3. The range for this type of job in industry (ask recruiters).
4. The reputation of the company for salaries plus benefits.
5. Your objective (120 percent of your last salary).
6. Your perfect salary (140 percent of your last salary).
7. How long have they been looking—urgency.
8. Their policy on salary reviews.
9. How your experience measures against their need.
10. How much in a hurry are they for you to produce?
11. How long do you intuitively feel it will take you to produce?
12. How difficult is it to find people with your comparable skills and experience in the area?
13. What impact will this job have on profits?
14. The salary of the person who had this job before (if you can find out).

Keys to Good Negotiations

1. Try to get an offer.
2. Never say "I need at least...dollars."
3. Relax; do not get excited.
4. Remember, the other person knows what the market is worth, too.
5. Act as if you both are working on the same problem—searching for a common solution.
6. Do not overstate your importance beyond what the job is worth.
7. Use accomplishments (again) to push your value to the high end of their range (SAY IT—ASK IT).
8. Try to settle the base salary first and then go on to the benefits.
9. A commitment for an early review can make up for a lower initial salary (a chance to show your worth).
10. If you are very qualified, explore whether more responsibilities can be added to increase the job's worth.
11. Always ask for time to review their offer—but make an appointment on the spot for the next meeting.
12. If you have studied their offer and feel that it is good for you, accept it graciously (ask for a letter confirmation).
13. If you have more than one offer, review your job preference criteria in Chapter 2 against each.
14. Do not become aggressive, cocky or arrogant.
15. Be flexible—never forget the company has options just as you do.
16. Acknowledge your acceptance with a positive letter.

THE COMPLETE MANUAL FOR CAREER-CHANGERS

ACTION PLAN

You now have all the tools and techniques for your job search. As you have seen, your greatest opportunities lie in the hidden job market. Your first priority should be concentrating on developing contacts and spending at least 70 percent of your time meeting people.

Now we come to the point of managing your time. With all the different avenues you can explore, you must be organized in the use of your energy.

What comes first?

1. If you have not yet set up your home office, now is the time. You need to have a place to work for writing letters, filing, making phone calls. It should be quiet. If there are small children in the house, you will need to lay down some rules when you are in your home office. Set up your files in the beginning so you will not have lots of stray papers. You will need to maintain some discipline so that when you have met more than 200 people you will have no problem in going back over your files to recall when you met them and what was said.

2. The work you did in Chapter 2 is the backbone of your search. Review it from time to time.

3. Know all your accomplishments by heart—even the ones not listed on your resume. When interviewing, you will want to draw upon specific accomplishments to match an immediate need. Needs will vary from company to company and person to person. Be prepared.

4. You should now have your resume completed and either stored on a word processor or printed, with matching printed stationery. Your resume will vary according to the position you are seeking. With the help of a personal computer, you can tailor your credentials to the specific needs of your target companies.

5. You have prepared your network list. This will be your data base of initial contacts. You will add to it as you move forward.

6. Your target companies list also should be completed. This, too, will grow.

Your First Stop

After reading this book and digesting its contents, your first stop should be your public or business school library. You should take as much time as necessary to familiarize yourself with as many of the reference books listed in Appendix C as possible. These reference materials are an important part of your search and

will provide you with the knowledge about people and companies essential for your personal campaign. Invest the time now so you can go to the right source for details when a question arises.

A mailing to recruiters has been discussed in Chapter 5. Now is a good time to get this behind you. The earlier this goes out, the sooner you can move on to other aspects of your program.

Every Day

When you had a regular job working for someone else, you rose every morning and probably were out early on the job. You now have a new job, though it is a temporary assignment, in finding a new position.

You must apply the same personal discipline to yourself as you did when you were employed. This means:

1. Get an early start on the day...every day!

2. Dress smartly—even if at home.

3. Keep yourself in shape, physically and mentally.

4. Keep your sense of humor.

Networking/meeting people is where the action is in terms of approaching the hidden job market. Begin your networking calls each day, gradually expanding your efforts. Your objective is to generate 10-20 or more interviews a week. You will make mistakes. So what? Everyone does. But as you move forward you will improve. Begin your calls with those people you know, and mix in others from referrals. Maintain good records of calls made and when to call back. Remember, calling back is preferable to leaving a number.

Take good notes when you have an interview. Every interview is important. At the end of each day, review your notes and, if necessary, summarize them for follow-on action. Read past reports from time to time. Do not rely on memory.

Record your expenses and be sure to have all receipts stored properly.

Do your correspondence at the end of the day, not during time that could be spent meeting people. Develop a routine for sending out thank-you letters after EVERY interview...good or bad. They do not have to go out the same day, but do not wait more than one week. Your letters should thank the person for his time and suggestions. You might add some new information in your letter based on questions that were raised. If you are to call back again, make sure you have noted this on your follow-up call list.

Prepare for the next day's telephone calls and visits. In the beginning, try to make your calls early and mix in interviews as you generate appointments. Your calendar should be always up to date.

Keep your address book current including the date you encounter each new person. Where appropriate, cross reference the name of your referral and his telephone.

Write on each business card you receive the date you obtained it. Store your collection of business cards in an album (available at most stationery stores).

Maintain files of all mail (thank-you letters, replies to ads and broadcast letters). It will make researching information an easy operation. Set a time during the day to read trade magazines, newspapers and mail. Cut out pertinent articles and file them by company or person. Cut out classified advertisements that you intend to answer and tape them into a spiral notebook for your pre-reply analysis. For your mail campaign, select no more than a dozen companies at a time. Why a dozen? It is a manageable number. Remember, you will be calling each to follow-up with a personal meeting. Too many and you will not be able to keep control.

Out of Town

Suppose some of your target companies are in another city or state. In this instance, use of a mail campaign is helpful, but sometimes you will have to travel for an interview. If a company is paying for the trip, use the opportunity for other calls as well. If you cannot get an invitation to see a company at its expense, you might consider paying your own way and combining your interview with some on-the-spot networking. To control costs, consider staying with a friend or relative. Watch airline rates for bargain fares to your target area.

Planning a trip is a good reason to call the people you have written in that area, advising them that you will be in their city and would like to drop by for a brief chat. Most people will appreciate the effort you are making, and your success rate in getting in to see people will be higher than that of others living in the city. Try to fill up your program at least 50 percent of the time with scheduled interviews, leaving the other 50 percent free for interviews you will generate by local networking. A well-planned, one- or two-week visit can bring to the surface quite a number of opportunities. Keep a record of all your expenses.

When traveling away from home, be sure to keep in touch with your answering machine. If you have someone at home to open mail, you can keep in contact with your mail network, even while you are on the road. Use your travel time to read newspapers and magazines and stay current.

Take your networking list and address book along in case you need to make calls. Of course, take resumes, stationery and business cards.

When traveling, be sure to take enough business clothes. Even though the person you visit may be dressed casually, you should dress the role you expect to assume.

If you need to rent a car, you can save up to 50 percent or more on rental costs by using off-airport rental agencies. Consult the local Yellow Pages, preferably before leaving.

If you plan to stay in a hotel, always ask if they have a business or commercial rate. Many hotels offer discounts to business travelers. Call 800 numbers of hotel chains in the area you want to visit beforehand, and shop their room rates before leaving. You can save 25 percent or more.

Recent college graduates should ask if the hotel has a student rate. If there is a college nearby, call and see if it has accommodations for visiting students. If none of the above works, and you are on a very tight travel budget, you can always try for a room at the local YMCA/YWCA.

The point is, if you are thinking of relocating, even with phone calls and letter campaigns, sooner or later you must make an appearance. Do not be afraid to finance your trip if you see that you are not getting the invitation you want. Always ask the question: "Is it worth a few hundred dollars of my money to create an opportunity?"

Pacing Yourself

Watch for burnout. While there are some who will need prodding to put in a full day, others will try to do everything in one day. This creates frustration and anxiety, and can result in depression when things do not happen as fast as you would like.

Even when you have been doing everything right, there will be days when the telephone will not ring. Other days, you will be hard-pressed to schedule all the people who want to see you. Patience is the rule of the day—every day. Your progress cannot be measured in one day or even one week. Job-hunting is a cumulative process.

There is an old rule of thumb that says for each $10,000 in salary, allow at least one month for search. However, some candidates searching for jobs with salaries in excess of $100,000 have found high-paying positions in three months or less. If you do your work diligently each day, you will have results sooner than you think.

Avoiding Monday Blues

One of the toughest times for an unemployed job searcher is Monday morning. You are accustomed to getting up every day at a set time and going off to work. Now life is different. Your office is most likely your home, and there is no peer group to talk to. You are all alone in your problem. Whatever appointments you make, set a few for Monday morning. Get out of your house and have someone to see. You will enjoy your weekends more, and Sunday evening you will have something to look forward to.

As you develop your networking program, you will find that your interviews will be planned from a few days ahead to as far as a few weeks. This gives you a chance to fill up your calendar on an even basis. Try not to have one interview on top of another. Give yourself a few minutes in between to collect your thoughts, review your notes and relax. Remember, the quality of an interview is more important than the quantity, though you should increase the quantity to as many as you can comfortably handle.

Summary Check List

1. Resumes.

2. Stationery.

3. Spiral notebook for notes during telephone calls and interviews.

4. Spiral notebook for classified ads to answer (note date and newspaper or magazine).

5. Spiral notebook for taping receipts for tax deductions.

6. Answering machine.

7. Network list.

8. Target company list.

9. Calendar for noting all appointments.

10. Follow-up call list.

11. Weekly expense report.

12. Interview call report.

13. Letters (thank you, confirmation, additional information).

14. Scripts for telephone practice.

15. Your answers to difficult questions.

16. What you do not want to discuss in an interview.

17. Your list of accomplishments.

18. "SAY IT—ASK IT" exercises built on accomplishments.

19. Your reference list.

20. Telephone credit card number.

21. Low-cost, long-distance telephone service.

22. A good dictionary.

23. General and trade newspapers and magazines.

Pay special attention to the following:

- Plan your program on a weekly basis though you will be adding to it as you move ahead each day.

- Keep good records on a daily basis. At the end of the day, summarize call reports either manually or on your computer.

- Continue to develop contacts from your network all the time.

STAGES IN JOB SEARCH

PREPARATION/RESEARCH

- Assessment Data
- Resume (Chapter 4 & Appendix A)
- Library (Appendix C)
- Recruiters
- Network Contacts
- Target People
- Target Companies
- Newspapers/Magazines
- Advertisements
- Associations
- Chambers of Commerce
- Research Interviews
- Clubs
- Schools

NETWORKING

- Calling—learn to telephone correctly (Chapter 7)
- Follow-up letters (Chapter 5 and Appendix B)
- Recalling
- Keeping good records
- Social/Professional events
- Meeting with other SUPER SEARCHERS (register today)
- 10-20 interviews a week…no less

INTERVIEW DYNAMICS (For information, names, a job)

- SAY IT—ASK IT (Chapter 8)
- ABC Principle
- Six Magic Steps—use them
- Take notes (manually or with SUPER SEARCH software)
- Close → another interview → referrals
- Post Close → eliminate any possible second thoughts
- Listen 51 percent of the time

BACKUP

- Keep accurate records
    + a good address listing of all people
    + references that got you in, references they give
    + dates, what happened, follow-up letters
- Watch what you write in letters (break down of a good letter—do you know it? Chapters 4, 5, Appendix B)
- Be organized (confusion breeds rush and frustration)

PRACTICE & UPGRADE YOUR TELEPHONE AND WRITTEN SKILLS

- Script out what you want to say—memorize it
- Practice with a friend or another SUPER SEARCHER
- Record your conversations and review techniques
- Know ALL your accomplishments by heart and use them at appropriate times (SAY IT—ASK IT)
- Refer to your list of what not to discuss
- Upgrade everything as you develop experience

WHEN YOU ARE GETTING AWAY FROM YOUR SEARCH…CHAPTER 9.
WHAT IS GOING WRONG? MAKE CORRECTIONS, TODAY.
DO NOT JUST READ SUPER*JOB*SEARCH, FOLLOW IT EVERY DAY.
ARE YOUR OBJECTIVES REALISTIC? IF NOT, MAKE CHANGES.
EVALUATE YOUR PERFORMANCE VS. YOUR ATTITUDE.
LET OFF STEAM…FIND YOUR WAY.
FIND SOMEONE TO TALK TO.
MAKE A LIST OF ALL POSITIVES IN YOUR WORLD AND READ IT OFTEN.

CHAPTER 9

When Clouds Hang Overhead

If you have been out on the job market for some time—this chapter is for you. You have been doing a little of everything and perhaps have had some good interviews—but are unconnected. If you have gone through the SUPER SEARCH Program and feel that you are still not getting results—this chapter is for you. In both cases the bottom line is to reassess your present position.

First, are you really working at your search? If you have done the SUPER SEARCH Program but are not devoting at least six full hours a day to your search, your problem could very well be one of inactivity.

If you are devoting six or more hours a day to your search on your own but without a structure—then your problem is lack of direction.

When up to proper networking speed, you should be meeting people almost every day; that is where 70 percent of opportunities come from. Proper use of telemarketing techniques will facilitate getting appointments. If you are having trouble getting to see people, you need to practice more.

However, if you are doing all of the above and still are not discovering opportunities, then you must take stock of your gameplan and re-evaluate which techniques are right for you and your market. If you have a cloud hanging over your program, these factors should be examined:

GENERAL REMEDIES

You have been looking for quite a while and have run out of people to call. Personal contacts no longer work, search firms are not interested in you and you do not receive responses from your target companies or ads you have answered. What next?

Job Objective

Ironically, it is sometimes easy to forget what job you are searching for. If you have not done the entire program as outlined in this book, BEGIN AGAIN

and go through it thoroughly. Act as if you were just laid off yesterday. Complete each phase with care. Have you indicated all jobs of interest and ranked them according to your preference and your skills? Are you being realistic? Are you looking for a job that no longer exists for you? This exercise, done correctly, will help get you refocused on your objectives.

Maybe you have to rethink what type of job you want in today's job market. Everything is relative; what sold well five years ago may be outmoded today.

Look at some classic examples:

You are an executive with an oil company. You have been earning a high salary. The oil crises promised you a golden career. Suddenly, there is an oil glut and you find yourself out of work. All you know is the oil business but there are no jobs—worldwide! What do you do?

You immediately move into the horizontal market described in Chapter 2. Find other industries that are not suffering where you can apply your experience.

You have to be realistic and recognize that maybe a salary cut will be needed to get you started again. You may have to prove yourself and move up the ladder in a fresh environment. You did it before.

Another case:

You have been a marketing manager and have looked high and low for a marketing job. You are 50 years old and, without anyone saying it, companies are hiring people in their 30s at salaries below yours to do the same job. You are at a dead end.

On the way up to your marketing manager's job, you were a good salesman. Your experience in selling has not been lost. A smart move might be to get back in sales. If you sold once and did well, you can do it again. A job transition may be indicated. Top salesmen are never obsolete!

Maybe it is time to take a fresh look at market needs and adjust your job objective.

Some examples:

Former Activity	A New Objective
Appliance sales	Personal computer sales
Financial management	Public accounting

Former Activity	A New Objective
Market research	Direct sales
Computer production	Computer service
Travel agent	Hotel management
Real estate sales	Real estate management
Export management	Purchasing
Production	Maintenance
Maintenance	Repair service

Use brainstorming techniques with friends and family to come up with new alternatives for you. Nothing remains the same, and you should be flexible. You have to think differently about your problems.

Career Change

Making a career change is not always for the other person. We often classify ourselves based on early training and fail to see how we have developed in terms of skills, knowledge, interests and accomplishments. This may apply to you. How can you tell?

The first question you have to ask is, "Am I really happy in what I want to do or am I doing it because it's the only thing I think I know?" Has the joy gone from your work? It is time to reassess your goals.

Get back in touch with your skills and interests. Identify what type of activities need these skills. On the other hand, maybe you want to begin a business of your own or develop something with another person. One of New York City's finest restaurants was created by a dentist!

The beginning of a career change comes with admitting that maybe this is for you and then doing plenty of research so you are sure of your ground. The research interview will permit you to explore other ideas.

You need to discuss with other people already in that activity: how they got involved, what skills are needed, what training is required and where you can get it, what earnings you can expect in the beginning and later, how they feel about the work after being in it for a while, what advice they have for you, what companies you should approach for further information, what questions they suggest you examine, whether you can observe what they do and see if it measures up to your expectations and—what steps you need to take now.

Your Network

As long as there are people in your city, you will never run out of networking prospects. To get back into networking, try research interviews. Bankers, lawyers and accountants know lots of people in industry. Similarly, service people such as stockbrokers, real estate agents and local merchants have many connections. Go to meetings in your community and practice meeting people. Your newspaper will tell you what groups meet in your area. Get back in circulation. That is where the hidden job market is!

Watch what you say. If people feel that you are asking for a job, it is a big turnoff. Refer to your list of what you do *not* want to say. How many times have you said these things anyway? Become conscious of the elements of good research and advice interviews.

Stay in contact with people you have not spoken with for a while. Call to let them know that you appreciated their introductions and inform them of what has happened (in terms of meeting new people). This renewed contact can often bring forth new suggestions.

Work your network in reverse. As you meet people and learn about their needs, help them solve a problem via your network. In doing a favor, you will be remembered and add players to your team.

Sometimes your prospect will not be able to come up with any referrals. Showing your target company list can help. Also, discussing your career in general terms rather than a tight objective will permit your prospect to suggest more people.

The bottom line is to be relaxed and open with the world so that your personality shows. People want to help people they like.

Your Target List

Have you maintained and upgraded your target company list? This will change as you learn about other companies in your area.

If you are seeking employment in companies that are not open to recruitment, you cannot move the mountain or change the course of the river! You must come up with a new list of companies of interest. For example, as this book is being written, employment is improving across the nation, yet there are fewer jobs available in manufacturing. Importing manufactured goods is less expensive than local production. On the other hand, the need for people in service industries is on the rise.

If you are a financial professional, instead of prospecting hard-goods producers, why not look at accounting service firms? What service industries parallel your particular skills? What companies in those industries have possible needs for your know-how? With the answers to these questions, you will have a new target list to prospect with greater potential for you.

Joining with Other Job-Seekers

You need someone to talk to. If you can get together in a group, the feedback will help provide some checks on your program.

Rejection goes with job search. You may have to approach people who have no time to help you. BUT there are others who will, and you only need one job offer!

Part-Time Work

If you have been devoting full days looking for work, have had no success and are hurting for income, get a part-time job. Try to leave at least half of each day free for job search. In looking at the part-time job market, take into account your overall skills and see which are the most salable in today's market. Make this a priority.

Part-time work does not have to follow exactly what you were doing full time. If you were a vice president of finance, you have basic accounting skills. You do not have to be a vice president to sell these talents to someone needing an extra hand with financial overload. Similarly, if you are an engineer or technical person, back off the management side of your skills and see what could be immediately valuable to another firm on a short-term basis.

Your help could be in replacing a permanent person on leave of absence, consulting, teaching, assisting with trade shows or helping on a specific project.

Suppose you are a computer professional. You know programming inside and out. You have advanced into management and have other programmers working for you. You now need a job. Go back to what you did well to get to that level. Take your programming skills and detail them on a single-page brochure in the form of a flyer. Do a mailing to heads of computer departments offering your assistance on a part-time basis (by the hour, day, week).

Use the same concepts of telemarketing and interviewing for obtaining a part-time job. Follow each mailing with phone calls for an interview.

Do not use a resume. Summarize your skills and what you can do for that person NOW, TODAY! If you have a friend in advertising, ask him to help you make a one-page brochure that can speed you to a part-time situation.

Register with every temporary agency in your area.

To find out the best way to market your part-time skills, try to be a buyer first by tracking down other people offering similar part-time services. Finding the right person will then show you how you must promote your services to reach your market: answering classified ads, doing a brochure mailing with a telephone follow-up, advertising in trade magazines, registering with temporary agencies, contacting service people who have knowledge of where there could be needs for the skills you are marketing, contacting professional associations.

The big difference in looking for a part-time position is in isolating your skills so that they are easily identified for your market. Do not forget, you then must continue on your main mission of finding a permanent situation.

Your Resume

Maybe your resume is stale. If it has not helped you produce job interviews, something may be wrong. Do it over. Get a new look. If you used a performance format, try a functional resume, or vice versa. Tie this into a fresh job objective. With a new job objective and resume, you can even re-apply to the same target companies you have prospected before and answer appropriate old ads for positions that still may be unfilled. Your new letter will reflect someone who is enthusiastic and tenacious. While you may not get many replies, just one will make it worthwhile. Keep writing new resumes until you find one that produces. Test your resume on business friends.

Moving to Another Area

Everyone wants to work in Southern California or Florida! So, at times, good jobs are hard to find in those locations. The more people looking, the more competition you have. One of the things you and your family might want to reconsider is moving to an area where your skills are still in demand.

Learning more about other cities requires research. You need to have as much information as possible about the types of industries in the new area and the companies within those industries where your skills apply. As you will note in Appendix C, your sources of information are rich. You must read the local newspapers, get lists of companies from Chambers of Commerce, get information on professional associations that you can contact by letter and phone, identify and attend trade shows that may be pertinent to your skills and interview people in your immediate network who know people there.

Finally, you can wait just so long and then it might be wise to make some exploratory trips. Use all the techniques in Chapter 5 to generate interviews.

Get a Checkup

There are outplacement professionals who can help you, and the cost does not have to be out of sight. Many commercial outplacement firms, i.e., those that work for corporations, use independent consultants to work on an individual basis with clients.

To locate a good consultant, call one of the commercial outplacement firms (that work exclusively for companies) in your area and ask if they can suggest a few independent counselors who might work with you privately. These firms cannot work directly with you but can make recommendations.

Rates can vary from $50 per hour up. If you do decide to discuss your problem with a consultant, you must make it clear that either of you can stop at any time. Insist on seeing references from candidates they have counseled personally and talk to these references. Make sure you will have a comfortable working relationship. A reliable consultant will be happy to work with you under these conditions. Once arrangements have been made, you will want to discuss the following:

> Attitude
> Objectives
> Accomplishments
> Your Resume
> Networking Techniques
> Target List
> Role Playing in Telemarketing & Interviewing
> Expanding Your Alternatives

If you find the fee on a one-to-one basis too expensive, you might form a group of candidates who are in a similar position and hire a consultant to work with you collectively.

Consider using the services of a nonprofit organization like FORTY PLUS. FORTY PLUS is run by people like yourself—out of work—but following a well-designed self-help program. It assists any executive who is over 40 years of age and looking for work. It is a serious, friendly and dedicated organization. Check your phone book for the nearest office.

Form your own support group to discuss individual problems and get back on track. Sharing experiences and network lists can make a big difference.

Lastly, if your company offers personal outplacement as part of your parting package, take it!

AFTER THE SEARCH

Network Maintenance

You have landed the job you wanted and will begin shortly. What about winding down your search? Unfortunately, many candidates just say "amen" and let all the work they have put into building a network drop by the wayside. What a waste! You have invested a lot of time, energy and money in developing your network. There are several things you can do to maintain most of your contacts, just in case something goes wrong with your new job, as well as using your network for further career advancement. Here are some suggestions:

1. Do not stop your networking or advise any prospective employers about your new situation until you are on the job. You may have to stall by saying that you are in negotiations.

2. Once the new job is moving forward, you should send out letters to any companies you have been in discussion with, informing them that you have accepted a new job, but stating that you still would like to maintain contact. To do this, call your contact every few months just to say "hello." Give him an update on what you have been doing and ask what is new in his world, company and work. If you ever need to start your network again, this relationship will be invaluable.

3. You should send a personalized letter to everyone on your network list indicating that you have found a new position and thanking them for their interest and help.

4. By now you have been in contact with a number of recruiters and agencies. They will be interested in the fact that you have landed a new position. It is good public relations on your part now to tell them about your success and your new position. Send personalized letters to as many as possible. You now become a part of their "employed" data base. Also, if you have any new accomplishments or successes, use that bit of news to continue contact with your recruiter and agency network. They will now use you as a networking source, and this will automatically keep your name and file alive.

5. Organize all your receipts and make printouts of your expenses week by week during your search. Depending on the new tax law, much of this may be tax deductible. You should save your calendar, letter files and computer disk to provide proof of job-search expenses. Discuss this with your accountant now.

6. Call and write thank-you letters to your reference list. Let them know what you decided and how much you appreciate their support.

7. Over time, many people let their network list dissolve. They become preoccupied with other things. A smart networker will separate his network list into different categories, such as:

- People I want to keep in touch with.

- Companies I want to maintain contact with.

- Recruiters and agencies I want to know about me.

If you want to be set apart from the crowd, think about this idea: You can send personalized newsletters to each of these people at least once a year with your Christmas cards. You will be remembered and appreciated.

8. There is another thing you should do concerning your network. You will be reading the news and following industry activity. If you spot news about any of your network contacts, write and acknowledge it. They will be glad to hear from you, and you will have further cemented your relationships.

AFTERWORD
SOME COMMENTS ABOUT YOU AND YOUR NEW JOB

In the course of looking at yourself over these past weeks and considering your strengths and weaknesses, you probably have acquired a lot of new knowledge about yourself and how you fit into the job market. As you begin your new position, it is a good time to review what you have learned and apply this knowledge to personal growth and career advancement.

About You

1. Do you now understand fully what went wrong at your previous job?

2. Can you improve anything in your personality that will make you a better employee and colleague?

3. Do you know your present capabilities and how to use them effectively?

4. Are you following a career path based on long-term goals (see Chapter 2)?

5. Can you learn new skills through seminars and outside research that will enable you to be a more valuable employee and create increased job security based on performance?

6. How can you follow changes occurring in your industry and profession?

7. Are you prepared to devote time to keeping yourself visible by writing articles, giving talks, appearing at professional organizations and becoming more expert in your field?

8. Are you a good communicator? If this can be improved, consider taking some outside courses and reading more books on the subject.

About Your New Job

1. Corporate politics are dangerous. Do not take sides in political issues. You have at least a 50 percent chance of losing!

2. Avoid being critical of anything from your past. If you do not have something nice to say, keep quiet.

3. Devote time to understanding what is expected of you. Ask for clarification if you do not understand something. Be discreet with your questions and your comments.

4. Do not be in a hurry to remake the world. Take time to get to know the company, its policies, your fellow employees and the rules of the game. Find out who the shakers and movers are. Learn and use the names of your co-workers.

5. Do not give in to the temptation to make suggestions for improving your job or someone else's until you fully understand what you are talking about and the implications concerning cost, personnel and company policies.

6. If you can get closer to your fellow employees by joining any groups or committees, do it. You now know the value of friends. To have friends, be one.

7. Make every effort to get feedback from your supervisor. Do not wait for criticism. Try to get regular performance reviews that can be discussed.

8. While you may have a job description, make sure you and your supervisor understand what it is you are to do. Know his priorities and make sure they become yours.

9. Be organized. You have seen the organization we have applied to your job search. Follow the same principles in attacking your work.

10. If you need to discuss something with your supervisor, ask for an appointment and organize your questions beforehand. Be at least as prepared as you were for your interviews!

11. Most supervisors do not like surprises, since most surprises are not good. If you see something going wrong, report it and advise what you are doing about it. Your supervisor may have nothing to add, but he should at least know what is going on. Above all, do not put your boss in the position of hearing it first from someone else!

12. Remember your loyalties—to the company and to your supervisor.

13. If things do not go right, do not wait for the roof to fall in. Try to get on the right track in your job and make every effort to make it work. If you see that it will not, you take the initiative to make a change. You will be very glad you have maintained your network!

14. Be on time—if not early. If it is necessary to work late, do it cheerfully.

15. Continue using SAY IT—ASK IT to sell ideas. It is one of the easiest ways to further your communications. You can see that now, can't you?

APPENDIX A

Sample Resumes

WILLIAM B. STRONG
2345 Market Place Court
San Diego, California 98999-0909

(619) 555-7777
e-mail: abstrong@loop.com
Home Page: www.billstrong.com

A highly successful consumer marketing professional who has contributed to the growth of $750 million in sales and $64 million in operating profit through the development and implementation of marketing programs and introduction of 20 new products.

A dependable and talented team player with exceptional leadership, marketing, idea development and product launch skills.

EXPERIENCE

Largest Food Chain Company of America, Del Mar, California   1992-1996

Senior Director, National Programs (1994-1996)

Developed and implemented the annual marketing plan for a $2.8 billion quick service restaurant chain including program development and testing, new product development and testing and sales analysis.

- Coordinated with media, advertising, merchandising, market research and field marketing to put together a master plan that supported corporate sales objectives.

- Directed a staff of 10 professionals and managed a $16 million production budget that provided radio and television commercials, point of purchase materials, market testing and consumer research to support an annual growth of 14% in 1990 and 16% in 1991.

- Developed the concept of 'layers of value' that was the cornerstone of the highly successful "59/79/99" pricing structure. This provided a net sales growth of more than $135 million with an operating profit of over $12 million.

- Directed the staggered launch of 19 new products that produced up to $15 million in sales each during the first four weeks.

Director, National Programs (1993-1994)

Developed the annual marketing plan and implemented selected programs.

- Directed the launch of The Instant Burger resulting in $16 million incremental sales during the first four weeks.

- Developed and implemented a promotion using more than 20 million Superman cups that resulted in a $12 million sales increase over a four-week period.

- Achieved a 16% increase in average store sales ($275 million) for 1993 using a combination of pricing, promotions and new products.

Director, New Products (1992-1993)

Managed new product development from concept generation through launch.

- Managed the reformulation of two existing products, The Largest Salad Ever and South of the Border Tacos, lowering the cost to achieve a reduction in sales price and an improvement in value rating.

The Great King Corp., Miami, Florida   1991-1992

Senior Manager, Menu Planning and Development

Managed new product development from concept generation through national launch.

- Took Super Dessert Treats from concept and product prototype to national launch within five months of assignment.

- Launched The 2-Minute Burger in two months. The product became a regular promotional product.

WILLIAM B. STRONG   **Page Two**

Kellogg Company, Battle Creek, Michigan   1988-1991

Product Manager, New Product Development

Managed new product development from concept through first year in market.

- Launched Sunshine cereal, an orange juice flavored breakfast cereal, within 10 months of assignment.
- Developed and implemented the marketing plan for Raisin Square cereal, achieving a 1.1% market share.
- Managed Apple Cinnamon Squares cereal from concept development through launch.

Kraft, Inc., Glenview, Illinois   1985-1988

Brand Manager, Parkay margarine (1987-1988)

Managed advertising, consumer and trade promotions, pricing, packaging product improvement and cost reduction to achieve annual and long-term volume and profit goals.

- Reversed share loss trend within eight months through targeted use of coupons and trade promotions.
- Managed Kraft Touch of Butter spread from concept development to test market launch. Product was subsequently launched and is still available today.
- Changed the pricing and deal structure on the Parkay margarine line to a lower everyday price on stick margarine and capitalized on higher relative brand loyalty.
- Redesigned the Parkay line's package graphics to update product image.

Associate Brand Manager, Kraft Confections (1986-1987)

Managed the Kraft confections line including marshmallows, marshmallow creme, candy, ice cream toppings and malted milk.

- Convinced management to redirect consumer spending from high volume marshmallows to high margin caramels, increasing volume and profits by 11%.

Brand Assistant, Kraft Confections (1985-1986)

Implemented and analyzed consumer and trade promotions. Developed a new trade promotion program for ice cream toppings that tested successfully and was used nationally.

EDUCATION

Harvard Graduate School of Business Administration, Boston, Massachusetts

Master in Business Administration, 1985

United States Military Academy, West Point, New York

Bachelor of Science, 1978

AFFILIATIONS

Harvard Business School Club of Southern California

MILITARY

U.S. Army, Captain, multiple line and staff assignments. Army Commendation Medal, 1978-1983

THOMAS WILLIAMS
2222 Walnut Street
Sunny Day, California 91000

Residence: (818) 555-7777
Office: (818) 999-8888

A human resources executive with exceptional experience and achievements in public and Fortune 100 companies who has created and managed human resource departments, providing full services for thousands of employees.

- Saved more than $21.6 million in potential litigation expenses and judgments through various management transitions.

- Established an in-house executive recruitment service that saved more than $1.2 million in search fees annually.

- Hired 1,200 professional and support staff in 1990 and 1,400 in 1992, supporting the company's rapid growth and performance.

- Created the office of College Relations for a student body of 27,000.

A highly motivated and energetic professional with strong creative, arbitration, negotiation and counseling skills.

EXPERIENCE

Giant Entertainment Company, Glendale, California   1981-Present

Director of Human Resources (1991-Present)

Provide human resources and employee relations services for a group of companies generating $3 billion in revenues including film entertainment, corporate administration, consumer products and a full service record company serving 6,300 employees worldwide. Administer a human resource budget of $1.5 million.

- Assume the Vice President of Human Resources function in his absence.

- Designed, developed and implemented a flexible benefit program for all employees that saved the company more than $5.2 million without cutting back on benefits nor charging the employees additional expense.

- Co-authored the Personnel and Policies Manual and designed a company-wide college relations recruitment brochure.

- Provided transition counseling for more than 800 exiting employees.

Manager of Employee Relations (1988-1991)

- Trained more than 400 managers in employee performance evaluation and employee discipline documentation.

- Negotiated a three-year contract with the Office and Professional Employees International Union (OPEIU) covering 700 employees.

- Successfully avoided two union organizing attempts.

THOMAS WILLIAMS   **Page Two**

Giant Entertainment Company *Continued*

Manager of Personnel (1986-1988)

- Convinced top management to put in a new qualified pension program for all salaried employees, eliminating an obsolete, unprotected discriminatory plan. This affected 1,500 employees.

Manager of Employment and Professional Staffing (1983-1986)
Senior Professional Staffing Recruiter (1981-1983)

- Successfully recruited 45 top MIS and data processing professionals and hired more than 500 professionals for the Starlight Theme Park.

- Established internships that encouraged an increase in quality minority employment.

California State University, Long Beach, Long Beach, California   1973-1981

Director of School and College Relations (1975-1981)

- Negotiated articulation agreements with 35 community colleges.

- Created a multimedia campaign that increased student enrollments by 7,000 in seven years.

- Conducted training programs for 1,000 faculty and staff supporting the university's Outreach Relations Program.

- Acted as spokesperson to the President's Advisory Board on all student enrollment issues.

Placement Counselor, Office of Career Planning and Placement (1973-1974)

- Counseled more than 1,500 students in career and academic issues.

American Hospital Supply, Irvine, California   1973

Western Area Sales Representative

- Sold more than 60,000 cataloged items to a market of 40 hospitals.

EDUCATION

California State University, Long Beach, Long Beach, California

Master of Science in Counseling and Psychology, 1978
Bachelor of Science in Psychology, 1973

AFFILIATIONS

Personnel Industrial Relations Association, California State University Alumni Association, Western College Placement Association, Employment Management Association

JOHN SUCCESS
123 Valley Street
Van Nuys, California 90055-7898

Residence (888) 555-9999
Messages (444) 777-8888

A highly successful and versatile corporate finance professional with exceptional skills in sales, marketing, financial analysis, management and business development.

- Generated $10 billion in new profitable commercial and investment banking activity, managed $30 billion in assets and produced more than $500 million in revenues for America's fifth largest financial institution.

- First recipient of the Top Producer award, chosen by peeers from among 3,000 professional bankers for the Great Pacific Merchant Bank.

- Developed outstanding client relationships throughout the energy, utilities, entertainment, media, communications and technology industries.

A natural leader who knows how to get things done. Excels in a client-focused team environment.

EXPERIENCE

Great Pacific Corporation   1976-1996

Senior Vice President, Special Industries Department (1995-1996)
Corporate Banking Group, Los Angeles, California

Responsible for the marketing, sales and credit underwriting activities of the Special Industries Department which included the energy, utilities, project finance, entertainment, media, communications and technology industries. Represented $8.5 billion in commitments with revenues of $38 million and a staff of 33 professionals. Authored the five-year strategic plan for the Corporate Banking Group.

- Originated $2 billion of new fee-based business in 12 months, generating $20 million in revenues.

- Exceeded revenue, profit and cost containment goals by 10%.

- Enhanced the quality of a $1.6 billion loan portfolio through the reduction of $400 million in troubled loans and less profitable relationships.

- Generated $2 billion in sales of the project finance loan portfolio without a single loss.

Managing Director, Corporate Finance and Banking Department (1994-1995)
Great Pacific Merchant Bank, Los Angeles, California

Responsible for the marketing and sales of general corporate finance and banking activities in the 25 Western states. Represented $11 billion in commitments and revenues of $70 million with a staff complement of 55 professionals.

- Produced pre-tax income of $45 million, exceeding goals by 10%.

- Led the bank's team in a group of eight principal banks that successfully restructured a $7 billion media financing, generating $100 million in fees.

JOHN SUCCESS   **Page Two**

Great Pacific Corporation *Continued*

Managing Director, Energy/Utilities Group (1990-1994)
Great Pacific Merchant Bank, Los Angeles, California

Held sales and marketing responsibilities for the energy and utilities industries for North America, represented by $5 billion in commitments and $20 million in revenues.

- Earned $10 million in banking fees for the successful management of $4.5 billion agented transactions.

- Met and exceeded revenue, profit and cost containment goals for five years.

Vice President and Managing Director (1986-1990)
Great Pacific Southwest, Inc., Houston, Texas

Responsible for marketing and sales of banking services to energy companies located in Texas, Louisiana and Oklahoma.

- Opened up the bank's marketing to the natural gas industry that resulted in a $1 billion new activity that produced $10 million revenues over three years.

- Restructured a severely troubled $1 billion loan portfolio, eliminating its major risk profile.

Vice President and Department Manager (1983-1986)
Stone National Bank, Seattle, Washington

Responsible for setting up the energy and general Southwest banking practice. Generated $300 million in quality loans in less than three years, producing $10 million revenues for the bank.

PRIOR EXPERIENCE

Great Pacific National Bank, Los Angeles, California (1976-1983)

Held various positions in Energy/Utilities, Credit Review and Retail Departments.

EDUCATION

California State University, Long Beach, Long Beach, California

Master of Business Administration, 1982
Bachelor of Science, Finance and Management, 1976

AFFILIATIONS

American Petroleum Institute   American Gas Association   Town Hall

PUBLIC OFFICE

Elected Board Member of the Valley Municipal Utility District, 1988-1989

MARIE MILLER   Residence (310) 555-6666
123 Materials Road   Messages (310) 555-9999
Santa Monica, California 91234

A versatile materials manager with 12 years' expertise in systems and project management for high volume, repetitive consumer goods and custom electronics manufacturers. Provided leadership for master scheduling, inventory planning, purchasing, production control and cost accounting for Fortune 100 and Fortune 500 companies.

An analytical professional with excellent teambuilding, research and planning skills with a proven track record in cost-efficient problem solving.

ACCOMPLISHMENTS

- Implemented a production planning and master scheduling system utilizing Just-In-Time principles and reduced inventory from $26 to $13 million in one year.

- Reduced material on order from $6.2 to $1.2 million and order turnaround time from 60 to 20 days while improving quality with supplier partnership programs.

- Reduced excess and obsolete parts inventory by $3.5 million through development efforts with Engineering and Marketing.

- Improved on-time delivery performance from 75% to 96% for the production of $100 million in consumer goods.

- Led the redevelopment of a scanner for a $12 million Air Force project and improved first yield from 25% to 80% within eight months.

- Led four MRPII software implementation projects: Dataworks, COPICS, ASK and MSA.

PROFESSIONAL EXPERIENCE

Automobile Parts International, Chatsworth, California   1994-1996

Director of Materials

Directed materials management for the final assembly of professional and home entertainment stereo speakers for a $120 million manufacturer. Worked with customer organizations to improve the master scheduling process and forecast accuracy.

- Coordinated supplier transition to a Just-in-Time environment, improving production flow and reducing inventory. Implemented KANBAN Systems utilizing EDI.

- Within two weeks after a major earthquake and the loss of $4 million of inventory, replaced purchased materials necessary to resume a $10 million monthly production.

Datatape Incorporated, Division of Kodak, Pasadena, California   1989-1994

Materials Manager/Program Manager

Served as Materials Manager with responsibility for inventory and production control, warehouse and scheduling for a manufacturer of military flight instrumentation recorders.

- Consolidated standard products and program planning organizations and eliminated duplication of services, reducing staff from 123 to 65.

MARIE MILLER   **Page Two**

Datatape Incorporated *Continued*

- Developed surface mount assembly capability that included point-of-use storage and date-coded locator system.

- Managed ATARS Scanner redesign and implemented productivity improvements and TQM projects.

Allegretti and Company, Chatsworth, California   1988-1989

Materials Manager

Directed materials management for a $100 million manufacturer of electric motors, retail lawn and garden equipment, a major supplier to Sears department stores.

- Coordinated production of three plants while improving new products introduction and developing a master planning system.

- Conducted weekly sales bookings review with marketing, improving forecast accuracy and reducing customer lead time.

Unitek Corporation, Subsidiary of Bristol-Myers, Monrovia, California   1985-1987

Manager of Manufacturing Systems and Scheduling

Led the development of a computerized inventory control and planning system for the orthodontics division of a pharmaceutical company.

- Improved on-time delivery of assemble-to-order pre-weld orthodontic products from 56% to 95% and enhanced customer service.

- Created and implemented a computerized project management software system for new product introduction.

PRIOR EXPERIENCE

Held management positions in cost accounting, warehouse, scheduling, production and inventory control for leading healthcare, furniture and aerospace companies. Provided consulting and project management support to aerospace and electronic manufacturers in the development of optimum software solutions, specializing in procurement and cost management.

EDUCATION

University of Southern California, Los Angeles, California

Graduate studies towards MBA in Finance (32 units)

California State University, Los Angeles, Los Angeles, California

Bachelor of Arts Degree

AFFILIATIONS

American Production and Inventory Control Society, Certified Practitioner in Inventory Management (CPIM); APICS, Los Angeles Chapter - Chairman of the Board, 1985; President, 1984

PETER NUMBERS	**Residence (818) 555-0000**
1234 Calculator Lane	**Messages (818) 555-2222**
Figures, California 91001	

A Financial Manager/Controller with 15 years of diversified experience in systems, financial operations, acquisitions, divestitures and cost improvement for domestic and international divisions of Fortune 100 companies.

- Designed and standardized the financial and management reporting for a $250 million company which reduced the financial close period by 33% down to six days and eliminated 2,000 man hours of manual reporting annually.

- Installed a company-wide general ledger system for 11 corporations.

- Created a new corporation by relocating a packaging operation to Mexico saving $3 million annually. This included construction of a new facility, staffing and installation of automated systems.

A proven CPA with exceptional skills in corporate finance, setting up companies and advising senior management on planning, forecasting and performance.

EXPERIENCE

International Healthcare Corporation   1982-1995

Scientific Division, Pasadena, California (1992-1995)

Assistant Controller
Directed accounting operations for a $300 million global manufacturing/distribution division. Presented senior management with financial operating reports.

- Orchestrated the company's 1993 financial audit preparation which resulted in a no-point audit.

- Integrated financial operations of a $9 million acquisition into the company.

- Converted 12,000 account numbers as part of a new project management system.

- Reduced the division's management capital base by $5.4 million, increasing its return on capital by 2%.

- Conducted the year-end close for three consecutive years.

- Managed the conversion to a new payroll system processing $30 million annually.

- Updated the financial and management reporting systems to reflect changes in an organization with 150 cost centers.

Disposable Products Division, Van Nuys, California (1983-1992)
Formerly a division of the Great Healthcare Products Corporation, acquired in 1989

Group Plant Controller (1989-1992)
Directed accounting operations for five domestic and two offshore manufacturing facilities with $500 million sales. Trained 28 accounting professionals in financial management. Interfaced with all levels of manufacturing concerning operations and cost containment programs.

PETER NUMBERS   Page Two

Disposable Products Division (continued)

- Exceeded the company's goal for controlling inventories by realizing an inventory adjustment of 0.3% covering $100 million of inventory.

- Organized and presented needed financial support for the successful divestiture of a $10 million business.

- Created a training program for 80 accounting/finance professionals.

- Realized a $334,000 cost savings through a personnel reduction program while improving accounting operations.

- Saved $400,000 by arranging an international debt swap agreement.

General Accounting Manager (1986-1989)

Consolidated the financial statements of a multi-company division. Managed general accounting, transaction processing and taxation.

- Proposed and installed an automated telecommunications system for ten remote operations as the forerunner to an automated accounting system. Received the President's Award for Outstanding Achievement.

Business Center Controller (1986)

Managed financial operations of three business centers generating $180 million in sales.

Plant Accounting Manager, Tucson, Arizona (1983-1986)

Responsible for accounting operations of a 100-employee manufacturing plant.

Great Healthcare Products Corporation, Chicago, Illinois (1982-1983)

Internal Auditor

Conducted worldwide financial and operation audits.

Square Company, Palatine, Illinois   1980-1982

Audit Supervisor

Performed first audits of company divisions in Central and South America.

EDUCATION

University of Chicago, Chicago, Illinois

Bachelor of Science, Accounting, 1980

CERTIFICATION

Certified Public Accountant, 1981

AFFILIATIONS

American Institute of Certified Public Accountants

GARY L. CARE   Residence (213) 555-8888
4567 Willow Lane   Cellular/Messages (213) 555-9875
Hartsdale, California 92345   e-mail: garylcare@pobox.com

A versatile administrator with more than 20 years of progressively increasing responsibilities who has managed 67,000 physician visits and 180,000 ancillary encounters annually for the largest privately held academic/teaching medical center in the West.

Expertise includes program management, quality improvement, business development, finance, managed care relations, human resources/employee development, marketing and strategic planning.

EXPERIENCE

Great Healthcare Medical Center, Hartsdale, California   1980-1997

Service Line Director (1988-1997)

Directed the Ambulatory Care Center and Clinics representing 45% of all outpatient activity for the Medical Center.

- Directed a primary and subspecialty care multi-group practice employing 250 faculty and attending physicians, residents and fellows-in-training. Disciplines included family practice, internal medicine, obstetrics and gynecology, pediatrics and surgery.

- Managed the Employee Health Service providing occupational and industrial medicine services to 6,200 permanent Medical Center staff.

- Developed and managed the Procedure Center providing outpatient diagnostic, infusion, treatment and surgical services.

- Administered the Executive Registry Program, the first and most successful corporate medical access and referral system, for the Southern California and Nevada Regions in concert with renowned hospitals throughout the world.

- Headed a freestanding dental center providing all forms of general dentistry and oral surgery.

- Implemented a mobile medical unit, Help for Kids, serving more than 2,000 homeless children and families every year.

- Administered a Medical Center-wide interpreter service program in sixteen key languages resulting in over 80,000 voice and written translations. The program was recognized as a healthcare industry benchmark.

- Achieved JCAHO accreditation in ambulatory care areas through three separate surveys.

- Participated in the planning that achieved an integrated continuum of patient care between acute-inpatient and ambulatory care services.

- Implemented an enterprise-wide computerized scheduling system for outpatient appointments.

- Coordinated the Master Facility Plan for future expansion of outpatient services.

- Redesigned the delivery model in the Employee Health Service to achieve 95% employee compliance with annual health evaluations.

GARY L. CARE   **Page Two**

Great Healthcare Medical Center, Continued

- Established improvements for outpatient medical record management, organization and accessibility of documentation processing of 72,000 records annually.

- Oversaw the reconstruction of the Pediatric Clinic Pavilion that has 8,000 patient visits annually.

Manager of Diversified Services (1984-1988)

Provided administrative management for the Mental Health, Physical Medicine/Rehabilitation, Chemical Dependency and Anesthesia Pain Departments.

- Directed a staff of 500 that maintained facilities for each department including equipment, construction, medical supplies and overall maintenance.

- Developed capital renovations and operational budgets amounting to $12.8 million annually. Managed purchasing materials activities and oversaw inventory control.

Senior Administrative Supervisor (1980-1984)

Worked off-hour tours of duty functioning as the Shift Administrator for the entire Medical Center which had licensed capacity of 1,196 beds. Managed a staff of 1,000 assuring all after-hour patient-care services and support operations functioned properly. Coordinated all patient air transportation inbound and outbound.

- Conducted rounds of the entire two million covered square feet which included 12 intensive care units, four step-down units, 26 nursing units and a Level One trauma emergency department.

- Established a 24-hour, seven-day-per-week hospitality program for inpatients.

- Developed new systems that captured more than $800,000 in lost revenues.

- Collaborated with local government and law enforcement agencies in handling decedent affairs and emergencies.

PRIOR EXPERIENCE

Began healthcare career as an I.V. Laboratory Technician supervising eight phlebotomists in adult and micro-pediatric techniques for the Great Healthcare Medical Center. Subsequently, completed an administrative residency at Thomas Healthcare System in Sacramento, California. Upon completion of the residency, became a Staffing Coordinator for Stoneville Memorial, a 178-bed acute-care hospital scheduling 24-hour, seven-day-a-week nursing resources.

EDUCATION

The Ohio State University
Columbus, Ohio

Master of Health Services Administration, 1982

Bachelor of Public Administration, 1979

BRENT MONTANA
123 Sweet Street
Los Angeles, California 90023
(213) 555-5555

More than 20 years of diversified data and telecommunications experience covering network planning, installation of equipment and software, maintenance, monitoring and problem resolution for Fortune 100 companies and a 1,200-bed acute-care medical center.

Hands-on technical knowledge of data communications networking including Ethernet, fiber optics, X.25, circuit switching, IBM 3270 protocols and asynchronous protocols.

EXPERIENCE

Great Healthcare Medical Center, Los Angeles, California   1989-1996

    Assistant Manager, Network Services

    Managed the Data Communications Group responsible for planning, installation and maintenance activities for a network that grew from 1,000 Ethernet and IBM drops to 6,000 drops. The Medical Center's network consisted of async dial-up and dedicated access for async, DECnet, SNA/SDLC, TCP/IP and Novell PC LANs to Internet, DEC VAX and IBM computer systems.

    •   Provided on-the-job-training for Data Communications personnel and ensured cross-training for the Medical Center network environment.

    •   Originated network documentation and vendor databases that increased operating efficiency.

    •   Planned and managed the networking portion of the relocation of the Computer Center without interruption of services.

    •   Planned, installed, programmed (CCL) and managed a 54-line MicroFrame DataLOCK 4000 remote access security system that processed 3,000 accesses a month.

Super Computer Service Center, Anaheim, California   1987-1989

    Senior Network Control Specialist

    Responsible for data network planning, installation, configuration, maintenance, equipment and vendor selection. The network supported Marketing, Manufacturing and Administrative user groups with 800 drops.

    Environment was an international data communications network supporting dial-up and dedicated access for async, BSC, SNA/SDLC and X.25 through the CompuServe network, to Prime, IBM and DEC computer systems.

    •   At the end of the first year, network down time had been reduced by 90%. Remote access costs were also reduced by 200-300%.

Major Software Corporation, El Segundo, California   1978-1987

    Senior Technical Support Engineer

    Responsible for coordinating the installation phase of VAN (Value Added Network) accounts on a network-wide basis. Environment was an international data communications network supporting dial-up and dedicated access for async, BSC and X.25 to Univac and IBM computer timesharing systems and VAN services for customer provided computer systems.

    Performed configuration, installation and repair to the board level of network hardware. Coordinated with customers to resolve communications problems related to circuit, equipment, software, protocol and/or procedures.

PRIOR EXPERIENCE

Served in the U.S. Army Communications Command and ITT-Federal Electric Corporation as a Fixed Ciphony Repairman and Senior Technical Controller.

EDUCATION

NCR COMTEN Field Training - 3690 Level 1 Course
U.S. Air Force FTD - Digital Techniques
U.S. Army Signal School - Fixed Ciphony Repair 32F20
U.S. Army Signal School - Fixed Station Transmitter Repair 32C20
East Los Angeles City College - Electronics Mathematics Course

APPENDIX B

Sample Letters

BRIAN JAMES
156 Eighth Avenue
Los Angeles, CA 90023

(213) 555-9022

(DATE)

Mr. Grant Green
President
Grant Distribution Company
23 Grant Street
Los Angeles, CA 90022

Dear Mr. Green:

I noted in yesterday's <u>Los Angeles Times</u> that your company received an export award from the Department of Commerce, and I want to congratulate you. Your success in selling computer components to Asian countries has been something few companies have achieved in the last few years. With your knowledge of export, I would appreciate your advice.

Having had more than 15 years' experience in export sales, including electronic, computer and military components, I am now seeking a career change.

Some of my key accomplishments have been:

* Locating new lines of products and developing international sales for them.

* Selecting and working with local distributors throughout the world.

* Increasing sales by 26 percent in one year when the dollar was at its highest exchange rate.

I do not expect that you will have a job for me, but I am sure that your advice and suggestions on my career change could be very helpful. If you could spare a few moments, I would appreciate meeting you personally. I will be calling your office next week for a mutually convenient time.

Sincerely,

Brian James

Brian James

Jack Smith
156 Washington Blvd.
Mt. Vernon, NY 10588

(914) 555-6777

(DATE)

Mr. Norman G. Henry
Chairman of the Board
Great Savings Bank
123 Savings Plaza
Bronxville, New York 10766

Dear Mr. Henry:

I note that the Great Savings Bank has yet to begin using Automatic Teller Machines (ATMs), and, on the chance that this subject interests you, I would like to introduce myself.

For the past 12 years, I have been responsible for all data processing of America's 15th largest savings and loan. I was instrumental in establishing ATMs for this firm, and today we have more than 110 branches scattered throughout New York. These ATMs handle 9,000 transactions a day with daily activity levels between $400,000 and $450,000.

My company has decided to relocate its operations to New Mexico, and my family and I would like to stay in the New York area. I am interested in locating a bank or financial institution that would like to benefit from my expertise in computer technology and particularly ATMs.

I would be delighted to meet with you and explain how I set up this network of ATMs. I will be calling your office in a few days to arrange a mutually convenient time, and I look forward to talking with you.

Sincerely,

Jack Smith

Jack Smith

Review:

1. Introduce yourself and state the purpose of your letter.

2. Present one or more accomplishments that let the reader know your skills.

3. State your reason for making a change and your objective.

4. Make him an offer he cannot refuse and get your interview.

JOHN STEVENS
23 Villa Drive
Mount Vernon, New York 10588

(914) 555-6767

                                        (DATE)

Mr. Paul Rivers
45454 Collins Drive
Los Angeles, California 90056

Dear Paul:

It has been some time since we exchanged news, and I hope this
letter finds everything well at your place. We often talk about
our get-together last year and the fun we had with you, Mary and
the children.

As you know, I've been working at Radio Electronics Inc. for more
than five years. Last week I learned that due to poor quarterly
results they are closing down their installation in our area.
After thinking it over, we now feel that it presents a good
opportunity to look at other industries and see where I can use
my computer skills.

I'm in the process of preparing a resume and will send you a copy
for your comments. In the meantime, I know you have many friends
who are involved in data processing, and I would certainly
welcome your introductions.

My goal is to find a small- or medium-size company in need of
someone to either update or begin from scratch a DP operation. I
am familiar with all mainframe IBM equipment as well as most
popular business software.

I'll give you a call next week.

Betty joins me in wishing you and the family all the best.

Regards,

John Stevens

John Stevens

JANET JAMES
123 SANTA MONICA BLVD.
SANTA MONICA, CA 90403

(310) 555-1234

(DATE)

Mr. Terry Jackson
Blink Sleep Products, Inc.
245 Pico Blvd.
Los Angeles, CA 90025

Dear Mr. Jackson:

Mary Moran mentioned your company is expanding into new fashion
products and suggested I get in touch with you.

My experience in fashion design began in Europe where, after
finishing studies at the Paris School for Design, I served as
apprentice for the House of Dupont. After only six months, I
created a whole line of ready-to-wear fashions.

Since returning to Southern California in January, I have been
freelancing as a designer for a number of local firms. However,
my goal is to locate a company where I can become a permanent
member of the design team.

Since pictures speak more eloquently than words, I am enclosing
some photos of my designs which were successfully sold in Japan
and the United States. I would like the pleasure of meeting you
and at the same time showing you other examples of my work. I
will call your office next week to see if we can arrange a
mutually convenient time.

Sincerely,

Janet James

Janet James

Enclosures

JOHN KENT
23 DALLAS ROAD
HOUSTON, TEXAS 77009

(713) 555-6767

(DATE)

Mr. Bill Franklin
President
Ajax Industries
23600 Olympic Blvd.
Los Angeles, CA 90024

Dear Mr. Franklin:

Charles Beene of the law firm Beene, Thompson and Stern suggested
I contact you concerning opportunities in the home appliance
industry in Southern California.

By way of introduction, I am enclosing a copy of my resume. My
experience in manufacturing has been extensive in high volume/low
cost appliances, electro-mechanical products and, more recently,
computer components.

My objective is to relocate in Southern California. I am
interested in obtaining a position in manufacturing either in
production, planning or design for a small- or medium-size company
needing someone with diversified talents.

Your comments and suggestions of any people or situations I
should pursue would be most welcome. I am planning to be in Los
Angeles for a few weeks in the middle of May and would be
delighted to meet you personally during my stay. I will be
calling you next week to see if a brief get-together might be
arranged.

Sincerely,

John Kent

John Kent

Enclosure

JOHN BLACK
235 FIFTH AVENUE
PASADENA, CA 91109

(818) 555-8934

(DATE)

Mr. Thomas P. Kane
Vice President
Second Interstate Bank
444 S. Flower Street
Los Angeles, California 90023

Dear Tom:

It has been a while since we exchanged greetings and even longer since my days with Second Interstate. I hope that in the intervening time all has been well with you and the family.

You may recall that when I left the bank I joined the investment banking group of Smith, Jones and Jones. The job has been an excellent experience, and I managed a portfolio of $56 million.

We have had a recent reorganization, and, in spite of the good work I have been doing, my position has been eliminated. I have begun to look around at banking and financial investment institutions and recall that you have a very keen knowledge of both sectors.

So that you can be current on my career, I am enclosing a copy of my resume. I would welcome the opportunity to get together with you and at the same time hear your suggestions regarding my career change.

I'll call you next week so we can arrange a time, and I want to thank you in advance for any assistance you can render.

Best regards,

John Black

John Black

Enclosure

CAROL FRANKLIN
23 Farm Lane
Hartsdale, New York 10556

(914) 555-6066

(DATE)

«Data Carol.DOC»

«title» «fname» «IF mi»«mi» «ENDIF»«lname»
«IF pos»«pos»
«ENDIF»«IF co»«co»
«ENDIF»«address1»
«IF address2»«address2»
«ENDIF»«city», «state» «zip»

Dear «title» «lname»,

Are you looking for a versatile and successful consumer marketing professional?

I am seeking a new opportunity where I can use my 11 years of experience in:

- **Launching new products** - provided marketing support for the launch of two subsidiary companies that generated $3 million in profits within 18 months.

- **Increasing sales** - helped create $325 million in sales growth and $43 million in pre-tax operating profit for Wilson Products, Inc.

- **Marketing packaged goods** - designed the marketing plan for the Sweet Biscuit breakfast cereal launch that achieved a 2.2% market share for NBC, Inc. Reversed a share loss on No-Fat-Ever Cheeses for the Greenstone Dairy Company.

If you are working on a client assignment requiring excellence in marketing, I would welcome your call.

Sincerely,

Carol Franklin

Carol Franklin

Enclosure: resume

MARY MORGAN
1200 Sixth Street
New York, NY 10017

(212) 555-7890

(DATE)

Mr. Jack Robbins
Jackson and Robbins Management Consultants
18990 Avenue of the Americas
New York, New York 10023

Dear Mr. Robbins:

For more than seven years I have been an account executive in advertising and public relations. I have had successful experience in the publishing, cosmetics, household products and fast food industries. Two of my most recent clients have been in the Fortune 500.

I am now seeking a professional change and am sending you my resume on the chance that you may be working on an assignment that could use my skills in developing new products, increasing brand and product acceptance and copywriting.

I would welcome hearing from you.

Sincerely,

Mary Morgan

Mary Morgan

Enclosure

Letter from a student in search of a summer job—no resume but maybe a nice, clean-cut photo

BETTY FAIRCHILD ✿
324 Wilson Avenue
Brea, California 92621

(714) 555-4567

(DATE)

Mr. Jack Howard
President
Fairplay Industries, Inc.
23456 Sixth Street
Los Angeles, CA 90023

Dear Mr. Howard:

Summer is approaching and I am one year away from completing my degree in marketing.
Being very interested in consumer products for juveniles, I am now seeking a summer
job where I can use my sales and marketing skills.

My grades last quarter were:

Business 4 (Advanced Marketing Techniques)	A
Accounting 3 (Cost Accounting)	B
Economics 4 (Demographics)	B
English 4 (Writing)	B
French 3 (Intermediate)	C

Advertising and promotion projects have been my main activity this past year, and I
would welcome your comments on some creative work I did concerning juvenile products.
I will be calling you next week so that we might set a mutually convenient time.

Sincerely,

Betty Fairchild

Betty Fairchild

JIM WHITE
2345 Evergreen Way
Santa Monica, CA 90405

(310) 555-4444

(DATE)

Mr. Terry S. Dale
Business Management Inc.
234 Jackson Avenue
Los Angeles, CA 90023

Dear Terry:

It was a pleasure meeting you and learning about the projects you are working on.
Your company certainly has grown in the last few years.

Since we spoke, I have also added Dale Electronics and Honeywell to my target list. I
mention this just in case you know anyone at either of these firms.

Your offer to discuss my background with your associate is very much appreciated, and
I will be calling you next week concerning other people you feel I should meet.

Kindest regards,

Jim White

Jim White

Betty Jones
23 Havers Court Road
White Plains, New York 10655

(914) 555-6868

(DATE)

Ms. Jenny Robinson
Robinson Realtors Inc.
234 Grand Street
White Plains, New York 10657

Dear Ms. Robinson:

Thank you so much for the time we spent yesterday.

Your explanation of real estate sales and how I might get started was most interesting. Many of my sales experiences in networking and meeting people could tie directly into real estate.

As you learned from our conversation, what I like most is the way you described how you can set your own pace. It is impractical to try to raise a family working full time, and yet I do not want to give up my sales experience.

Your offer for me to accompany you on sales calls will be a great help, and I look forward to going out with you next Monday, May 19th. I will be at your office at nine a.m.

Thank you again for all the detailed answers (and great coffee)! I look forward to our next meeting.

Kindest regards,

Betty Jones

Betty Jones

KEN MAY

234 Sixth Avenue
Pasadena, CA 91109

(818) 555-9330

(DATE)

Mr. Jeff Frank
Vice President – Marketing
Blatt Computer Products
234 Seventh Street
Burbank, CA 91503

Dear Mr. Frank:

I appreciated our conversation yesterday and the chance to meet Jane Smith.

Your sales program for the XR-124 line sounds like a real challenge, and while you only mentioned sales to dealers and service centers, there could be a market for OEM applications. This is something I developed for the TR-120 line for the Collins Memory Products Company.

Perhaps we might discuss this when we meet next Tuesday, March 31st, at nine a.m.

I feel confident that our time will be well spent.

Sincerely,

Ken May

Ken May

Review:

1. "Thank you" and acknowledge your meeting.

2. Summarize what was said. Show that you listened.

3. Introduce a new idea, thought or a new skill that you can tie into your discussion.

4. Confirm the next step (an interview or a follow-up call).

SCOTT ADAM
156 Bedford Road
Marina Del Rey, CA 90291

(310) 555-8888

(DATE)

Ms. Janice Green
President
Green Publishing Company
345 Reading Drive
Los Angeles, CA 90012

Dear Ms. Green:

It was indeed a pleasure meeting you yesterday to discuss your need for an Industrial Engineer.

Your planned expansion is most interesting, especially your ideas concerning streamlining existing production before gearing up for the new product line.

My experience in plant layout, equipment selection and manpower planning would tie in well with your needs. In addition, my knowledge of microcomputers and industrial engineering software could help meet your September deadline.

I am very much interested in discussing this further and feel confident that my skills would be a good addition to your team. I'll give you a call next week to get your thoughts.

Thank you again for your hospitality.

Sincerely,

Scott Adam

Scott Adam

GEORGE HOWARD
234 Edwards Street
Brooklyn, New York 11208

(212) 555-5676

(DATE)

Mr. Dan Jefferson
Vice President
Handy Electronics Inc.
2 Sixth Street
Brooklyn, NY 11208

Dear Dan:

As you can imagine, I was disappointed in not being chosen as your final candidate for Production Manager. I am sure that the decision must have been a tough one, as you indicated on the phone today.

I was very much impressed with my visit last week and the people I met. My search continues for a company like Handy Electronics where I can use my skills in production planning and management. I would be most grateful if you could suggest any other business executives I might contact in your industry. Who knows, I just might bump into an opportunity!

I hope we can stay in contact and will give you a call next week concerning the above.

Kindest regards,

George Howard

George Howard

JACK LEE
2314 OLYMPIC BLVD.
LOS ANGELES, CALIFORNIA 90023

(213) 555-9090

(DATE)

Mr. Jim White
World Personnel Services Co.
200 Olive Avenue
Pasadena, CA 91109

Dear Jim:

I was glad to have had the chance to meet with you, and later with Jack Andrews of the Sandex Company.

Jack and I had a long discussion, and while he was most interested in my candidacy for the position of Manager of Export Sales, I feel that this job is not for me.

My reasons are:

1. The company is too small and my responsibilities would not take advantage of all my skills.

2. Jack Andrews indicated a salary range that was below my last position, and, even with an incentive, it would take quite a while for me to meet my present objective.

3. This would not be an advancement in my career.

I wanted you to know my reasons for not pursuing this situation, and hope that we can keep in contact should you run into another opportunity that matches my background.

Thank you again for thinking of me.

Kind regards,

Jack Lee

Jack Lee

A P P E N D I X   C

Reference Materials

our public library is a rich and marvelous source for background data. If you have a university nearby with a business school or graduate school library, you already have access to a tremendous wealth of information. Invest some time in discovering what these reference books can do for your search.

Many companies are classified by SIC number (Standard Industrial Classification). These four-digit numbers indicate the principal activity of the company, and cover the entire field of its economic activity—products to services. While these numbers can be of great help, there are two major problems: 1) Some companies do not indicate all their products and so the number shown is not truly representative of their activity. 2) Some companies have more than one activity, but in many cases only one number is listed by the directory. If a reference book uses SIC numbers, you will often find an explanation in the manual. Otherwise, refer to the *U.S. Government SIC Manual* as a separate reference.

Proper use of these resources will provide you with essential background to permit you to zero in on companies that interest you, supplying the names of the people who run them, their addresses and telephone numbers, along with personal information about individuals you may wish to approach.

Product data and addresses of divisions will permit your networking to be at any level you wish, from senior position to entry-level job.

RECOMMENDED RESOURCES

The Big Three Directories

The Million Dollar Directory
(Dun & Bradstreet.) Includes the four-volume "Series" and the "Top 50,000 Companies." Companies are listed alphabetically, geographically and by industry classification. The "Series" volume includes 160,000 businesses with net worths of more than $500,000. The "Top 50,000 Companies" are the largest, with net worths of more than $1,850,000.

Register of Corporations, Directors and Executives

(Standard & Poor's.) This three-volume set includes 1) Listings of approximately 45,000 corporations providing complete data on management, products, addresses, as well as names of each company's accounting, banking and legal advisors, covering more than 450,000 key executives. 2) Individual listings of directors and executives with complete personal history on each from birthdate to schools attended, covering more than 72,000 people. 3) Corporate "Family Tree" indexes covering the Standard Industrial Classification Index (SIC numbers), Geographic Index and other pertinent information about individuals, including New Company and Individual Additions. [These volumes are invaluable for setting up advice and research networking referrals.]

Directory of Corporate Affiliations, "Who Owns Whom"

When you cannot locate a company which may be a division of another group, this reference can help. It covers all companies listed on the New York and American Stock Exchanges, the *Fortune 1,000* and companies traded over the counter as well as many privately owned firms.

Other Valuable Resources

Dun's Employment Opportunities Directory—The Career Guide

A description of career opportunities in more than 5,000 U.S. companies including information on the requirements and hiring practices of these employers.

The Guide to American Directories

This offers descriptions of more than 6,000 directories which will lead you to addresses, membership names and titles of people covering a wide range of industrial and professional activities throughout the United States. An excellent resource for the networker.

Encyclopedia of Associations

Lists more than 14,000 national associations with all contact details. These groups are invaluable for names of networking contacts.

Standard Directory of Advertisers and Supplements

If you are interested in advertising, this guide covers 17,000 national and regional advertisers along with 80,000 executives. Addresses, telephone numbers, products, advertising agencies employed, media use, etc. are provided.

Thomas Register of American Manufacturers

Here you will find full information on a wide variety of products and companies which are leaders in their fields. Many of these companies are not listed elsewhere.

Annual, 10-Q and 10-K Reports

When you want to know more about a publicly owned company, request these reports directly from the company if your library does not have them already. You will gain many important details and insights as to the company's operations.

Additional References

Business Periodicals Index
Chamber of Commerce Directories - By City
Consultants and Consulting Organizations Directory
Directory of Occupational Titles
Directory of Agencies
The Directory of Directories
Directory of Management Consultants
Directory of Women-Owned Businesses
Encyclopedia of Job Descriptions
Encyclopedia of Careers and Vocational Guidance
Madison Avenue Handbook
North American Register of Business & Industry
Occupational Outlook Handbook
Taylor's Encyclopedia of Government Officials
Yellow Pages, Business to Business
[Ask your librarian for any special state or city directories.]

Some Important Magazines

Barron's
Business Week
Business World
Dun's Review
Entrepreneur
Forbes [*Annual Directory Issue]
Fortune [*Annual Directory Issue]
INC.
Nation's Business
[Plus specific trade magazines and newspapers covering your particular product interests or profession.]

International Reference Materials

Directory of American Firms Operating in Foreign Countries
More than 4,000 American companies with foreign subsidiaries are classified by product and country, indicating key corporate managers.

Directory of International Recruiters
(Consultants News, Templeton Road, Fitzwilliam, NH 03447.)

The Financial Times
(Printed in London, England.) Found at many international newsstands in the U.S.A.

ICA International Executive Search Newsletter
(International Classified Advertising, 3, rue d'Hauteville, 75010 Paris, France, telex: 260 380 BUREAU PARIS ICA. By subscription only. Ask for a sample copy and their rates.) World-wide jobs with emphasis in Europe.

The International Herald Tribune
(International Herald Tribune, S.A., 181, Avenue Charles de Gaulle, 92521 Neuilly Cedex, France. Call toll free in U.S. at 800/572-7212.) A world-wide publication.

International Listings
(Dun & Bradstreet. For locations of library holdings, call toll free 800/526-0651 or in New Jersey 800/624-0324.) Listings of international companies are available under the following titles:

"America's Corporate Families and International Affiliates." Lists more than 22,000 American companies—1,800 U.S. parents with more than 16,000 Canadian and foreign subsidiaries and 1,400 Canadian and foreign parents with more than 3,200 U.S. subsidiaries.

"Canadian Key Business Directory." Covers 14,000 Canadian businesses with 60,000 executives listed.

"Guide to Canadian Manufacturers." Covers the top 10,000 firms.

"Guide to Key British Enterprises." Covers 21,000 British firms representing one-third of the country's employment.

"Europe's 10,000 Largest Companies." Key data on the top 8,000 industrials and 2,000 trading companies in the Western bloc market in Europe.

"Exporters' Encyclopedia." This is a guide on every phase of exporting to more than 220 world markets.

"Principal International Businesses." Covers 133 countries reporting in excess of 50,000 companies.

Kompass
This is an industrial listing of all companies within a given country and can be

found in most American Chamber of Commerce libraries. Listings include classifications by industry and geographic location as well as products and services along with the key management of each company. There are Kompass Directories for France, West Germany, Belgium/Luxembourg, Denmark, Spain, Great Britain, Italy, Norway, Holland, Sweden, Switzerland/Liechtenstein, Australia, Brazil, Indonesia, Morocco and Singapore. For more information write: SNEI, 22, Avenue F.D. Roosevelt, 75008 Paris, France.

Other International Resources

Chambers of Commerce

Some International Chambers of Commerce publish newsletters which indicate local employment opportunities. When visiting a city of interest, be sure to inquire at the local Chamber office as to what reference materials are available and where jobs are listed which could be of interest to you.

Overseas American Chamber of Commerce offices where you can write for information and directories are as follows:

Argentina
American Chamber of Commerce in Argentina
Avenida Leandro N. Alem 1110
Piso 13, 1001
Buenes Aires, ARGENTINA
Executive Director: Mr. Felix Zumelzu

Australia
American Chamber of Commerce in Australia
Level 1, 123 Lonsdale Street
Melbourne, VIC AUSTRALIA 3000
State Manager - Victoria: Ms. Robyn Larson

American Chamber of Commerce in Australia
Suite 4, Gloucester Walk
88 Cumberland Street
Sydney, NSW AUSTRALIA 2000
National Director: Mr. Charles W. Blunt

Austria
American Chamber of Commerce in Austria
Porzellangasse 35
A-1090 Vienna, AUSTRIA
Secretary General: Dr. Patricia A. Helletzgruber

Belgium
American Chamber of Commerce in Belgium
Avenue des Arts 50, Boite 5
B-1040
Brussels, BELGIUM
Manager: Ms. Jo Ann Broger

Bolivia
American Chamber of Commerce of Bolivia
Avenida Arce No. 2071
P.O. Box 8268
La Paz, BOLIVIA
President: Mr. Edward Derksen

Brazil
American Chamber of Commerce-Sao Paulo
Rua Alexandre Dumas, 1976
04717-004
São Paulo, SP BRAZIL
Executive Vice President: Mr. John E. Mein

American Chamber of Commerce for Brazil
C.P. 916, Praca Pio X-15, 5th Floor
Rio de Janeiro 20.040, BRAZIL
Executive Vice President: Mr. Augusto de Moura Diniz Jr.

Chile
Chilean American Chamber of Commerce
Avenida A. Vespucio Sur 80
9th Floor Casilla 82
Santiago 34, CHILE
Manager: Ms. Maria Isabel Jarmillo

China
American Chamber of Commerce in Beijing
Great Wall Sheraton Hotel, Rm. 301
North Donghuan Avenue
Beijing 100026, CHINA
Office Manager: Ms. Mary Liu

Colombia
Colombian-American Chamber of Commerce
Apartado Aereo 8008
Calle 35 No. 6-16
Bogota, COLOMBIA
Director: Mr. Joseph Finnin

Cote D'Ivoire
American Chamber of Commerce-Cote D'Ivoire
01 B.P. 3394, 01
Abidjan, COTE D'IVOIRE
Mr. E.T. Hunt Talmage

Dominican Republic
American Chamber of Commerce of the Dominican Republic
P.O. Box 95-2
Ave. Winston Churchill, Torre BHD, 4th Floor
Santo Domingo, DOMINICAN REPUBLIC
Executive Director: Mr. Authur E. Valdez

Ecuador
Ecuadorian-American Chamber of Commerce
Edificio Multicentro, Piso 4
La Niña y 6 de Diciembre
Quito, ECUADOR
Executive Director: Mr. Roque A. Miño

El Salvador
American Chamber of Commerce of El Salvador
87 Avenida Norte, #720 Apartado A
Colonia Escalón, San Salvador, EL SALVADOR
Executive Director: Ms. Patricia Allwood

England
American Chamber of Commerce of the United Kingdom
75 Brook Street
London W1Y 2EB, ENGLAND
Director General: Mr. Robert E. Brunck

France
The American Chamber of Commerce in France
21, avenue George V
75008 Paris, FRANCE
Executive Director: Mr. W. Barrett Dower

Germany
American Chamber of Commerce in Germany
Roßmarkt 12
60311 Frankfurt/Main, GERMANY
President: Mr. Fred B. Irwin

Greece
American-Hellenic Chamber of Commerce
16 Kanari Street
106 74 Athens, GREECE
Executive Director: Mr. Symeon Tsomokos

Guatemala
American Chamber of Commerce in Guatemala
12 Calle 1-25, Zona 10, Edificio Giminis 10
Torre Norte, 12 Nivel, #1206
Guatemala City, GUATEMALA
Manager: Ms. Rossana De Rodriguez

Honduras
Honduran-American Chamber of Commerce
Centro Bella Aurora
6 Avenida 13-14 Calles N.O.
San Pedro Sula, HONDURAS
Manager: Ms. Ingrid Delgado

Hong Kong
American Chamber of Commerce in Hong Kong
1030, Swire House
Chater Road
Central, HONG KONG
President: Mr. Frank Martin

India

American Business Council - India
Mohan Development Building, 11th Floor
13, Tolstoy Marg
New Delhi, 110 001, INDIA
Chairman: Mr. P.M. Sinha

Ireland

United States Chamber of Commerce in Ireland
20 College Green
Dublin 2, IRELAND
Administrative Assistant and interim Executive Director: Ms. Geraldine McNamara

Israel

Israel-America Chamber of Commerce & Industry
America House
35 Shaul Hamelech Boulevard
P.O. Box 33174
Tel Aviv 64927, ISRAEL
Executive Director: Ms. Nina Admoni

Italy

American Chamber of Commerce in Italy
Via Cantù 1
20123 Milano, ITALY
Managing Director: Ing. Sergio Minoretti

Japan

American Chamber of Commerce in Japan
Bridgestone Toranomon Building, 5F
3-25-2, Toranomon
Minato-ku, Tokyo 105, JAPAN
Executive Director: Mr. William R. Farrell

Korea

American Chamber of Commerce in Korea
Room 307, Chosun Hotel
Sokong-Dong, Chung-Ku
100-070 Seoul, KOREA
Executive Vice President: Mr. William Oberlin

Malaysia

American Malaysian Chamber of Commerce
11.03, Level 11, AMODA
22 Jalan Imbi
55100 Kuala Lumpur, MALAYSIA
Executive Director: Mr. John Hawes

Mexico

American Chamber of Commerce of Mexico-Monterrey
Picachos 760, Despachos 4 y 6
Colonia Obispado, Monterrey, Nuevo Leon, 64060 MEXICO
Executive Director: Mr. John Barrett

Morocco

American Chamber of Commerce in Morocco
18, Rue Colbert, 01
Casablanca, MOROCCO
Executive Director: Mr. Rabea El Alama

The Netherlands

American Chamber of Commerce in the Netherlands
Carnegieplein 5
2517 KJ The Hague
THE NETHERLANDS
Executive Officer: Mr. Kees Burgersdijk

New Zealand

The American Chamber of Commerce in New Zealand
Quay Tower, 10th Floor
29 Customs Street West
Auckland 1001, NEW ZEALAND
Executive Director: Mr. John W. Lavelle

Nicaragua

American Chamber of Commerce of Nicaragua
Apartado 202
Managua, NICARAGUA
Executive Director: Ms. Susan de Aguerre

Panama

American Chamber of Commerce and Industry of Panama
Apartado 168
Estafeta Balboa, Panama, PANAMA
Executive Director: Mr. Fred Denton

Paraguay

Paraguayan-American Chamber of Commerce
General Diaz 521
4 Piso
Asuncion, PARAGUAY
Manager: Mr. George Murphy-Lee

Peru
American Chamber of Commerce of Peru
Avenida Ricardo Palma 836
Miraflores, Lima 18, PERU
Executive Director: Mr. Michael Donovan

Philippines
American Chamber of Commerce of the Philippines
P.O. Box 1578
Manila, PHILIPPINES
Executive Vice President: Mr. Robert Sears

Portugal
American Chamber of Commerce in Portugal
Rua De D. Estafania, 155, 5 ESQ, 1000
Lisbon, PORTUGAL
General Secretary: Dr. Henrique Brito do Rio

Singapore
American Business Council of Singapore
1 Scotts Road #16-07 Shaw Centre
0922 Singapore, SINGAPORE
Executive Director: Mr. Donne Petito

South Africa
American Chamber of Commerce in Southern Africa
P.O. Box 1132
Houghton
2041 SOUTH AFRICA
Executive Director: Mrs. Luanne Grant

Spain
American Chamber of Commerce in Spain
Avenida Diagonal, 477
08036 Barcelona, SPAIN
Executive Director: Mr. José A. Manrique

American Chamber of Commerce in Spain-Madrid
EuroBuilding
Padre Damian, 23
28036 Madrid, SPAIN
Assistant Executive Director: Ms. Maria Nieves Hermida

Sri Lanka
American Chamber of Commerce of Sri Lanka
P.O. Box 1000, Lotus Road
Colombo Hilton, Third Floor, 1
Colombo, SRI LANKA
Executive Director: Mr. Sarath Devapura

Sweden
American Chamber of Commerce in Sweden
Box 5521, 114 85
Stockholm, SWEDEN
Executive Director: Ms. Marianne Raidna Wali

Switzerland
Swiss-American Chamber of Commerce
Talacker 41
8001 Zurich, SWITZERLAND
Executive Director: Mr. Walter H. Diggelmann

Taiwan
American Chamber of Commerce in Taipei
96 Chung Shan North Road
Room 1012, Section 2
Taipei, TAIWAN
Executive Director: Ms. Lynn Murray Sien

Thailand
American Chamber of Commerce in Thailand
140 Wireless Road, 7th Floor
P.O. Box 11-1095
Bangkok, THAILAND
Executive Director: Mr. Thomas Seale

Trinidad and Tobago
American Chamber of Commerce of Trinidad & Tobago
Hilton International
Upper Arcade
Lady Young Road
Port-of-Spain, TRINIDAD & TOBAGO
Executive Director: Ms. June Maharaj

Turkey
Turkish-American Businessmen's Association
Fahri Gizdem Sokak
No. 22/5
80280 Gayrettepe, Istanbul, TURKEY
Vice Chairman: Mr. Haksever Suner

Uruguay
Chamber of Commerce Uruguay-USA
Calle Bartolome Mitre 1337
Casilla de Correo 809
Montevideo, URUGUAY
Manager: Mr. Carlos Boubet

Other Resources

If you or members of your family belong to political, professional, fraternal or alumni associations with affiliations abroad, be sure to ask the U.S. offices for their overseas addresses and key contacts.

Glossary

ABC Formula: One of the key factors of a successful interview occurs when a candidate identifies an interviewer's need and matches one of his accomplishments against that need. The accomplishment then becomes a benefit for the interviewer and shows how the candidate's skills can solve a particular problem of concern to the interviewer.

Accomplishment = Benefit (need), with the Conversion being made by the candidate.

Advice Interview: A means of obtaining professional referrals (bridges) to individuals who may help you meet people in your target companies, suggest a particular job opportunity, suggest a new target company and/or share other contacts that will expand your network. The advice interview begins with your friends and business associates and branches out in both random and structured directions. This interview shows the real power of networking as you add people to your "team."

Bridge: People who will refer you to other people and help you develop a new contact. Without "bridges" in human relations, including job search, a lot less would be accomplished.

Broadcast Letter: This letter (without a resume) is used to provoke an interview. It is made up of elements from your resume and, primarily, your 20-Second Resume. Often, when a candidate does a mailing including a resume, the targeted recipient does not see the letter or the resume. A well-intentioned secretary, following instructions, routes the letter to the personnel department for reply. However, when a personal letter arrives without a resume but uses certain key resume elements to provoke interest, the chances that the target person will read the letter are greatly improved.

Chronological Resume: This is one of the original resume formats. It lists jobs, usually in reverse chronological order, showing the name of each employer, their city and state, the time period you were employed, your title(s), responsibilities and key accomplishments.

Direct Interview: This is the moment every job searcher seeks: the face-to-face meeting with someone who can use your services and provide you with gainful employment. The direct interview can come from quite a number of sources. Along with research and advice interviews, the direct interview is something that each candidate must prepare for.

Functional Resume: This resume focuses attention on skills and accomplishments rather than individual jobs. It is particularly effective when the candidate has had a number of job changes or has had a long career.

Horizontal Job Market: Industries that parallel the industrial sector in which a candidate is presently working. It refers to opportunities outside of what may be a dry industry. For example, many banks at this writing are going through a shakeout with mergers followed by cost reductions and layoffs. Parallel industries that could absorb people coming from banking institutions comprise the horizontal job market. In making the transition to a new industry, a candidate may move up (or down) in the hierarchy depending on the size of the company, his experience and the job's responsibilities.

Networking: Networking is one of the oldest and surest ways to get a new job. It involves meeting people on a one-to-one basis and enlisting their assistance in introducing or referring you to people in a target company or who can expand your contacts. Everyone should be networking all the time—not only for job search, but to develop friends and expand individual worlds.

Outplacement: Relatively new, outplacement deals with helping people review their skills, resources and objectives while developing know-how in self-marketing their way to a new job or career. Based on the concept that the best qualified do not necessarily get the best jobs, but the best candidates do get the best offers, outplacement is concerned with taking people who are on the verge of making a job change and making them into the best candidates to complement their professional talents.

Performance Resume: This resume takes elements from both the functional and chronological resumes and focuses on those skills and abilities that complement a specific job. The performance resume looks at the candidate from the buyer's point of view. "What can this person do for me and my company?"

Research Interview: This interview is just what it says: You are going after information. It could be about a new career, a company, a person, a business or service. The people you approach are usually expert in their particular fields and can provide information that will help you in meeting more people or making a decision. Of course, this interview, like the advice interview, can turn into a direct interview and you should be prepared.

Salary Package: The salary package includes not only take-home pay, but all the extras that can come from a job, ranging from a company car to stock options.

SAY IT—ASK IT: You make a statement and from that statement introduce a question related to your objective.

> Suppose you are in the midst of an interview and learn from your host of a company problem that you have already solved in another job situation. At the appropriate time, you can bring up your accomplishment (SAY IT) and follow your statement with a question (ASK IT): "Would such a solution to your problem help?" or, "Would you like to know how I achieved those results?" or, "Is that the sort of know-how you are looking for?"

> Another use for SAY IT—ASK IT is when you do not want to answer a question immediately, such as, "How much money do you want?" In this case the candidate can reply, "You can see that I have more than eight years' experience to bring to this job." (SAY IT) "What range do you have in mind?" (ASK IT)

> For telemarketing: The candidate is trying to get an appointment by telephone. He has just been told that there is no need for any new people. He replies, "I can understand that you do not need any new people (SAY IT), yet, do you have enough sales people who have more than ten years' experience selling radio time?" (ASK IT) Or, "I can appreciate that you're fully staffed. Does that include experienced Pascal programmers as well?" The SAY IT—ASK IT technique is explained in detail in Chapters 7 and 8.

Severance Pay: When a candidate is let go, a settlement of his account is usually made. This exiting pay package will include pay up to the agreed time of termination of services, accrued vacation pay, any bonuses due, outplacement and any other indemnity pay that may be a function of time of service, performance or special circumstances surrounding the person's leaving. Many times a person is paid up to a certain date even though he is free to search full time to locate another job. Sometimes the severance package also includes the use of an office and/or secretarial services to help the candidate through his transition. This package is sometimes negotiable at the time of termination.

Telemarketing: Selling by telephone. While we have all been solicited at one time or another in the past by a telephone salesperson, more attention now is being placed on such sales. The largest retailers in America even use robots to make calls advising that their catalog is ready to pick up or a special sale is on. Telephone companies, realizing the power of telephone sales, have become much more active in helping companies develop departments for this type of activity. Job seekers can use these techniques to become better networkers in making interview appointments by telephone.

20-Second Resume: The opening part of the performance resume—the part that gets the reader's attention. What goes into this part of your resume is critical, and your statements and accomplishments should be tailored to your objective. The 20-Second Resume is so powerful that it can, by itself, become the basis of a broadcast letter.

Vertical Job Market: Other opportunities in your industry where you can apply your skills in a new job. A salesperson in one company could become a sales manager in another. A production supervisor could be a director of manufacturing. The vertical job market is important when a candidate is considering a move from a small- or medium-size company to a large one, and vice versa.

Index

About the Author

A graduate of The Ohio State University with Bachelor and Master of Science degrees in engineering and business, Peter K. Studner served as a United States Air Force officer and later became a licensed professional engineer.

Early in his career he moved to Paris to head up the European operations of H.K. Porter Company. Since then he has been C.E.O. and served on boards of publicly and privately held companies in England, France and the United States. He has been responsible for a number of key international marketing and sales operations as well as turnarounds.

Upon his return from Europe, he completed research on new techniques for speeding the job transition process. He currently practices outplacement in Los Angeles. He has helped thousands of men and women make successful career changes and has trained both independent consultants and corporate human resource professionals in how to deliver effective outplacement programs.

Mr. Studner appears regularly on television and radio, has been a feature editor of a career magazine, and contributes articles to business newspapers and magazines. He conducts regular career transition seminars at local universities and colleges and has been on the faculty of University of California at Los Angeles (UCLA Extension).

Super•Job•Search® received the Benjamin Franklin Award for the Best "How to" book, presented by the Publishers Marketing Association at the American Booksellers Association Convention. It has also won awards from the American Library Association as the "Best of the Best" and an award from Quality Books.

Mr. Studner is the author of *Objectif Emploi—Guide complet du CV jusqu'à l'embauche*, published in France by MAXIMA and in North America by Jamenair Ltd. He is also the author of five children's books and one business thriller. He is currently a member of the Publishers Marketing Association, Independent Writers of Southern California, Maxim's Business Club, French-American Chamber of Commerce, The Society of Authors (UK) and the Société des Gens de Lettres in France. He resides in Los Angeles.

REGISTRATION FORM-SUPER*JOB*SEARCH

(please print or type)

JAMENAIR LTD.
Post Office Box 241957, Registration
Los Angeles, CA 90024-9757 USA
Telephone (310) 470-6688

Name _____

Address _____

City _____ State _____ Zip _____

SUPER*JOB*SEARCH MANUAL PURCHASE:

From: _____

Date: _____

Dear Friend:

Practice makes perfect. This becomes crystal clear as you read through the **SUPER *JOB*SEARCH** Manual. Recognizing that SUPER SEARCH techniques lend themselves to practice either in groups or with a partner, we will be happy to help your SUPER SEARCH NETWORK by putting you in touch with other people in your area who would also like to practice.

We will do this at NO CHARGE to you provided we receive this ORIGINAL REGISTRATION FORM (**sorry, no copies accepted**) along with your signature below authorizing us to try to match you.

To be effective, we would like to know your salary group so we can put you together with someone close to your salary level. Circle one figure group below:

ENTRY LEVEL	$20K-29K	$30K-39K	$40K-49K	$50K +

YOUR AGREEMENT

I agree practice makes perfect. Please give my NAME and TELEPHONE NUMBER to someone using SUPER SEARCH in my area so I may perfect my SUPER SEARCH techniques. I understand and agree to indemnify and hold JAMENAIR LTD. and Peter K. Studner harmless from any liability resulting from use of this service. All contacts and practice will be entirely at my discretion and responsibility.

_____   _____

Your signature is required for this free service.   Area code + tel. no.

While every attempt will be made to match you with someone in your area, we cannot guarantee how soon this will be done as it depends on incoming registrations.

THE COMPLETE MANUAL FOR CAREER-CHANGERS

SUPER SEARCH™ SOFTWARE

VERSION 4.0

Power Networking Software™ for Career People On The Move

A diligent job searcher needs to maintain good records in order to control necessary search information. Throughout SUPER•JOB•SEARCH®, I have presented various forms to help you facilitate organizing this information.

SUPER•JOB•SEARCH® is complete as a manual alone. However, since there are millions of microcomputers in use today, it is more practical to use a personal contact manager designed to lighten the administrative load connected with career transition for the job-seeker and career-changer.

The first version of SUPER SEARCH™ Software was released in 1986. At the time, it was alone on the market and was created for job-seekers and career-changers to keep track of their many contacts. For several years, Version 3.0 did just this. However, with the advancement of both hardware and programming languages, Version 4.0 of this personal contact management program has evolved. Though loaded with many new exciting features, Version 4.0 permits even the most novice computer user to safely record all professional and personal contacts, generate lists, mail merge letters and maintain control over a wide range of events.

Having worked with thousands of professionals on their way to better careers, one thing became evident. It is the people in our lives who open doors to opportunities. Maintaining control over a network with several hundred contacts needs some degree of automation. SUPER SEARCH™ Software, Version 4.0 answers this need. While there are a number of excellent personal information management programs on the market, SUPER SEARCH™ Software has endeavored to stick to its original concept of providing an easy-to-use menu driven contact manager program that will complement any career-minded professional's efforts to expand his network.

TECHNICAL SPECIFICATIONS

SUPER SEARCH™ SYSTEM PROGRAM
SUPER SEARCH™ FINANCIAL ANALYSIS PROGRAM

Requires

CPU 286 or higher
At least 4.5 MB hard disk space
DOS 3.3 or higher

475K free RAM
Mouse optional
Windows compatible

SUPER SEARCH™ WORDPROCESSING FILES

Available in ASCII, Word and Macintosh formats.

In writing SUPER SEARCH™, it was inevitable that there would be a need for forms to fill out, as well as sample letters and model resumes to illustrate each point. This information would be invaluable to a job searcher if it could be brought up on his PC monitor, modified to individual needs, printed and stored for future reference.

The following is a list of everything provided in these files. I have indicated the chapter and page number where you will find each document and form in this manual.

All of these files are spaced at 65 characters to a line EXCEPT those marked *, where the line is 85 characters long. To accommodate a line with 85 characters, the resume was printed in "Courier" type to make it fit on 8-1/2" x 11" paper. If your printer will not produce "Courier" type, you should adjust the * sample by reformatting down to 65 characters per line.

SUPER SEARCH™ SYSTEM PROGRAM

Features of the program:

- Create unlimited separate databases—no longer are you limited to one database. From your program, you can create as many databases as you wish—all accessible through your Catalog of Databases.
- Unlimited entries—create a database of all your contacts including call reports with up to three pages of notes for each contact.
- Company addresses recorded for future data entry—as you enter company names, addresses and phone numbers, they are recorded to automatically repeat for new contacts from the same company.
- Multiple addresses can be created for the same company at different locations.
- SIC code referencing—built-in library of more than 1,500 listings—comes complete with Standard Industrial Code listings that pop up as you enter your data. Additional listings other than SIC numbers are easily created.
- Double sort by any of seven fields—not only can you sort on one field, but multiple field sorts are possible. For example, you can print out the names and addresses of recruiters for the city of San Diego.
- Built-in utility to change area codes throughout any database—no longer is it necessary to edit each Master List entry. With this utility, you can easily modify changes to area codes on a selective basis throughout your database.
- Fully compatible with all dBase software—data files can easily be used with other database programs.
- Write a quick letter or memo including an envelope or label from the Master List entry—while browsing through your Master List of contacts, you can generate a letter or memo along with an envelope or label.
- Search on any field—search possibilities now make it possible to search on any of your Master List fields easily and accurately.
- Data Import/Export—import other SUPER SEARCH™ databases into your Master List as well as dBase or ASCII text data. Create ASCII files which can be easily imported into wordprocessors or other database programs.
- Automatic phone dialing—no need to leave the program to make calls. Dial from within the program while you are working on your data.
- Editing utility for company names, SIC code and database catalog tables—modify your library of company names, SIC code and database tables.
- Create multiple call reports for each master listing including expenses—up to three pages of notes, key people contacted and follow-up action. Reports can be sorted by company or name of contact.
- Each Master List entry shows date of entry and date of latest update—selections can be sorted on either.
- Easily change return address.

- On-line help using the F1 key—help is built into SUPER SEARCH™ with just a key stroke.

Wordprocessing

- Contact notes, memos, letters—generate letters and memos from your database without retyping addresses.
- Mail merge—both in and out of the program. The program's wordprocessor has mail merge capability or you can generate a selected list of names and addresses for use in another wordprocessor.
- Envelopes and labels (laser or dot matrix)—envelopes and labels are easy to produce.
- Model networking letters—form letters are provided to get you started with mail campaigns to both companies and recruiters.
- Spell checker—a 60,000 word modifiable dictionary is included.
- Prepare form letters in advance—create your own form letters for any occasion.
- Advanced features—for more sophisticated users, query capability is included.

Reports

- Can be sorted by multiple specified fields and dates.
- Master directory lists—based on your selections.
- Call reports—keeping track of your contacts has never been easier.
- Expense reports for any period of time—valuable for preparing tax deductions.
- Contact follow-up to do lists for any time period—always be in control of who you have to contact and when.
- Telephone lists—never be without your personal telephone directory.

Plus!

- Mouse support—program can work with or without a mouse.
- Built-in backup of data—never be caught without backups.
- Will run as a DOS application in WINDOWS™.
- Printers: dot matrix or laser.
- Color monitor support.
- Easy word and phrase searches.
- Compatible with previous versions.

The end of each day is the best time to sit down with your computer, collection of business cards, receipts, notes and diary. In a matter of minutes you can enter pertinent information into your database so that you need not worry that you will forget some follow-on action that could lead you to your next job.

You are about to go on a trip to Chicago. From your data you can request a listing of all names, addresses and telephone numbers in your directory for specific industry or professions sorted up to the minute. From this information you will be able to plan efficiently.

You call your answering machine from the field and get a brief message from Sue Smith to call her back right away. No need to wonder who Sue Smith is when you carry a short telephone list of key people selected from your directory along with their company name.

Meeting people who can help you means not forgetting what transpired at the time of your contact. Creating a call report where you show who you met, their positions, matters discussed, other key items plus your follow-up action, can make the most out of your networking. Having your information sorted and protected means that nothing will be forgotten, especially when you need it most!

Networking expenses need to be controlled. Using the expense report built into the program will help you stay within budget and will prove invaluable when reporting job-search expenses in your tax deduction if you qualify.

One of the most important things a networker must do is follow-up after contacts are made. Meeting people everyday means that there will be a lot of future follow-through and calls to make. The follow-up report will keep you on track. You will not leave anyone out and, more importantly, be able to get the most out of each contact.

Surprisingly, few job-seekers remember to send thank-you letters to the people they are asking to help them. A short thank-you note with a reminder of what was said, or a future action to be taken with perhaps some new information, will keep your name in the mind of your contact. Appreciation goes a long way. With the thank-you follow-up report, you will not leave anyone out.

One of the most valuable features of this program is its ability to prepare selected lists of names and addresses for mail campaigns. Suppose you want to send to all the recruiters in your list news about your new job or a promotion you received. Nothing could be easier. Perhaps you have written an article on banking. From your list you can do a mailing to all bankers. If you ever wondered how to maintain your own public relations for future career moves, this is the way.

A database would not be complete without the ability to easily produce labels and envelopes from your data. Formats have been provided to create address labels and envelopes using domestic and international addresses.

You have been away on a business trip or vacation and have forgotten what is in your database. You can either display or print out all the components in your directory for maximum control.

Some people already have databases and would like to use SUPER SEARCH™ Software without having to re-enter all the names and addresses. From either a text file (ASCII list) or an existing dBase file, you can import any number of names, addresses and telephone numbers into your directory with a touch of a few keys.

SUPER SEARCH™ Software is designed to make your work easier. You can search and edit or delete listings, update mileage costs and change the program set-up, all at the touch of a key.

SUPER SEARCH™ DEMO PROGRAM

To get ahead in a career or job change, you need to meet people—the right people and decision makers who can put you into the best jobs. Keeping control over all the contacts you make, both before and after a career change, does not have to be a chore.

To facilitate your introduction to the SUPER SEARCH™ System Program, I encourage you to order a free copy of our DEMO program that contains all of the program's key features less the importing and data backup functions. It will permit you to enter, delete or edit a maximum of 10 entries using the full capability of the program directly from your hard disk.

FREE OFFER:

To obtain your FREE DEMO copy of the SUPER SEARCH™ Software System Program, call 310/470-6688 and ask for DEMO Version 4.0. Or, FAX us at 310/470-8106 or write to:

Jamenair Ltd.
Software Division/DEMO OFFER
Post Office Box 241957
Los Angeles, California 90024-9757 USA

SUPER SEARCH™ FINANCIAL ANALYSIS PROGRAM

This program will enable you to:

1. Prepare your FAMILY NET WORTH and revise it as necessary.
2. Prepare your ESTIMATED JOB SEARCH CAMPAIGN COSTS and revise them as they change.
3. Prepare a MONTHLY CASH FLOW for a 12-month period that will help you maintain better control of your personal finances as you go through your search and beyond.

Peter K. Studner Associates

Los Angeles ▪ Glendale ▪ Westlake Village ▪ Irvine
Mailing Address: P.O. Box 241957, West Los Angeles, California 90024-9757
310/470-6688 ▪ FAX 310/470-8106

Peter K. Studner Associates outplacement counseling produces Black Belt Candidates_{SM}.

If you want to be a winner, you will be! Every job offer is a competition where only one person will emerge on top. Our training not only gives candidates an edge in this competition, but the confidence to win.

The Black Belt Candidate_{SM} Program is divided into three key components:

Strategic Planning: We analyze and define what the candidate wants to do in the next chapter of a career path with long term objectives in mind. This includes in-depth career assessment that ties in with the candidate's life values. If appropriate, other members of the family are included in the strategic plan. The candidate develops a personal campaign that is pro-actively organized to go after jobs in companies that meet defined objectives and values.

Techniques:

- Defining and building a competency inventory.

- Identifying where the jobs are for each candidate.

- Creating successful resumes and/or entrepreneurial marketing materials. A resume or brochure must reflect a candidate's best benefits to a future employer in an interesting, original and attractive manner. It must be unique to each candidate and create a demand for interviews. It must immediately show a candidate's potential worth.

- The art of successful networking. Black Belt Candidates_{SM} learn how to be comfortable and competent on the telephone, obtaining interviews and meeting the right people and decision makers. PKS Associates' training includes constant video and audio reinforcement of interviewing skills where the candidate learns the art of successful interviewing, becoming an effective listener and an excellent presenter of benefits.

- Testing the job market through advice and research interviews. The candidate begins with networking and discovers how to locate the best jobs before they are made public. Feedback is constantly analyzed with a professional counselor every step of the way.

- Finally, when a job offer is in view, the Black Belt Candidate_{SM} is prepared to discuss and negotiate a win-win salary.

Services:

- Comprehensive secretarial services — unlimited resumes, stationery, business cards, mailings and facsimile transmissions.

- As needed, individual FAX machine installed in the candidate's home.

- A complete set of Super Job Search® Software.

- Personalized corporate and recruiter data bases.

- 24-hours per day live operator message service.

- Inclusion and access to the national Black Belt Candidate_{SM} Network.

- Lifetime guarantee and career support.

Your success is our reputation.

Career Transition Management
Programs for Corporate Sponsored Outplacement

Executive/Black Belt Candidate_{sm} Outplacement Program
This program offers a complete one-on-one counseling program covering every aspect of career transition. It includes all our services: counseling, testing, candidate use of executive offices, secretarial support, telephone and message center, resumes, stationery, business cards, follow-up, sharing in our networks, Super Search® Software, FAX, job leads and continued support into a new position and beyond.

Mixed Group and Individual Counseling
Mixed programs of group and individual counseling include group workshops on job-search strategies, resume preparation, marketing, interviewing techniques with individual counseling for personal assessment, resume completion and action plan. Continued support and follow-up counseling are provided into a new position. The cost will vary depending on group size and level of candidates involved.

Entrepreneurial Counseling
Some candidates wish to organize a business of their own instead of searching for another job. Counseling is offered to help with financial planning, funding, product/service design, business plans, budgeting, marketing, action plans and actual start-up or acquisition.

Train the Trainer Workshops
Super•Job•Search® manuals and software are ideal for companies wishing to provide in-house outplacement. We provide two-day workshops for human resource staff covering all aspects of Super•Job•Search® materials for in-house programs. We suggest that groups be limited to six or fewer.

Workshops-Preretirement
Sometimes it is prudent to introduce eligible employees to a company's early retirement program through a two-day workshop. The first day covers all the possibilities should they accept an early retirement. Professionals discuss financial and healthcare planning. Career changes for both profit and non-profit activity are included. When employees sign up for the company's retirement program, a continuing one-day workshop deals with the actual career transition. Groups should be limited to 30 participants.

Workshops-Outplacement
This program offers one- or two-day workshops covering all the aspects of job search. In the two-day workshop we strive to have candidates complete individual resumes. All materials are provided. Groups are limited to 20 participants and are consistent in terms of work classification (non-exempts or exempts). Continued counseling is provided by telephone at no additional charge.

Accelerated Outplacement Program
It's true! You never get a second chance to make an outstanding first impression. That's why our Accelerated Outplacement Program is geared to get you up and running quickly with job skills and resources to meet the competition head on. In sessions of individual counseling, candidates receive help with determining a career path to assure they are on track with today's job market. Plus...an initial supply of resumes, stationery, business cards, reference materials on recruiters, companies, agencies, hot lines, associations and more. Always: on-going support by phone. Each candidate's job-search questions will have answers.

Mid-Career Check-Up Program
When an employee's performance, communications and effectiveness deteriorate, it is usually the result of changes which have gone unheeded, unobserved or unreconciled. These changes can be in the job, supervision, company policies and objectives as well as an employee's value system. The benefits of a Mid-Career Check-Up Program include salvaging years of corporate experience, insight to larger problems, avoidance of potential litigation, elimination of dysfunctional situations, reduction of stress claims, guidance and assistance to troubled employees with a total revaluation of an employee's career direction. Through the use of a combination of psycho-diagnostic instruments with counseling, the employee can confidentially review what changes are needed. If an outplacement program follows, the cost of the Mid-Career Check-Up Program will be absorbed into the outplacement program. Confidentiality: All personal information including test results remain between the psychometric professional and the employee.

Manuals and Software
The Super•Job•Search® Manual and Super Search® Software are available for in-house counseling. Qualified corporations can purchase these materials at a discount.

A plan for every need. We invite your inquiry. Telephone (310) 470-6688

A Special Message for Human Resources Professionals

CONSULTANTS:

Do you work with people in career transition? Would you like to help your clients obtain faster results in setting realistic, attainable career goals followed by perfected strategies and techniques to win any job or career objective?

If you would like additional information on how you can become a Certified *Super•Job•Search*® Counselor, contact me for details about the *Super•Job•Search*® Training Program. There is no obligation.

COMPANY HUMAN RESOURCES EXECUTIVES:

Outplacement is here to stay. For all the reasons: legal, moral, humane, morale, contractual, government—it makes good sense.

More and more companies are providing in-house career counseling for leaving employees that often includes setting up temporary or permanent career transition centers.

With *Super•Job•Search*® as your manual, your company can have its own Outplacement Department for even greater control and significant economy.

If you would like more information on this subject, please contact me.

Peter K. Studner
Jamenair Ltd.
Training Seminars
Post Office Box 241957
Los Angeles, California 90024-9757

Telephone: (310) 470-6688
FAX: (310) 470-8106
e-mail: SuperSearch@pobox.com
Internet: www.SuperJobSearch.com

ORDER FORM

Jamenair Ltd., Post Office Box 241957, Los Angeles, California 90024-9757
Telephone: 310/470-6688   FAX 310/470-8106
e-mail: jamenair@pobox.com

Please send me the following manuals and software:

_____ copies of SUPER•JOB•SEARCH® Manual @ $22.95 each

_____ copies of SUPER•JOB•SEARCH® Manual (UK Edition) @ $22.95 each

_____ copies of OBJECTIF EMPLOI, in French for Canada & France @ $22.95 each

_____ copies of SUPER SEARCH™ SYSTEM & FINANCIAL
ANALYSIS PROGRAMS (Version 4.0) @ $79.95 per set

_____ copies of SUPER SEARCH™ WORD PROCESSING FILES for
❏ WORD™ - PC (1 Diskette = 62 documents)
❏ WORD™ - MAC (1 Diskette = 62 documents)
❏ ASCII (1 Diskette = 62 documents) @ $24.95 each

Total cost of Manuals and Software $_____

Shipping and Handling Charges $_____

Appropriate California Sales Tax $_____

Total Order Amount $_____

Software Requirements:

CPU 386 or higher | 475K free RAM
At least 4.5 MB hard disk space | Mouse optional
Operating system: DOS 3.3 or higher | Windows compatible

California Residents: Please add appropriate sales tax. **Shipping & Handling:** $5.00 for first manual plus unlimited software, $1.00 for each additional manual. Software alone: $5.00 per shipment. Outside U.S. add additional 20% on value of merchandise. Payment must be in U.S. currency by international money order or check drawn on U.S. bank. We accept Visa and MasterCard. In the continental U.S., we ship by UPS; please give us a street address for UPS delivery. Delivery: One week to ten days. International orders take longer.

Please Print

Name: _____

Address: _____

City: _____ State: _____ Zip: _____

Telephone: _____

___ Enclosed is my check for $ _____ (payable to JAMENAIR LTD.)

___ Please charge my: _____ MasterCard _____ Visa Account

Card No.: _____ Exp. Date: _____

Signature: _____